MAX WEBER ON ECONOMY AND SOCIETY

ROBERT J. HOLTON

and

BRYAN S. TURNER

London and New York

First published in 1989 by Routledge
Reprinted in paperback in 1990 by Routledge
11 New Fetter Lane, London EC4P 4EE
29 West 35th Street, New York, NY 10001

Typeset in Baskerville
by Pat and Anne Murphy, Highcliffe-on-Sea, Dorset

Printed and bound in Great Britain by
Biddles Ltd, Guildford and King's Lynn

British Library Cataloguing in Publication Data

Holton, R. J. (Robert John), *1946–*
Max Weber on economy and society.
1. Sociology. Theories of Weber, Max
I. Title. II. Turner, Bryan, S. (Bryan Stanley), *1945–*
301'.092'4

Library of Congress Cataloging in Publication Data

Holton, R. J.
Max Weber on economy and society
Robert J. Holton and Bryan S. Turner
p. cm. Bibliography: p. Includes index.
1. Weber, Max. 1864–1920. 2. Sociology — Germany — History.
I. Turner, Bryan S. II. Title.
HM22.G3W4435 1989   301'.0943 — dc 19   88-30646 CIP

ISBN 0-415-05433-8

CONTENTS

ACKNOWLEDGEMENTS

The chapters by Bryan Turner were completed at the University of Bielefeld (West Germany) where he was guest professor in the Faculty of Social Science in 1987–8. The period of study was made possible by the Alexander von Humboldt Foundation, which was generous in its research support.

Earlier versions of Chapters 2 and 5 were delivered by Robert Holton and Bryan Turner respectively at the Max Weber Colloquium held at the William Paterson College of New Jersey in 1986. We are grateful to Professor Ron Glassman for organizing this important gathering of Weber scholars.

A version of Chapter 3 was given by Bryan Turner at Bielefeld University and St Maartens, French West Indies, in 1987. We are grateful to Roland Robertson for criticism of an earlier version.

Chapter 4 was a conference paper at the Law and History Conference held in Melbourne, Australia, in 1986.

A number of arguments in Chapter 6 were outlined in a paper given to the Sociology of Consumption Conference at the University of Oslo in 1988. Robert Holton is particularly grateful to Peter Saunders and Bert Moorhouse for helping to clarify many issues pertinent to this paper.

Chapters 3, 4, and 5 were finally assembled in 1988 in the Algemene Sociale Wetenschappen, Rijksuniversiteit te Utrecht. Bryan Turner would like to thank the staff at Utrecht for their support, especially Professor Hans Adriaansens.

We should also like to thank Sue Manser and Ina Cooper for their assistance in turning our often confused manuscripts into final copy.

Robert Holton
Bryan Turner

INTRODUCTION

There is a definite revival of liberalism under way within western thought. This revival is in one sense rather surprising since much academic opinion had supposed liberalism to be in retreat if not vanquished and discredited. Political economy, it seemed, had been intellectually if not institutionally triumphant over neo-classical economics, critical legal studies were taken to have undermined the liberal theory of law, while Marxism had demolished liberal-democratic political theory, and Frankfurt School critical theory had rendered obsolete Enlightenment notions of liberal rationalism, and exposed the shallow repressiveness of consumer society, leaving radical sociology for its part to destroy the theoretical pretension of liberal Parsonian sociology. While liberalism remained institutionally entrenched in many of the core institutions of academia, its ideologues could be regarded for the most part as a discredited and largely atavistic bunch of cold-war warriors living out a curious sort of decaying intellectual half-life on the margins of intellectual progress. From today's viewpoint, however, this set of putative victories seems increasingly precarious and in some cases illusory.

There are a number of indicators of the scope of the liberal revival. In the first place, many of the influential stars in the post-war Marxist firmament such as Althusser and Poulantzas, Lukács and Gramsci, are on the wane, while names like J. S. Mill, T. H. Marshall, Talcott Parsons, and Robert Dahl are increasingly to be found as intellectual reference points. Second, many of the weaknesses and residual problems in political economy, critical theory, and Marxism have by now achieved an intolerable scale, prompting interest in alternative social-theoretical paradigms. Many of these difficulties stem from the growing realization that the period from 1950 to 1986 has been

1

INTRODUCTION

characterized not by a crisis of capitalism, but by a crisis of communism and those forms of socialism based on a *Gemeinschaft* model of social organization. Many of the critical positions advanced against the liberal world-view effectively asserted the superiority of *Gemeinschaft* over *Gesellschaft*. This superiority was claimed by asserting the merits of community over individualism, public collectivism over private self-interest, and an organic theory of political participation and consent over representative democracy and individual citizenship rights.

It now seems that *Gemeinschaft* is dead in the western world and world communist movement, though not within the resurgent Islamic world. Crises of communism as a system of government are reflected in economic mismanagement and the inability to satisfy consumer demands on the one hand, and in political repression and totalitarianism on the other. The difficulties of economic planning by command mechanisms are reflected in the shift of some eastern European societies like Hungary, and more recently China, towards a greater element of market-based resource allocation. This in turn has engendered a loss of confidence in many circles in social planning strategies based solely on state initiative. The overall record of communist societies has helped to erode any a priori claims as to the moral superiority of communism over capitalism and liberal individualism that once may have existed.

The death of *Gemeinschaft* within the west is reflected in the decline of class-based politics. Within the climate of effective individual autonomy and value pluralism engendered by the secularization process and the dynamic economic performance of the capitalist economy, there is little attraction for *Gemeinschaft*-based conceptions of class — except in a few declining occupational communities. The rationale for collectivist strategies such as nationalization and the welfare state has also wilted in the face of electoral support for privatization projects such as sale of publicly owned industries through access to share-ownership, sale of public housing to tenants, and the expansion of private medical care systems.

These developments do not signify a complete collapse of support for public service provision, but they do reflect a characteristically modern *Gesellschaftlich* commitment to the autonomy of personal choice. Although the balance of public to private provision varies considerably between western nation-states, making sweeping generalizations difficult, even the much-vaunted Scandinavian

2

welfare-state systems appear to have reached the limits of electoral support for social-democratic interventionism. All this does not represent a return to a mythical free market minimal state system, since levels of public intervention remain high, and certain public schemes popular, especially where choice is encouraged. But it does signify the inauspicious context in which class-based socialist movements seek to build successful electoral coalitions of support.

One of the fundamental residual problems left unanswered by Marxist thought, radical sociology, and political economy was the robustness of the market model of social exchange as a means of co-ordinating relations between producers and consumers. While it is very clear that markets are not self-regulating, that markets sometimes fail to deliver a just distribution of goods, and that markets are prone to problems of monopolistic control, it remains the case that the market-place has been seriously underestimated as a social institution by opponents of liberal-democratic thought.

This underestimation has developed in part because the problem of producer domination has been taken to be so fundamental as to reduce consumers to alienated purchasers of fetishized commodities or simple dupes of advertising and public relations. The net effect was to deny the authenticity of consumers' choices and searches for use-values, or, when faced with effective consumer resistance, to resort to the charge of sectional middle-class self-interest — distinct from the universalistic, organic *Gemeinschaftlich* interest of the working class as potential free producers.

Along with this neglect of individual autonomy and consumption went a hostility to the spatial organization of consumers within suburbia. The patrician disdain for the plebeian semi-detached with its back yard and washing line was typified in the dismissive comment on the suburban home as 'Heaven and a Hills Hoist'. (The Hills Hoist is a form of Australian washing line exported around the western world.) There is still comparatively little research into the instrumental and symbolic significance of the suburban home, though what there is testifies to its popularity as a form of housing. Exchange of 'private' housing through the market may well be mediated through financial institutions like banks and building societies. Yet it has proved both a more flexible means of allowing individual access to preferred locations than bureaucratic public housing mechanisms, and a way for home-owners to accumulate capital, thereby enhancing life chances. In the housing market as in

3

other markets, autonomous individuals and individual households can make choices under constraints of resource scarcity within an impersonal system relatively free of ascriptive discriminatory elements.

One of the interesting general features of the current liberal revival is the emergence of a post-Marxist form of democratic liberalism, with origins distinct from the older classical liberal schools. This post-Marxist position, more evident in sociology than economics or history, appears to have learnt from both the strengths and weaknesses of the Marxist tradition, such that its post-Marxism cannot be regarded as some simplistic conversion to unreconstructed liberalism. In other words, Marxist-influenced alertness to problems of private capitalist power or of the use of liberal rhetoric to justify illiberal practices are blended with a growing post-Marxist respect for 'democracy', 'the individual', and 'the market-place'. Democracy is seen as an unambiguous good, the very foundation of effective citizenship, not something to be tolerated at best as the terrain for 'reformism', pending some fundamental social change. The individual and individual household meanwhile are seen as a basic unit of social action. Individual freedom, whether from ascriptive discrimination or bureaucratic domination, is a major social and political point of reference for mass society. Although 'liberal' freedoms to privacy, private property ownership, and egalitarian citizenship rights do not exhaust current social definitions of freedom, they have turned out remarkably robust, enduring to confound their previous opponents.

One of the interesting questions in the current liberal revival is whether post-Marxist liberal-democratic theory will merge with classical liberalism. Another way of putting this is to ask whether post-Marxist liberal democratic theory, aware of the residual problems facing *both* Marxism *and* liberalism, will be able to find much common ground with classic liberals. One of the major problems of this kind concerns the place of the public sector and public interventionist strategies in a liberal-democratic social order.

The project of a minimalist state may at times be little more than a caricature of the classical position, in the sense that there always was plenty of scope for liberals to approve public initiatives in such areas as foreign policy and defence, public utilities unable to generate adequate private profit potential and social services for those without the resources to operate within private, market-based systems. Public choice theorists also justify public provision where negative private externalities cannot be otherwise offset. In addition, the liberal premium on education as a positional good, for which maximum social access should be encouraged, offers a special justification for optimum and not merely minimum standards of public provision. Even those most committed to current privatization of public services call for relatively modest cuts in the scale of government spending on the whole (for example, from 40 to 35 per cent of GDP in Australia). This reflects not merely major residual public functions within liberal political philosophy, but also an awareness of electoral support for certain services. In other words, the climate of privatization and liberal revival does not signify a wholesale abandonment of the idea of a public sector.

This situation may then make it easier for post-Marxist liberal democrats to find some kind of accommodation with more general liberal traditions, including classical liberalism. One such *rapprochement* is evident in Peter Saunders' courageous essay 'The New Right is half right' in a collection of essays published by Economic and Literary Books under the title *The New Right Enlightenment*.

Saunders' argument is that many instances of public provision of goods and services in Britain have tended to be bureaucratic and inefficient, undermining individual or class autonomy and leaving the population in a greater state of dependency on the administrative apparatus (for instance, housing, education, and medicine). He also points to the hidden history of working-class attempts at private provision through the market-place (such as in medical care) and their conflict with and eventual domination by the state. These data justify the view that the 'New Right' is at least 'Half Right'. The major residual difficulty with the liberalistic version of New Rightism is the existence of large numbers of the population too poor to express their preferences within the market-place and too powerless to influence the democratic polity. Saunders' view is that rectification of these problems would require a massive level of state intervention to redistribute resources in such a way as to redress the balance. Yet this conflicts with the New Right commitment to privatization. Here we find a classic statement of the liberal-democratic dilemma in relation to the unreconstructed liberalism of *laissez-faire* economics.

There may of course be no dilemma here if it can be demonstrated that there exist 'liberal' ways of handling the redistribution required — such as by means of a guaranteed minimum income secured in part through negative income tax benefits to the poor, or through voucher systems of access to private services. It is in this kind of policy area that the possibility of some greater degree of accommodation between classic liberalism and post-Marxist liberal-democratic theory may exist. However, the policy options required to redress other structural imbalances, such as that between the corporate power of big business and the workforce, or even more between big business and consumers, or big business and small business, seem to imply even more draconian inroads into private property rights than those requiring fiscal redistribution through the taxation system. In this sense the scope for *rapprochement* with the New Right may turn out to be rather limited.

One of the most interesting intellectual challenges to the post-Marxist liberal-democratic position is that provided by what might be called the public sector theory of communicative rationality. Drawing on Habermas' theories of moral learning and communicative rationality, and/or feminist theorizing on the conditions for discursive freedom, there is a view extant that sees the core analytical units in liberalism as epistemologically disprivileged forms of possessive individualism. Habermas has argued that inter-personally negotiated models of rational communication oriented to truth, authenticity, and rightness represent a higher form of 'learning' than monologic strategies of individually based purposive or instrumental rationality. This distinction has been taken by some as coterminous with the divisions between public and private domains and hence to divisions between state and civil society. It is but a short step from here to locate communicative rationality within the social programmes of the public sector where communicative inter-personal competence is required — for example, by welfare professionals — and to identify this sector as the locus of the emerging new class (though this latter inference goes beyond Habermas). It only remains, from this point, to universalize the relations engendered in this context within social life generally.

The problem with this challenge is that it does not give sufficient attention to the continuing functioning of those impersonal relations of social co-ordination, such as markets and bureaucracies characteristic of modern society. Markets, as a mode of resource allocation, remain the most intractable problem for collectivist thought since they show no sign of diminishing in importance. The collectivist strategy is to rely on public planning strategies as a means of bringing collective solutions to the privatized networks of possessive individualism that link producers and consumers. What has not been shown as yet is the capacity for large-scale planning organizations to find a democratic manner in which to ascertain human needs and deliver appropriate services. Such mechanisms can at best do little more than provide their own interpretation of such needs, mediated by interest-group pressure from the more powerful clients. This is scarcely a communicatively rational process, and it certainly violates the liberal conception of the integrity of individual knowledge. Beyond the market, it is also unclear as to how far bureaucracies may be democratized with respect to their internal functioning and inter-face with clients. Although it is true that work groups of professionals may well shift to a communicatively rational basis for action, it is not clear where else this model could be applied, and whether it would entirely subordinate the possessive individual model or the conventional bureaucratic line-management model. In this respect, it is not at all clear that communicative rationality is coterminous either with the actually existing public sector or with any recognizable potential public sector. Reviewing this challenge overall, it may be seen, in Weberian terms, as yet one more instance of conflict between an enduring model of formal rationality — that is impersonal, calculative, and yet efficacious and enabling — and the substantive rationality of those committed to a value-position stressing the transcendental importance of participatory decision making through inter-personal consensus. Like all transcendental moral theories, the difficulty here from a liberal viewpoint is the claim to have grounded a substantive ethics in social scientific knowledge of immanent social trends.

WEBER AND LIBERALISM

We can also approach the issue of liberalism in Weber's sociology via a commentary on his methodological presuppositions. It is well known that Weber's methodological perspective was heavily influenced by neo-Kantianism, especially in the work of Windelband, Rickert, and Lask. In this tradition, reality is perceived to be a complex flux of events and processes which can never be reproduced in knowledge. We can only know a slice of reality through the intel-lectual process of concept formation (especially the ideal-type construct). Knowledge is an approximation to the manifold nature of real phenomena. Furthermore, this conceptual apparatus is not simply offered to us as a determinate, coherent mental map of the world. We are inevitably forced to choose between competing intellectual frameworks. These choices are determined by issues of value relevance; our intellectual equipment will inevitably reflect our own values, our political commitments, and the purpose of our research. At the same time, a scientist attempts to maintain value neutrality by exposing his or her own values to dispute, criticism, and empirical evaluation. It is through this uncertain and unreliable process that a sociologist aims at causal adequacy by causal attribution and counterfactual theory (Wagner and Zipprian 1986).

The point about Weber's methodology is that it cannot guarantee truth or validity, because it does not aim at absolute or exhaustive knowledge. It suggests or promises an approximation to reality within certain limits. Furthermore, we cannot as sociologists hope to achieve any knowledge of social laws. History is merely a contingent collection of processes; our knowledge of the future can at best be stated in terms of certain possibilities and probabilities. The sociologist proceeds somewhat like a courtroom judge in the face of contradictory evidence, conflicting advice, and incomplete information. Both sociologist and judge are forced to make reasonable guesses and to justify their conclusions by reference to moral traditions, concepts of individual responsibility, and legal precedent.

Weber's methodological stance was thus far removed from the positivism of Comte and Spencer, and from the historical materialism of Marx and Engels. Rather than searching for social laws and moral conviction, Weber offers us a realistic statement of the limitations of social scientific knowledge. Furthermore, his attempt to maintain a division between factual knowledge and moral evaluation (between 'is' and 'ought') removed his formal sociology from the world of political campaigns and moral debate. Of course, he thought that sociology might be relevant to politics, but he was convinced that ultimately a vocation in politics was an alternative to a vocation in science. These methodological assumptions explain much of the intellectual conflict between Marxism and Weberian sociology. Whereas Marxists have regarded historical materialism as a science which, in displaying the underlying logic of history, provides tools of analysis relevant to the working class, Weberian sociology is characteristically anxious about the status of scientific knowledge and reluctant to engage in political guidance of any special group. In Weberian sociological discourse there is no analytical space for a privileged epistemology. While in Weber's Protestant ethic thesis the Calvinistic bourgeois was the carrier of rational values, he was highly ambiguous as to the human value of the capitalist world and western rationality. He admired the heroic values of the Calvinist entrepreneur, but described the world they helped to create as an 'iron cage'.

Weber does not, therefore, provide us with a clear moral message by which we could guide ourselves through social reality. He does not provide us with a clear calling in the world. Whereas Marxism saw the working class (as the bearer of universal reason) as an onto-logically privileged class in capitalism, Weber saw historical change as the unintended effect of endless social processes and contingent circumstances. The difference here is partly explained by the fact that Marxism is a secular version of Hegelian philosophy of history, whereas the principal influences on Weber's world-view came from Kant, Rickert, and Nietzsche. We have suggested that this world-view is a social liberalism which asks us, given the complexity and uncertainty of knowledge, to behave responsibly — that is, as agents with 'personality' who are forced to make choices in conditions of unreliable knowledge.

Weber's neo-Kantian view of knowledge has an interesting relationship to the contemporary debate over 'the condition of knowledge' between J-F. Lyotard and Jürgen Habermas. In the tradition of Hegelian Marxism, Habermas has argued (in *Knowledge and Human Interests* and *The Theory of Communicative Action*) that objective knowledge of social reality is possible. Objective understanding of reality can only emerge out of situations which permit open, endless, and free discourse. The role of critical theory is to expose those features of social life (such as unequal power and economic exploitation) which make communicative competence unlikely and which distort communication (by ideological mystification). Discursive freedom is both the normative standard by which to evaluate social relations and the descriptive statement of how valid truth claims emerge. Within this epistemological tradition of enlightenment, Habermas has become increasingly associated with the defence of the project of modernity as a project of substantive reason.

Against Habermas, Lyotard in *The Postmodern Condition* (1984) has argued (by adopting aspects of Bell's notion of post-industrial society) that contemporary social change has rendered Habermas' world of unfettered, open discourse obsolete. We live in a fragmented world where the establishment of unambiguous truths about a unified reality is not possible. Technological changes (especially information storage and processing), a global consumer culture, the social role of universities, the complexity of knowledge and social differentiation have made the quest for a coherent, unified truth sociologically meaningless. Modern societies are too diverse, too complex, and fragmented to permit the emergence of a legitimate, single, reasonable world-picture. Lyotard argues that Habermas' philosophy has to assume the possibility of a 'noise-free' environment where truth messages would not be disturbed by outside interference or by channels on the wrong frequency. By contrast, Lyotard argues that we live in an age of noise. We have to come to terms with informational complexity and incommensurability of different knowledges.

Lyotard also detects a contradiction in Habermas' position which, although Lyotard does not make the point, bears closely on our view of the possibilities of a modernized version of liberalism. Lyotard claims that there is in fact a disguised but real authoritarian aspect of Habermas' emphasis on discursive consensus as the outcome of free debates. Lyotard sees no reason to assume that any real or lasting consensus is possible or desirable in contemporary society. Why should we seek agreements rather than creating conditions which permit the tolerance of necessary and permanent dissensus? Permanent dispute appears to be a more likely outcome of modern systems of communication and exchange. These problems are in fact the heart of the liberal dilemma: how to cope with illiberal opposition? Lyotard wants to suggest that (at least implicitly) Habermas' model may preclude the noise of dissent behind a monotone quest for discursive agreement over a normative consensus. In short, Lyotard claims that Habermas' modern project is no longer viable or desirable in a post-modern world.

These contemporary debates have been conducted in the context of a contrast between modernism and post-modernism, but they also bear a close relationship to earlier debates between Weber and his contemporaries. Weber was forced to digest a good deal of Nietzsche's message: the security which had been provided by an absolute authority (God) had disappeared, leaving behind a world of endless value conflict, and no new absolute basis for knowledge (the working class, society, or history) could fill the gap which had been opened up by God's death. The result is that we are compelled to live in a world of perspectivism. Weber's epistemological (as much as his political) liberalism was developed to respond to this world of competitive values. Liberalism recognizes diversity and dissent as inevitable features of a social reality without ontologically privileged entities — God, the working class, or universal history. In short, Weber's sociology both points to and anticipates the post-modern condition.

This study of Max Weber's sociology in relation to problems of economy and society should be seen as a direct sequel to an earlier study, namely, *Talcott Parsons on Economy and Society* (Holton and Turner 1986). Our study portrayed Talcott Parsons as the quint-essential sociologist of modernity. This portrayal involved three main exercises. The first defended Parsons' sociology against erroneous and often wilfully misguided criticism. The second demonstrated the empirical relevance, scope, and comprehensive theoretical dynamic of Parsons' work as a whole, rather than focusing on any one single dimension or element. Our final intention was to move beyond exegesis to attempt an application of Parsonian sociology to certain empirical features of contemporary social life. These included the relationships between economy and society, sickness and medical institutions, and value pluralism and social structure.

This study of the work of Max Weber follows a similar trajectory. We do not attempt to provide an over-arching interpretation of Weber's sociology. Such interpretations are in plentiful supply. Readers who wish to find contemporary and sophisticated interpretations of Weber's work should look elsewhere (Hennis 1988; Whimster and Lash 1987). In line with our previous analysis of Parsons, we take a very broad perspective on the work of Weber, looking in particular at his relevance to the analysis of economic relations, the law, religious systems, social class, and social stratification. These themes are linked by a common interest in the robustness of liberalism as an enduring world-view.

In exploring various dimensions of Weber's liberalism we have found it necessary to defend Weber against many artificial and misguided criticisms from Marxism and Marxist sociology. Against the Marxist critique, we seek to show Weber's ongoing relevance to many major issues of contemporary political, economic, and social life. These include the place of the market in modern society, and the possibility of individual moral responsibility in a secularized bureaucratic world. These interests have emerged both from our sense of the exhaustion and collapse of the intellectual and moral credentials of Marxism and state socialism, and from the interesting revival of interest in liberalism and libertarianism.

This study of Weber owes a good deal to our previous work on Parsons. We have found Talcott Parsons' sociology particularly congenial, because of his highly realistic view of contemporary social problems. Parsons did not indulge in any nostalgic, backward-looking analysis of contemporary society. Instead he embraced a moral vision of the possibility of human freedom within the necessary requirements of social order (Alexander 1987). Parsons was not a conservative apologist of American capitalism. Rather, he was committed to the idea of the moral autonomy of the individual. He saw the unrestrained impact of competitive capitalism as a threat not only to a civilized social order, but also to individual moral freedom. It was this notion of freedom he so much cherished and hoped could be defended within a contemporary industrial civilization. It was for this reason that Parsons defended the underlying values of professionalism against the naked economic forces of the market-place.

Although Parsons was often critical of economic arrangements within contemporary capitalism, he did in the 1950s come to see America as the leading illustration of the model of social order which he thought would maximize individual choice within the necessary constraints of communal life. It was the differentiation of the American social system in combination with moral individualistic values and a democratic political process that would maximize the liberal objectives which were either implicit or explicit within his sociology as a whole. Within a broader perspective, while Parsons himself was either secular or liberal in his religious values, Parsons' sociology was broadly compatible with the underlying humanistic values of liberal American Protestantism. This feature of his sociology was evident in his treatment of Christianity itself (1963), but it was also important in his treatment of the human condition in his final return to the problems of the relationship between biological and social systems in *Action Theory and the Human Condition* (Parsons 1978).

The major link between our work on Parsons and the present studies is the continuing interest in liberalism and the moral integrity of the individual in the modern world. In this study of Max Weber we explore a further range of economic, legal, and religious dimensions of liberal thought. These centre on the pervasiveness of the possessive individualism of *Gesellschaftlich* social organization even in the face of an expansion of the state and corporatism. For Weber as for Parsons, the problem was how to secure the integrity of personality and individual action in a secularized world of polytheistic, pluralistic meanings.

In this study, we wish to examine some of the moral and political dimensions of Max Weber's work in order to throw some sociological light on the political and economic problems of our times. This study is, therefore, premised on a certain frustration with any sociological theory which is merely bound to the exegetical study of texts. While George Homans expressed a critical view of Parsons' *The Structure of Social Action* (a view we do not share), we feel some sympathy for Homans' sense of exasperation over sociological textbooks which are 'another book of words about other person's words' (Homans 1984: 323). At the same time, we also intend to avoid the logical trap of pretending to avoid an explicit interpretation of a work while necessarily having to rely on an implicit interpretation of a sociological theory. In short, it is not possible to consider the relevance of Weber without adopting some value position towards Weber's own sociological theories. In our case this value position selects questions of liberal-democratic theory for attention. We will turn first to the problematic relationship between sociology and liberalism. This will be considered by way of a commentary on individualism.

Chapter One

SOCIOLOGY, INDIVIDUALISM, AND LIBERALISM

In very general terms, it is often assumed that sociology is profoundly hostile to individualism and liberalism, tending to collective perspectives or even collectivist responses to social issues. Within the French sociological tradition (connecting together the work of Claude Saint Simon, Auguste Comte, and Emile Durkheim), for example, there is often thought to be a complete opposition to the liberal-individualistic tradition of both classical Kantian philosophy and English economic theory. Indeed, it would not be difficult to find sources to support this notion, notably the attempt by Durkheimian sociology to destroy any individualistic assumptions in sociological theory. This attack on individualism appears to be most prominent in Durkheim's treatise on suicide. Within the German philosophical and sociological tradition, there was also an antipathy to English economic individualism, especially in the work of Karl Marx, who regarded the utilitarian tradition of writers like Bentham and J. S. Mill as merely ideological legitimations of individualistic capitalism. By way of contrast, it is often claimed that Weber's sociology was unambiguously committed to methodological individualism, providing a strong critique of collectivist concepts and the reification of concepts in sociology. The position is, however, seen as very much a minority one.

On closer inspection, it can be argued that in fact the whole tradition of classical sociology, far from being opposed to individualism *per se*, presented a well-established critique of economic utilitarian and hedonistic individualism while supporting an ethical or social notion of individualism. This argument is important because it shows that classical sociology was not necessarily opposed to individualism *tout court*, but merely opposed particular forms of individualism, namely those emanating from social utilitarian psychology

14

and the Manchester economic tradition.

Writers like Durkheim saw the utilitarian and egoistic tradition of Herbert Spencer's sociology as a corrosive element within the social structure. It represented a cultural environment in which suicide was more likely to flourish and in which self-seeking and self-interested actions would be incompatible with more collective or social goals (Abercrombie, Hill, and Turner 1986). In a similar fashion, we find in the philosophical doctrines of J. S. Mill an opposition to all Darwinistic forms of thought which he associated with hedonism, and worse still, with animality; Mill thought that what was essential for both society and the individual was the cultivation of virtue, individual taste, and sentiment (Semmel 1984).

We can detect at least some similarities between Mill's notion of individual perfection and Weber's ideas about the importance of personality. Weber feared that the iron cage of bureaucracy would obliterate individual autonomy, reducing the individual to a mere cog within the machine. Weber's ideas on individual virtue were derived partly from the work of Goethe and partly from the theological tradition represented by writers like Albrecht Ritschl (Ward 1987). For Weber, 'personality' meant the development of an individual plan or project for life, involving the regulation and control of sexual and emotional relations. Personality, therefore, was a calling in life in which the individual directed actions towards the achievement of a coherent project in the world. Finally, in the development of *The Structure of Social Action*, we find Parsons returning to rather similar themes in the idea of the individual autonomy of the agent requiring a certain degree of freedom from constraint and, through socialization, the development of a life project.

Classical sociology was, therefore, not fundamentally opposed to individualism and liberalism. And while classical sociologists might have associated utilitarian individualism with capitalism, they did not see moral individualism as necessarily coterminous with economic individualism or the simple product of an urban industrial society. On the contrary, this notion of moral individualism was derived via Kant from classical, Christian, and humanistic traditions, which were clearly very ancient and historically complex.

While classical sociologists were critical of utilitarian individualism, they saw the main threat to the moral coherence of the individual in terms of either bureaucratic rationalization, or socialist regulation, or from the blind opinion of democratic institutions. One of the most influential books of the nineteenth century was Alexis de Tocqueville's *Democracy in America*. We know that this work had a profound influence on Nietzsche and upon J. S. Mill, both of whom saw the threat of democracy in terms of the destruction of cultivated belief. For example, J. S. Mill wrote that

> M. de Tocqueville's fears, however, are not so much for the security and the ordinary worldly interests of individuals, as for the moral dignity and progressiveness of the race. It is a tyranny exercised over opinions, more than over persons, which he is apprehensive of. He dreads lest all individuality of character, and independence of thought and sentiment, should be prostrated over the despotic yoke of public opinion.

> (Mill 1977: 81)

We know that Weber was also profoundly ambivalent about the desirability of unregulated and undirected democracy. For Weber, both democracy and socialism would tend to increase the surveillance of populations through centralized bureaucratic mechanisms, precluding or limiting the possibility for moral autonomy and individuality. Socialism would be merely an extension of the bureaucratic tendencies within organized capitalism, merely another step in the great unfolding of rationality. Weber supported the notion of plebiscitarian democracy in which the ruled would occasionally give some support or legitimacy to leadership which would, in fact, be relatively autonomous and free from daily bureaucratic regulations (Mommsen 1987). Weber feared not only unregulated dominance by so-called democratic opinion, but also the domination of professional politicians who lacked any moral calling, and therefore he held out as the best hope a form of leadership democracy within a party machine. Weber's views on the problems of democracy have, of course, been closely associated with the work of Robert Michels, who developed the idea of the iron law of oligarchy as a necessary tendency within bureaucratic democracy which would result in the dominance of the party (Bentham 1977).

To summarize some aspects of the political sociology of classical sociology, we can argue that it was based upon a well-established criticism of utilitarian, egoistic individualism, while supporting a form of moral or institutional individualism guided by ethical norms. Second, the classical sociological tradition of Durkheim, Pareto, Simmel, and Weber was sceptical about the claims of socialism to be an alternative system to capitalism. Especially in the writings of Weber, we find the idea that socialism would be merely an extension, and indeed, application of the underlying principles of rationalization which would exclude and eventually destroy any notion of personal autonomy. While there was this critique of the collectivist version of socialism, there was also an anxiety about the growth of democratic egalitarianism as a system which would further destroy and undermine the individualism of the private citizen. Mill, in particular, thought of this unguided form of democracy as ushering in a period of 'Chinese stationariness'.

SOCIOLOGY AS 'BOURGEOIS SCIENCE'?

In contrast to the view of sociology as hostile to individualism and liberalism, there is an alternative viewpoint which links sociology to bourgeois social science. A version of this view surfaced in the 1960s and 1970s when British sociology and, more broadly speaking, social philosophy was profoundly influenced by French Marxist structuralism, especially by the work of Louis Althusser and Nicos Poulantzas. They attempted to show that Marxism was a science in contrast to sociology, psychology, and other social science disciplines. The latter were dismissed as individualistic and subjectivist. Because of sociology's often negative relationship to socialism, it was often possible to characterize sociology as a bourgeois science, because its principal concepts were said to reflect or to legitimize some of the underlying structures of the capitalist market-place.

This type of critique was also found in the famous debate between Ralph Miliband and Nicos Poulantzas. Here political sociology was criticized by structuralist Marxism as methodologically individualistic and epistemologically naïve because sociology merely accepted the everyday, taken-for-granted notions of social actors, rather than transforming these notions into the real concepts of science (Urry and Wakeford 1973). Fortunately, the contemporary view of the relationship between Marxism and sociology is a good deal more sophisticated and scholarly. There are now rather fewer polemics seeking to erect a divide between Marxism and sociology, and far greater common ground between various theoretical traditions. There is, for example, a consensus (however flimsy) that a certain parallel exists between Weber's views on rationalization and Marx's view of alienation, that there is much common ground between Marx and Weber in the conceptualization of capitalism, that Weber's view of social classes is not entirely incompatible with Marx's analysis of economic classes, that Weber's emphasis on power and conflict is an important addition to or complementary with Marx's idea of economic domination, and that their views of the progressive and revolutionary character of capitalism were, in fact, very similar. These parallels are significant even if a number of very profound differences separate Weber and Marx, particularly in terms of political prognosis, epistemology, and theoretical strategy.

Although orthodox Marxist theories are far less influential in the 1980s than they were in previous decades, the Marxist criticism of liberalism and sociology as ideological disguises for bourgeois interests probably still colours critical attitudes towards the liberal tradition. We would like to pick out three common criticisms of liberalism which owe much to Marxist writing but which have a wider currency in social and political thought.

The first criticism concerns the character of the individual within liberalism. For socialist social philosophy, the liberal concept of the individual is often thought to be artificial and unsociological by taking the autonomy and voluntarism of individual life either for granted or as excluding social relations. Collectivist thought criticizes liberalism for describing the individual in terms of an isolated Robinson Crusoe figure, somehow free from social relations and ahistorical in character. In C. B. Macpherson's famous study of the theory of possessive individualism (1962), it was argued that the liberal individualistic tradition of Hobbes and Locke was a possessive tradition in which the genuine individual was the property-owning individual. This line of criticism suggests that the liberal individual can only exist on the basis of private property, yet the social nature of private property remains disguised and unanalysed within the liberal philosophical tradition. Possessive individualism excludes those members of society who lack property, and thus may be said to lack the self-proprietorship necessary for individuality, and the other liberal values of individual responsibility and rationality.

The second criticism is that liberalism is merely an ideology of a bourgeois property-owning class which, through the doctrine of individual political rights, in fact legitimizes its collective class rule within the democratic system. Democracy is held to be a sham in western capitalism because the ritualized forms of opinion-formation and attitude testing via the mechanism of the vote obscure and block

18

opinion, rather than allowing opposition groups to shape the direction of government policies. Once again, there is the argument that real power lies in the hands of property owners and that formal liberal democratic rights act either as a mystification or as a safety valve rather than as a means of genuine opinion-formation and regulation of government by democratic processes. Liberal democracy is held to be a particularly suitable ideology for capitalism because it appears to allow for individual rights while, in reality, legitimizing indirectly the power of owners of property. In short, 'liberal democracy is the political form most compatible with the market place of industrial capitalism' (Hearn 1985: 130).

A third and related criticism of the traditional liberal political philosophy is that liberalism acts as a legitimation of ongoing inequality and blocks the development of superior or, at least, more desirable collectivist values such as equality and solidarity. Liberalism is often associated with the doctrine of opportunity (in particular the notion of equality of opportunity which allows people to compete in the market-place). Critics argue that this very competition favours the continuation of individual inequalities, because individuals entering the market-place already bring with them various assets which are both cultural and material. Against the idea of individual rights, socialist or various forms of humanistic philosophy tend to emphasize the equality of human beings *qua* human beings, or argue in favour of equality of outcome as opposed to equality of opportunity. Liberalism is seen to be the ideology of competitive capitalism, permitting the continuity of inequality. Doctrines about the importance of equality of outcome tend to be associated with various forms of socialism, but especially with centralized socialism, since the achievement of equality of outcome would require massive state intervention to regulate the market, education, and family life.

We accept that these arguments contain some powerful criticisms of elements of the liberal tradition. We do not advocate a return to some mythical unreconstructed liberalism on the model of Hayek. None the less, we wish to argue that the criticisms outlined here are not fatal objections to the broad traditions of liberalism as these have developed in the last two hundred years. While there may be other criticisms of liberalism, we will take these three to be characteristic of the core objection to liberalism as a political and philosophical tradition.

With regard to the first argument that liberalism adopts an artificial view of the individual, necessarily promoting the notion of the asocial individual, we would suggest that this does not apply to many significant strands of liberal thought. We have already seen that liberal writers within the classical sociological tradition objected strongly to the legitimacy or primacy of utilitarian, egoistic, and hedonistic individualism. On the contrary, they advanced the notion of a social individual, equipped with a social consciousness whose actions are oriented to other actors and towards moral (and therefore collective) goals and objects. The idea that the actions of the individual could or should be entirely monological without restraint or hindrance, or that the individual in some way preceded society may well be found in Locke, but it was alien to sociological liberalism as it developed in the nineteenth and twentieth centuries. Neither classical sociology nor liberalism required, theoretically, a doctrine of the isolated, egoistic, pre-social individual. On the contrary, it was largely through the further development of liberal traditions through Weber, Durkheim, and Parsons, that a more developed theoretical account has emerged of how individuals are socialized into the role of individual. Where Durkheim and especially Parsons went beyond Weber was in elaborating more clearly the inter-personal context of individual action.

Many critics of liberalism continue to rehearse Marx's critique of the asocial utilitarian thoughts of the 1840s and 1850s as if it was the last word on the liberal analysis of the individual. Marx, however, failed to discriminate between different varieties of liberalism, branding them all with the same brush. For example, Marx frequently criticized writers like J. S. Mill for adhering to egoistic individualism and for believing that the individual within capitalism in a way defined the characteristics of humanity as a whole. We know, however, from Mill's own autobiography that he rejected this whole position outright, arguing against the Benthamite tradition by insisting upon the social training of the individual into virtue and rejecting the Darwinistic idea of the survival of the fittest through an evolutionary struggle. Kant and the neo-Kantian tradition had a strong influence on sociology, leading sociologists like Weber to put a particular emphasis on the notion of personality which was not an asocial or pre-social conception. To argue for the existence of individual rights or for certain mechanisms to protect the individual against bureaucratic or state regulation is not *ipso facto* to take up an asocial conception of the individual.

One of the main problems with this critique is its elevation of the asymmetrical bargaining power of capital and labour within the market-place to the status of the over-arching power relation in society. The effect was both to diminish awareness of countervailing forms of bargaining power by labour, and to diminish the broader cultural and political economy of the mass of the population. While not denying the endemic existence of poverty and unemployment, this line of analysis took as abstract and asocial, types of individual autonomy, such as political citizenship rights or consumer choice that had an increasing, though often precarious and sometimes contested, *reality* for the majority of the population. Problems like 'commodity fetishism' or 'reification' were simply assumed on a priori theoretical grounds rather than demonstrated in careful empirical and historical research. One reason for the revival of interest in liberalism is that it highlights the cultural authenticity of individual autonomy and responsibility in modern culture.

With respect to the second range of criticism of the liberal tradition, it is clear that Locke and the nineteenth-century liberals held to a rather limited conception of democracy. The view of citizenship within this early liberal tradition was restricted to some notions of minimal legal protection and minimal political involvement. However, this conception of democracy was developed in a society in which the mass of the population had very limited literacy and a very elementary educational attainment. Mill's fears can be explained on the grounds that he held that democracy could only work in a society with a very extensive educational tradition. While in this respect Mill adhered to a somewhat limited conception of democracy, it is possible to present his argument in a more positive form, namely that democracy depends upon an educated public and that democratic freedoms can only operate in a society in which there is freedom of enquiry, communication, and expression. In turn, the existence of democratic publics requires a lively and democratic educational tradition capable of growth and development. There is nothing, as it were, indigenous to the liberal tradition which precludes radical democratization.

It is therefore possible to reformulate the liberal tradition via the work of T. H. Marshall (1977) to note that the twentieth century has seen at least potentially a major expansion of citizenship rights from the legal and the political through the social to the economic. An expansion of liberal citizenship through democratization would be perfectly compatible with the Mill tradition, provided that there were educational and welfare developments to accompany purely political advances. In other words, the liberal vision of individual autonomy is seen as resting upon political, legislative, and legal guarantee, underwritten by state power.

At the same time, both Mill and Max Weber feared that the expansion of democracy was simply one feature of a growing rationalization of society which would bring about a levelling of individual opinion and belief, reducing a democratic public to a collection of manipulated beliefs. For Weber, the expansion of democracy would be accompanied by an expansion of bureaucratic surveillance and control.

Of course, fear of mass society is not a fear exclusively confined to liberalism. The Frankfurt School and the critical theorists were also alarmed by the possibilities of manipulation of mass opinion through the media, and regarded this feature of modern politics as particularly threatening to a tradition of critical public debate. We realize, of course, that this is a provocative argument, given the fact that writers like Herbert Marcuse saw liberalism as the theory of industrial capitalism in which the individual person as the private entrepreneur is the representative of capitalism (Kellner 1984). The major weakness of this argument is the assumption of a necessary connection between liberalism and capitalism. It no longer appears to be the case that liberalism is the most suitable form for capitalism in its political arena, or that liberalism has anything necessarily to do with capitalism. Capitalism can flourish within a variety of cultural, ideological, and political systems. There is also an argument that capitalism might be better suited by more authoritarian, regimented, and bureaucratic systems of belief (Abercrombie, Hill, and Turner 1986). Liberalism can equally be seen as setting limits to capitalist monopoly power, or as an enabling factor in the historic transition to capitalism in western Europe.

The Marxist critique of liberalism as an ideological defence of capitalism no longer appears particularly forceful, in the absence of any significant development of socialism within the western industrial capitalist societies and electoral support for policies of home ownership and mass shareholding. On the contrary, the liberal defence of individual rights (as Weber anticipated) has become more important rather than less important with the development of corporatism in the west and growth of highly centralized bureaucratic forms of state socialism in east European societies. The problem of individual rights is not bounded by bourgeois conceptions of absolute private property rights within the economy, and guaranteed by law. It is far more than this. Its status is, rather, that of a basic issue within all human societies as such. The problem of how to achieve a just balance between private and public rights is generic and has clearly not been demolished by the advance of various forms of socialism (or corporatism) within contemporary societies. There is a very important role for public law in protecting individuals as citizens, customers, consumers, and parents (Hirst 1986). It is very easy to demonstrate that in democratic capitalism the rights of individuals are often very fragile and superficial, but this is not an argument against individual rights, only an argument against the inadequacy of their provision and defence. The final criticism of liberalism which we consider is the assertion of a higher value for equality as against personal freedoms. It is clear, again following the arguments of T. H. Marshall on citizenship, that there is a tension between the expansion of citizenship rights and the continuity of inequality in capitalist society. However, to argue that there is a tension between citizenship and capitalism is not to suggest that improvements in citizenship rights are impossible within capitalist society; for example, in the post-war period there was a very significant improvement in social and welfare rights under various policies of post-war reconstruction. Although the consequences of these changes may have been only relative, Marxists often go to extreme lengths to suggest that no changes are really significant within a capitalist framework.

These arguments usually fly in the face of evidence of popular support or consent for extended social and welfare rights. They also assume rather than demonstrate the possibility of constraint-free social orders. They often lead to a political fatalism, which rules out the possibility of successful social struggles in the interests of social rights. The problem with equality in any society is the potential conflict between equality and personal freedoms, especially where a social movement or a government espouses the aim of equality of outcome. To guarantee equality of condition or equality of outcome requires extensive political intervention, which may involve the increasing surveillance and subordination of populations to government regulation. We would not argue that there is an inevitable contradiction or opposition between freedom and equality, but there are certainly tensions and contradictions between these two social objectives, tensions which appear endemic to the human condition in a secularized, differentiated world.

Part of the problem with the Marxist or any radical critique of capitalism is the tendency to conflate and confuse the market with the capitalist mode of production. Indeed, one might say that the marketplace remains the most inadequately analysed institution in Marxist and radical thought. Historically, empirically, and theoretically, there are good reasons for distinguishing between the market and the capitalist economic system. Whether or not markets are universal, they have clearly played a massive role in world history, both in pre-capitalist societies and in more recent state socialist societies.

A number of writers, including Marx himself and Weber, have recognized that the market may have a radical and progressive role to play in human societies. For example, in market exchange relations it is typically the case that the particularistic characteristics of social agents become completely irrelevant, since trading relations are typically indifferent to the peculiar characteristics of individuals. This universalistic thrust to the development of market relations was, for example, recognized by Lucian Goldmann in *The Philosophy of the Enlightenment* (1973). For Goldmann, as for Marx and Weber, the extension of exchange relationships generates universalistic, egalitarian, and individualistic norms, because exchange relations flourish best where there are no limitations placed upon trade by questions of religion, race, or creed. The same argument was developed by Georg Simmel in *The Philosophy of Money* (1978).

Simmel had argued that the growth of abstract trading relations corresponded to the growth of institutionalized trust, and that the greater the extent of abstract exchange, the greater the extent of universalistic, neutral, social relationships.

We would wish to distinguish capitalism, as a system of production through the private ownership of the means of production, from the notion of the market, that is any social arena within which commodities are exchanged. Recent sociology has almost completely ignored the positive case for the market as a mode of co-ordinating in a universalistic and impersonal manner the detailed and complex wants, needs, and aspirations of individuals and households. Indeed, one might speak of a profound intellectual agoraphobia. While we do not subscribe to a teleological view of history as the progressive unfolding of the market, we do see its possessing an evolutionary advantage in terms of the capacity to co-ordinate individual wants with resources in a non-ascriptive, relatively non-coercive manner. While markets are never self-subsistent, it is arguable that many alleged market failures have more to do with monopoly or political constraints on individual autonomy than with the market principle as such. The problem is more that of universalizing access to market relations rather than abolishing markets in favour of some better allocative principle.

We would argue that it is wrong to assume that liberalism is a defence of capitalism, since there is nothing in liberal theory which necessarily requires inequalities of property ownership or necessarily a capitalist mode of production, but liberalism may have clear affinities with the existence of market-places, in so far as liberalism advocates universalistic individualism. In this study of Weber, we frequently focus upon his view of the historical importance of the emergence of open, associational relations as opposed to closed, communal ones. Weber was, if ambiguously, fascinated by the progressive but threatening potential of associational open relations as an effect of the emergence of markets as dominating features of modern society.

It is clear that in the contemporary world the rhetoric of liberalism and individualism is frequently used as ideological defence for quite reactionary political movements and nationalistic, reactionary social systems. Appeals to the rights of the individual can often mask quite cynical attempts to redistribute the common good in inegalitarian directions (Raskin 1986). An attempt to defend liberalism through a study of Weber's sociology does not, however, commit us either implicitly or explicitly to a neo-conservative or reactionary position. On the contrary, arguments in favour of liberalism are radical in relationship to both the bureaucratic centralism of state socialist societies and the authoritarianism and inequalities of the capitalist world. While Weber's form of liberalism appears particularly relevant both as a critique of bureaucratic socialism and of right-wing conservatism which, in our view, is anti-individualistic, we also believe that there is an important note of realism in Weber's evaluation of the inevitability of social stratification in societies, the permanence of conflict over values and of political violence, and, finally, the limitations of economic systems in providing for rising expectations and social needs.

MELANCHOLY, PESSIMISM, AND REALISM IN SOCIOLOGY

We may briefly outline three basic requirements which we believe are

25

essential to any modern moral-political orientation within sociology. The first is a necessary defence of the social individual against both the deadening regulation of bureaucratic systems within both state socialist and capitalist society, and against the more violent intrusion on social rights by authoritarian political systems of any particular political hue. We realize that ultimately the presuppositions of any sociological theory can never be fully justified, but we feel that the status of the moral individual within sociological theory has been eroded by an often naïve commitment to some intangible notion of absolute egalitarianism. We see such a defence of the social individual as both compatible with (indeed, the basis of) Parsons' action-system theory on the one hand and Weber's interpretive sociology of meaningful action on the other. Any sociological theory which undermines this basic notion of voluntaristic agency can scarcely count as a sociological theory at all. This emphasis on the individual, therefore, has both theoretical and moral connotations.

Second, we believe that any political-theoretical position within contemporary sociology has to be realistic as opposed to Utopian or nostalgic. We took great pains to criticize nostalgic theories of sociology in our earlier publication on Parsons, where we welcomed his open attitude towards both the problems and promises of modern society. To emphasize 'realism' of this kind is not to deny the social function of Utopian thought as a fertile source of social innovation, projecting alternative possibilities of social organization, not rooted in observable social trends. The sociological problem with Utopianism is its excessively transcendental standards of judgement. These tend to protect the core propositions of the Utopian viewpoint, against observable social trends which point in very different directions to those desired. To give one example, some versions of Marxist critical theory, equipped with a Utopian social ontology of the community of free producers, are forced to maintain a more or less permanent sense of the final crisis of capitalism (or late capitalism) to protect their transcendental assumptions against the disconcerting evidence of lack of mass resistance to capitalist social relations. It is equally possible of course to find transcendental liberal Utopias, such as Hayek's theory of spontaneous order in which the politics of legislative enactment is subdued before the mysterious wisdom of the common law (Hayek 1973–9). Hayek's liberalism, none the less, has its liberal critics, including those who find it possible to conceive of a theory of social order which rests on democratic consent expressed through the political process (Vaughan 1984).

By realistic, we mean that any sociological theory worthy of the name has to come to terms with the problems facing human agency in terms of dilemmas of how to balance competing ends.

The first type of dilemma is that posed by the problem of social order in a *Gesellschaftlich* society of autonomous individuals with heterogeneous ends. Sociological theories which seek to resolve this dilemma by invoking a new *Gemeinschaft* around notions of a general will or organic relationship between politicians and/or bureaucrats and/or intellectuals and the people, are forced to deny the heterogeneity of ends often in the name of some spurious communitarian ontology of the human condition.

A second type of dilemma is that posed by the conflict between competence and technical efficiency on the one hand, and equality of outcome on the other. The dilemma exists because excessive egalitarian measures can undermine competence and diminish the social surplus of resources available for distribution (witness the Chinese Cultural Revolution as an extreme example), while over-protective measures to privilege the competent and efficient produce particularistic sectional advantages which violate principles of universalism and social justice.

Not only is it the case that there is empirically no known society in history which achieved equality between its members, but there are also very strong theoretical arguments for believing that all human social systems must be inegalitarian, in the sense of being stratified. This realistic recognition of the social necessity of inequality is evident not only within structural functionalist theory of stratification, but also in Weber, and in reinterpretations of Marxism and structuralism in the work of writers like Pierre Bourdieu on distinction (1984).

Of course, to accept the inevitability of inequality is not to provide a moral justification for inequality or to commit the sociologist to a programme necessarily supporting inequality. Indeed, there are very strong arguments from the position of moral individualism to argue for equality of treatment of individuals and an enhancement of the conditions of equality in modern society through social reformism. But it is to downplay any Utopian or eschatological commitment to egalitarianism.

This argument leads us into our third requirement, which is for a theory of economic action and economic growth within sociology.

While many Marxist and radical positions within and outside sociology are committed to some doctrine of economic redistribution through taxation methods, nationalization of enterprises, or welfare benefits, these theories often fail to provide the supporting arguments which will demonstrate how economic growth can take place to provide a surplus which can then be redistributed. In this sense, much of contemporary sociology is frankly anti-business (Marsland 1987).

By contrast, classical economics and classical sociology saw the genesis of economic surplus in some form of pain or expenditure of energy. For Marx, the roots of economic accumulation lay in the iron heel of economic deprivation; for Weber, it lay in the life-denying doctrines of puritanism; for Schumpeter, it lay in the strenuous but creative activities of the entrepreneur. Unfortunately, most contemporary theories of social equality within sociology have no account of where the economic resources for growth will come from (other than in some theory of the redistribution of existing wealth or in terms of the reorganization of patterns of ownership).

The issues of social and economic reform also have to be set within an analysis of the location of the national economy within the global system of economic relations and political-economic inequalities. Since we currently live in a global economic recession which cannot be resolved without new international arrangements between Germany, Japan, and the United States, it is difficult to see how, in the short term, any rapid secular economic expansion can be sustained and hence where the resources for significant new forms of public redistribution will come from. Even with economic recovery, however, there will still remain the underlying economic problem of a finite scarcity of resources. In short, any contemporary defence of individual rights will have to be set within the realistic assumptions of inequality as a continuing feature of human society and of scarcity of economic resources as a more or less permanent state of affairs.

We believe that Weber's interpretive sociology provides some of the theoretical conditions which are necessary for meeting these three requirements. It is clear that Weber's anthropological philosophy of human nature provides a distinctive view of personality and a critical stance against bureaucratization and state management. However, Weber was also sceptical of the prospects of democracy without certain conditions and limitations on mass regulation of political leadership. Weber sought the socio-economic conditions which would make autonomous personality possible and protect personality in the future. It was for this reason that he was particularly realistic about political and economic issues. Weber once asked his colleagues what was the point of social and economic reforms when the Cossacks are coming. Weber, therefore, felt that in order to maintain standards of social welfare, democracy, and personal rights, it was necessary to secure one's boundaries.

Boundaries can be interpreted here in the widest metaphorical sense. Weber's liberalism sought secure boundaries both in the sense of individual rights and associational forms to secure the autonomous individual and geo-political boundaries to secure western liberalism from illiberal threats from the east. We would argue that a similar realism has to be adopted with respect to the possibilities of economic growth, redistribution and egalitarianism, and world peace, but there are further moral reasons for wanting to defend individualism against bureaucracy.

Although we feel that Weber's general sociology provides some very useful guidelines in this area, we would not wish to adopt his largely pessimistic assessment of the possibilities of social change. Weber once said that what lies in front of us is a polar night of icy darkness. This reflects very much Weber's German legacy of nostalgic pain which he shared with writers like Simmel and Tönnies. While, to quote Keynes, we are all dead in the long run, there is, we feel, plenty of scope in the short term for social change for egalitarian social reform for a more liberal international order and for the defence of the moral individual. In this sense the future is 'open' and the changing trajectory of relations between the market, the state, and the private household remains a matter for further empirical research. The research agenda that we propose in the following chapters is not formed exclusively within liberal parameters. It does, however, take many of its reference points from liberal and libertarian traditions, including the particular legacy of Weber.

Chapter Two

MAX WEBER, AUSTRIAN ECONOMICS, AND THE NEW RIGHT

The relationship between Max Weber's sociology and the development of economic theory has received a rather uneven and episodic treatment in the literature. Best known perhaps are Weber's comments on the late nineteenth-century *Methodenstreit* in German economics and history. These debates provided many of the reference points for his early work on the epistemology and methodology of the social sciences (Weber 1949a, 1949b, 1975). Another familiar focus is the substantive affinity between Weber's work on purposive rationality, the Protestant ethic, and the spirit of capitalism, on the one hand, and neo-classical marginal utility theory, on the other. For Weber, the 'this worldly' Quaker ascetics of the seventeenth century represented a 'living law of marginal utility' (Weber 1930: 277).

Such areas of convergence between Weber and neo-classical economic theory stem in part from the shared legacy of moral and economic liberalism. Weber's liberalism is evident not only in his neo-Kantian epistemology, and in the normative discussion of the emergence of the idea of the personal calling within European Protestantism, but also in his comments on the relations between state and society. Here may be found highly critical analyses of the efficacy and feasibility of centralized public planning, whether in the form of modern socialist nationalization (Weber 1971: 191–219) or of the statist empires of the ancient world (Weber 1976: 389–411). Weber's economic liberalism is, however, far from being an apology for unregulated market capitalism (Mommsen 1985). Although influenced by marginalist economics in constructing his ideal-type of purposive rationality, he remained committed, as is again well known, to the broader perspective of 'social economics'. This emphasized the institutional power configurations and distributional inequalities of the market economies, inequalities which tended to generate conflict.

Part of the problem of locating Weber's relationship with economic theory arises from the difficulty of balancing his anti-statist, and in many respects anti-socialist, liberalism, with his equally critical stance towards instrumentalized utilitarian reason. The search for such a balance has perhaps become unnecessarily protracted as a result of the adversary idiom of Weber interpretation. In this discourse, rival uni-dimensional interpretations stand opposed. The conflict between those who regard Weber as a radical critic of capitalism, linking Marx with Frankfurt School critical theory, and those who interpret Weber as a bourgeois or neo-liberal ideologist of capitalism, is certainly unresolvable in these simplistic terms.

Another unsatisfactory feature of existing commentaries that has received less comment is the neglect of Weber's impact on subsequent generations of economists. Since sociological commentators often write as if the development of sociological thought takes place within hermetically sealed disciplinary parameters, it is not perhaps surprising that we know far more of the impact of Weber's work on theorists like Schutz, Parsons, and Habermas than of its salience for modern economic theory in general and the modern Austrian and libertarian traditions in particular. This disciplinary tunnel vision is especially ironic in view of the close involvement of both Parsons (1931, 1932, 1934a, 1934b, 1935) and Schutz (1943, 1954, 1967a) with problems of economic theory, an involvement which has generally been neglected (but see Holton (in Holton and Turner 1986) on Parsons, and Prendergast 1986 on Schutz).

The neglect of Weber's impact on economics may also be a product of the tendency of interpreters to look backward ritualistically to the nineteenth-century *Methodenstreit* and the neo-Kantian revival. A major cost incurred in this concern with forebears is the failure to relate Weber's work, and the further debates it encouraged within the Austrian School and libertarian economics, to late twentieth-century debates centring on the challenge of the New Right to socialist planning and the welfare state.

The contemporary social and political revival of a liberal or neo-liberal world-view, linked, whether contingently or necessarily to the movement known as the New Right (Levitas 1986), provides one important reason for a re-evaluation of Weber's economic sociology. Mommsen (1985) is one of the few commentators to have picked up the issue of Weber's anticipation of the liberalism of von Hayek and Arendt, though he does not explore this problem in any great detail.

The unexpected robustness and staying power of the model of purposive rationality in liberal economics, libertarian moral philosophy, and rational choice theory has certainly to be better understood. Virtually none of the sociological theories of post-war corporatism and the welfare state predicted this development. While the idea of a 'free' market operated by sovereign individuals may be largely illusory in an epoch of private and public bureaucratic and technocratic domination, it is equally the case that the decline of 'civil and familial-privatism' and of 'possessive individualism', predicted by Habermas (1976: 75–92), has not eventuated. Even though the two variants of the liberal theory of social order — namely, social contract theory and the spontaneous theory of the 'hidden hand' — have proved inadequate as a means of comprehending corporatist power relations between organized interest groups, the liberal model of purposive rationality by sovereign individuals has endured to confound its more simplistic critics.

In this context, it is worth asking if there exist elements of a more adequate theory of social order, and of relations between economy and society within the liberal heritage. Although Weber has been portrayed, and saw himself, as a liberal in despair in relation to the onward march of rationalization and disenchantment, his economic sociology remains an important reference point in any contemporary re-evaluation of both the robustness and residual problems inherent in this heritage.

A second, more technical reason, for exploring Weber's relationship with economic thought arises from the re-emergence of a new *Methodenstreit* in contemporary social science. Developments such as game theory, and the application of rational choice theory to both market and non-market phenomena have raised a set of epistemological and methodological problems familiar to Weber and his German and Austrian contemporaries. What is at stake here is the role of concept formation and the place of rationality assumptions within the social sciences.

When rational choice theories are applied in non-market contexts, are we to suppose that the social actors and institutions involved actually operate empirically according to the assumptions and means–ends procedures specified? Or are these constructs merely heuristic, in which case we must ask which of the components in the logic of rational choice explanation are empirically testable, which are formal assumptions, and what properties are being claimed for such formal elements? Just as the marginalists and historical economists clashed in the late nineteenth century over the appropriateness of deductive and inductive strategies of explanation, so we now find debates over the legitimacy of applying axiomatic rational choice assumptions to such extra-economic issues as family life and crime (Becker 1976; Stigler and Becker 1977). The particular interest of game theory in this context is its ostensible extension of rational choice theory from individualistic Robinson Crusoe situations to n-person interactions between individuals who must take each others' purposes into account in developing their own purposes (Nozick 1977). It remains important within this new extended *Methodenstreit* to establish whether Weber's clarification of the heuristic character of the ideal-type construct is similarly appropriate to the operations of the rational choice in economic thought, and to the wider problem of theorizing general relations between economy and society.

All these operations are, of course, necessary components in any effective specification of the intellectual terrain upon which rational choice theory and economic liberalism might be evaluated. Are the 'substantive' economic anthropologists of the Polanyi School (Polanyi 1977) on target in criticizing economic thought for its abstract and ahistorical formalism? Or is abstract formalism a necessary component in any social theory? To the extent that this is so, it also becomes appropriate to offer a logical evaluation of economic formalism in general, and rational choice axioms in particular. On this terrain it is important to ask whether such meta-theoretical presuppositions are incoherent or incomplete, and whether a more adequate alternative to the generic methodological individualistic postulates of economic theory is available.

This latter strategy — which goes some way beyond Weber's own epistemological and methodological position — offers the prospect of a theoretical dialogue between sociology and liberal economics. The most successful attempt to advance this strategy to date has been articulated by Parsons and Smelser in their study *Economy and Society*, published in 1956 (Parsons and Smelser 1956). It was, however, advanced on the basis of a formal theory of action-systems rather than within traditions of methodological individualism. While Weber rejected the 'system' metaphor, his work served as an important reference point in the project of Parsons and Smelser. There is clearly some interest therefore in tracing why Weber did not develop his critical engagement with marginalist economists in this kind of synthetic or unified direction.

WEBER AND AUSTRIAN NEO-CLASSICAL ECONOMICS

Weber's intellectual and personal connections with the economists and historians of his day are relatively well known. These contacts and sympathies spanned both sides of the *Methodenstreit*, which should not be regarded as an absolute divide, in spite of the polemical heat generated (Hutchinson 1973). Weber's early methodological essays from the period 1897 to 1905 were in any case written some time after the onset of the debates over method. He was certainly critical of a number of elements in both the deductive theoretical method espoused by Carl Menger, originator of Austrian neo-classical economics, and of the inductivism of the historical economists led by Gustav Schmoller. Weber none the less kept open a wide-ranging set of intellectual exchanges among historians and economists of all viewpoints.

Interesting debates have taken place as to whether the 'historical' element in Weber's work declined over time in favour of abstract general theory (Antoni 1959; Rex 1971; Mommsen 1974). Whether any such change amounted to more than a shift of emphasis is, however, doubtful. It would certainly be unwarranted to subdue altogether Weber's abiding interest in the historical specificity of occidental rationalism, in any appreciation of his later work. At the same time there are good grounds for emphasizing the growing importance of his contacts with the Austrian neo-classicists in his later theoretical projects — notably the *Outlines of Social Economics* (*Grundriss der Sozialökonomik*).

Two important members of the Austrian School — Frederick von Wiese and the young Joseph Schumpeter — were invited to contribute to the outlines series, and it appears that Weber regarded their participation as quite crucial to the launching of the enterprise. Von Wiese, a student of Menger, is notable both for his development of the notion of opportunity cost — a central element in rational choice theory — and as a 'social economist' with an interest in the organizational power framework surrounding market exchange. This interest is reflected in *Sozial Ökonomiks Wirtschaft (Theorie des Gesellschaftlichen)*, which von Wiese contributed to Weber's series (von Wiese 1927).

Schumpeter's contribution, *Economic Doctrine and Method* (1954), represents an early version of his later and unfinished *magnum opus* on the history of economic thought. It appears that Schumpeter was influenced by Weber's rationalization thesis in his own theory of entrepreneurship. Schumpeter's comments on the decline of entrepreneurial culture and capitalism as a civilization read very much like an application of Weber's idea of the routinization of charisma to business enterprise.

In addition to personal contacts of this kind, Weber also read widely in contemporary Austrian theory. Of particular interest are his favourable comments on the early work of Ludwig von Mises, who, alongside Friedrich von Hayek, represents the leading Austrian economist of the twentieth century. Weber made particular mention of von Mises' 1912 volume *The Theory of Money and Credit* (von Mises 1934), and his 1920 essay on problems of economic calculation under socialism (von Mises 1935). It is of some importance, therefore, to locate Austrian neo-classicism more precisely within the development of economic thought and social theory.

In general terms, the relationship of the Austrian neo-classicism to other currents of economic thought may be conceptualized as follows. Whereas classical political economy had stressed the centrality of economic aggregates such as land, labour, and capital, and rent, wages, and profit, in the determination of costs of production and income distribution, the neo-classicists of the late nineteenth century centred their analyses on marginal changes in the micro-choices of sovereign individuals in the market-place. Neo-classicism gave pride of place to rational choices by consumers and producers, replacing the 'objectivist' labour theory of value with a thoroughgoing subjectivism concerning individual actors' 'ends'. One effect was to shift attention from aggregate costs of production to marginal changes in consumer demands, within the price-setting process.

Although sharing these basic propositions in common, neo-classicism was not an entirely homogeneous position. One important internal distinction was between the so-called Lausanne or 'equilibrium' approach associated above all with Leon Walras, and the Austrian tradition, begun by Carl Menger, and developed by Böhm-Bawerk, von Wiese, and later writers such as von Mises and Hayek. Although neither of these currents can be regarded as internally monolithic, there none the less existed clear general differences between the two, over issues of epistemology and the conceptualization of the market-place.

Walras had likened the market to the process of 'tatonnement', that is to the role of the auctioneer in clearing the supply of commodities offered for auction. In this model, equilibrium prices could be reached between utility-maximizing buyers and sellers following rational choice strategies based on perfect knowledge, such that the market reached an equilibrium end-state. For Walras there was no fundamental interest in the time dimension in market adjustments. For the Austrians, on the other hand, perfect knowledge is impossible in principle. Economic relations are characterized by uncertainty and risk-taking, with action often producing unintended consequences. From this viewpoint, the market-place is conceptualized as a dynamic *process* of search for equilibrium over time, rather than an entity tending to a series of equilibrium end-states. Unlike Walras' 'tatonnement', in which rational actors adjust to market conditions in an almost automatic self-regulating manner, the Austrian view, stressing the climate of uncertainty, gives far greater scope for heroic acts of judgement by entrepreneurial innovators. Such judgements were, however, based on expectations of the future, which could easily be faulty and overtaken by the hand of 'fate'. In this sense *ex ante* certainties are impossible, hence the Austrians' noted resistance to centralized public planning strategies on epistemological grounds.

It was Austrian neo-classicism which exerted a dominant influence on German economic theory during Weber's lifetime, and which had a particular influence upon Weber himself. Weber and the Austrian economists both shared a liberal world-outlook in which the 'subjective' value-judgements of individuals were regarded as authentic and sovereign. They could not be reduced to any naturalistic ethics or substantive rationality, such as that propounded by the state socialists and protagonists of a strong domestic interventionist state in welfare policy. Weber's defence of the separation between the scholarly vocation and the kind of political partisanship practised by the state-oriented academics of the *Verein für Sozialpolitik*, was in turn influential on subsequent generations of liberalistically inclined economists in their attempt to insist on a distinction between fact and values in economic life. In particular, Lionel Robbins' influential study, 'An Essay on the Nature and Significance of Economic Science' (Robbins 1935), served both to popularize Austrian economics and Max Weber's scientific methodology to an English audience. Weber's influence here was strong, even if his separation between science and politics has sometimes been bowdlerized by 'positivistic' social scientists as a plea for 'value-free' science. Weber's position was of course that all science is value-relevant and thus selective in orientation, but that there is none the less a distinction between value-judgements and value-relevant scientific propositions.

We can go further, however, to claim that Weber's liberalism, inflected as it was with the influence of Nietzsche, had strong affinities with the highly activist emphasis on action and entrepreneurship within the Austrian tradition. With the breakdown of traditional normative communities and the death of God, individuals were placed in the position of creating secular meanings for themselves, albeit in competition with others. Whereas the Austrians accepted as given a secularized world in which individual values were irreducible to any kind of normative contract within the community, Weber was still concerned to chart the historical pathways whereby the process of 'disenchantment' had first emerged in the western world. His own account of the psychological dilemmas of the Protestant ethic in which no certainty of salvation can be assured even in the context of a highly activist culture, is none the less mirrored in the neo-classicals' emphasis on the uncertainties of the market-place in which secular achievement cannot be assured within the highly activist process of economic competition.

Weber, too, was clearly influenced by the doctrine of the unintended consequences of action, which Menger had reasserted in the tradition of Mandeville and Adam Smith. At the same time, Weber found it impossible to accept that such unintended consequences could produce social order in a spontaneous manner. Thus, he explicitly rejected Mandeville's seventeenth-century formulation 'private vices, public virtues', as a means not merely of explaining market order, but of the development of social institutions such as the law (Weber 1975: 81–91). It was at this point that Weber's 'social economics' required an emphasis on the relations of power and domination surrounding the market-place, relations which were to be outlined systematically in the sociology of domination. Weber's sympathetic reception of Austrian neo-classicism involved the following areas of methodological convergence.

First, he shared the neo-classicists' objection to the epistemology and methodology of naturalistic induction as practised by the historical economics. Neither history nor economics could be grounded in a presuppositionless appeal to empirical data. The strong influence of neo-Kantianism on Weber, and on neo-classicists like von Mises, lay behind their common belief that the cultural sciences, in dealing with the meaning of action, were refractory to natural science methodology. There were no laws of history to be established by inductive proofs, and in this sense both Weber and the Austrian School rejected scientific positivism, whether practised by the historical economists or by the alternative Walrasian School of neo-classical economics.

One important consequence of this epistemological standpoint is that the appeal to data (whether historical or economic) cannot in principle solve moral problems. In the case of modern economic thought, a tendency has sometimes been observed for the smuggling of normative elements into the analysis of market choices. Hollis (1979) has pointed to the elision involved in the (usually implicit) assumption that what the rational man would do, the plain man should do. For Weber and the Austrians, by contrast, the appeal either to history or to reason could not solve moral problems. Solutions depended rather on voluntaristic choices, limited by constraints, but informed by subjective preferences and ultimate values.

One corollary of this position was of course the limits placed on the guiding hand of reason in human choice. Weber and the Austrian School both share an interest in the limits on knowledge available to human action and the consequent uncertainties that arise. Notwithstanding Weber's fateful comments on the technical efficacy of bureaucratic modes of domination, we should also note the constant reference in the basic building-blocks of his sociology, to 'probability', 'chance', or 'opportunity for advantage' in the definitions of social action, social relationship, and so on.

The historical analogue of this uncertainty and the consequent rational action schema generated is to be found, as Arnold Eisen (1979) has pointed out, in the Puritans' orientation to the overcoming of chance, and uncertainty of proof of salvation through purposive social action. Our fate as human actors is not then the inevitable construction of an iron cage, but rather that we cannot know for certain what our fate will be, and yet we must continue to act, search for meaning, and orient ourselves to others under this constraint.

A second convergence between Weber and the Austrians is the rejection of organicism in social theory, and adherence to an alternative methodological position generally known as 'methodological individualism', and first labelled as such in all probability by the young Joseph Schumpeter in 1908 (Machlup 1978: 472). Since there is so much confusion and ambiguity in what is actually meant by methodological individualism, it is important to point out the polemical foil against which the 'doctrine' was addressed. Certainly in the case of Weber and the Austrians this foil was represented by organicist emanationism. Just as the neo-classicist economists rejected naturalism — where history is represented as the emanation of natural law-like processes — so it rejected those forms of idealism where history is represented as the emanation of an organic ideal, such as a *Volksgeist* or national character.

To appeal to an organic totality or some super-organic conception of the 'social' was, for Weber, to retreat into epistemological incoherence. This was because no general or universalistic viewpoint existed which could yield a comprehensive account of 'social wholes'. One cannot comprehend society as a totality. All that is possible are insights into the endless flux of the 'social' from particular value-relevant positions. Weber also believed that very little had as yet been achieved in elaborating the nature of the 'social' given the predominant but illegitimate recourse to organicism on the model of Spencerian biological evolutionism. In a stern warning, Weber argued that 'those who are so contemptuous of the ''Robinsonade's'' [i.e., Robinson Crusoe premises] of classical theory, should restrain themselves if they are unable to replace them with better concepts' (Weber 1949b: 95).

In this context it is worth pointing out that sociology had as yet to emerge in Germany as a discipline distinct from 'economics', 'history' or 'law', and that Weber still regarded himself as a 'social economist'. How then should the commitment of Weber and the Austrian economists to methodological individualism be understood? This is a difficult question to answer in general terms because the Austrians were and are by no means united in their methodology.

Methodological individualism is premised on the notion that the individual actor is the central unit of analysis in social theory, and that organic totalities must therefore be disaggregated into their individual parts for purposes of explanation. It is, as it were, the methodology of a *Gesellschaft* society rather than a *Gemeinschaft* community. Beyond this point, however, serious difficulties arise in clarifying the nature of the individual unit, and its relation to the wider society. One influential strand of methodological individualism associated with utilitarianism asserts a psychologistic conception of the individual, whose ends are thus beyond social determination. Carl Menger's law of marginal utility was often expressed by economists in such terms. They involved a basic psycho-physiological law of want satiation as the foundation of the process of preference rankings and changes in marginal choices by sovereign individuals. Weber, however, was not a methodological individualist in this psychologistic sense, as he made clear in his essay on marginal utility (Weber 1908). His methodological individualism was set, rather, within a social context in which actors gave meaning to their actions, and in which individual actors oriented themselves to others. The more specific modern cultural context involved embodied value pluralism or heteronomy ends. This had emerged with the death of God and the challenge to natural law.

Another type of methodological individualism is what Stephen Lukes has called Social Atomistic Truism (Lukes 1968). Here individuals are socially rather psychologistically constituted, and the further claim is made that there are no other entities able to act in society than individuals. Lukes sees this approach as a self-evident sociological truism of little assistance in establishing the all-important general nature of relations between individual and society.

The disaggregation of the category Social Atomistic Truism, however, yields a variety of further options. One is that accounts of individual purpose provide exhaustive causal explanations of social phenomena. Although this viewpoint has been sharply criticized (Lukes 1968; Hodgson 1986), it is actually rather difficult to find anyone who holds to such an entirely voluntaristic position. Neither Weber nor the Austrian economists subscribe to this version of methodological individualism on two grounds. The first is that purposeful actors may fail to acknowledge or may misunderstand the conditions of action, such that actions may fail to yield the intended consequences. The second is that all purposeful actions, whether successful or not, may yield unintended consequences that no individual or set of individuals intended.

Another version of methodological individualism claims that causal explanations must necessarily include accounts of individual purposes, or as Weber put it, must be adequate on the level of meaning. Beyond this, scope remains for the analysis of unintended outcomes, but this analysis cannot be conducted in terms of organic entities that are regarded as causally effective, independent of human purpose or will. This proviso clearly leaves scope for the analysis of collectivities or institutions in at least two senses. The first involves the claim that institutions or collectivities exist in so far as individuals believe them to exist, and orientate their actions according to that belief. The second claims that some institutions exist, even though they are not the product of human design. The origins and persistence of such undesigned institutions cannot, however, be rendered intelligible without some reference to the activities of individuals.

This type of methodological individualism is that shared by Weber and most of the Austrian School. Many of its emphases derive from the work of Carl Menger. He saw institutions as divided into two types: those designed by legislation and those that were undesigned, such as language, markets, legal norms, and money. Menger sought to combat organicist theories of institutional developments because of their metaphysical idealist character, while at the same time criticizing liberal social contract theories on the grounds that they over-emphasized the importance of conscious design and consensus.

Weber took over Menger's approach in his sociology of law. Like Menger and von Mises, he was inclined to speak of many institutional developments as the undesigned resultant of social or cultural forces constituted by individual actors. In this respect he accepted von Mises' theory of the origins of money as undesigned rather than as an institution arising from social contract (Locke) or state intervention (Knapp). Although Weber believed that the norms governing institutions arose only in the rarest of cases by autonomous agreement, he none the less emphasized the centrality of 'new lines of conduct' in the evolution of institutional norms or rules. In this way his methodological individualism cannot be equated with pure voluntarism or be regarded as the obverse of pure structural determination. There is room in Weber for 'structural' influences on social outcomes, but only in so far as these are either points of orientation in individuals' action-schema (for example, the belief in capitalism as an over-arching compulsive system constraining individual freedom of action), or as a not necessarily intended resultant of the actions of many individuals.

On this account the main type of social theory excluded by the methodological individualism of Weber and the Austrian economists is that form of structuralism in which individuals are merely bearers of forces beyond their volition, and in which it is possible to conceive of 'history without a subject' as in the work of Althusser and Foucault. Otherwise there is considerable space left in this approach for the analysis of norms, rules, and collectivities, although it is only the minority of Austrian economists such as Carl Menger, von Wiese, Schumpeter, and, more recently, Ludwig Lachmann (1970), who have taken a systematic interest in these matters.

This state of affairs is serious, as Nozick (1977) points out, for two reasons. The first is the clear requirement that methodological individualism provide some general theory of how utility functions are shaped in different institutional environments. Second, there is the difficulty that it is not logically necessary that methodological individualism start from human action and work upwards, so to speak, to the macro-level in order to constitute social theory. Nozick also points out that there are no a priori grounds for accepting the reductionist proposition that no new, more challenging, and more adequate unreduced macro-theory cannot arise which might render Austrian a-prioristic action theory redundant or at the least reduce its explanatory plausibility. In all of this, it is quite misleading to argue that methodological individualism, either does, or must necessarily exclude institutions. There is equally no logical requirement that institutional accounts must necessarily be reduced to the intentional purposes of individuals.

Notwithstanding these difficulties, it remains the case that methodological individualism gives epistemological privilege to individual 'subjective' definitions of wants and rights. In common with neo-classical subjectivist value theory, Weber's own position is that objective evaluations of various individual values by the state, by classes, or by any other collective agency are impermissible and illusory. The individual remains sovereign as the unit of action capable of judging moral rightness and ethical authenticity. This privilege still leaves room for collective action by sets of individuals on the basis of adherence to shared rules or values, or, alternatively, as a result of the domination by one set of individuals over another on the basis of 'a minimum of voluntary consent'. It is possible, thereby, to conceive of the state as a form of social agency — not, however, as an organic transcendental force as in Hegelian political philosophy, but rather as a set of individuals acting in concert in a governmental manner. This Weberian formulation has recently been praised by libertarian economists like Murray Rothbard.

To sum up, Weber and the Austrian School are not at all obliged to deny the reality of institutions or the idea that actors may act under institutional constraint, or that this constraint may be experienced as an external compulsive force or imperative. Nor need they hold to a social contract or design theory of institutions. Only two propositions are excluded. The first is that social life can be explained without reference to the causal consequences of the meaning individuals give to their actions. The second is that institutions act as organic, causally effective entities through the structural imposition of rules or constraints on unwilling actors, and irrespective of the actions of such actors.

In the light of this clarification of the possibility of a non-psychologistic, non-truistic version of methodological individualism, it is not at all surprising to encounter recent debates claiming compatibility between Marxism and methodological individualism. Jon Elster (1982) in particular has issued a powerful challenge to Marxism to provide micro-foundations of a methodological individualist kind to prevent the degeneration of Marxism into unacceptable versions of organic functionalism. As he points out, methodological individualism is not incompatible with the views (a) that individuals often have goals that involve the welfare of others, (b) that individuals often have beliefs about supra-individual entities that are not reducible to beliefs about individuals, and (c) that many social properties of individuals are relational, and thus require reference to other individuals. Elster's argument, while apparently unconvincing to most Marxists, is most striking perhaps for its demonstration that methodological individualism need not entail political individualism, or a liberal capitalist world-outlook.

A final feature of the methodological individualist critique of aggregation that deserves some attention here involves what economists refer to as the 'index number' problem. This concerns the dubious or ambiguous epistemological status of specifically economic aggregates.

Unlike the positivistic schools of mathematical economists concerned with modelling aggregate magnitudes, the main thrust of the Austrian School was to produce an essentially qualitative account of the mechanisms of human action. Within a money economy, to be sure, one can try to measure the costs and benefits of different choices. The Austrian School, stimulated in large measure by the work of Schumpeter, also made enduring contributions to the quantitative analysis of trade cycles. Yet for the most part, the primary Austrian emphasis is on the uncertain and imperfect knowledge which actors must necessarily bring to economic life, and on the incommensurable subjective character of individual human wants. In this respect an essentially qualitative decision is required in making choices between various 'costed' means, or in deciding what constitutes welfare.

This approach offers a very radical challenge to the homogeneity and reality of conventional socio-economic aggregates, such as national income, capital, or labour. While Marx criticized the liberal world-view for its 'fetishism of commodities', the more far-reaching claim of the Austrians is that all economic aggregates are prone to fetishism or reification.

In the case of capital theory, to take one distinctive area of Austrian economic theory, the claim is that capitals are heterogeneous entities which are not capable of simple aggregation. The problem here is not so much that of the diverse physical characteristics of capitals, since all are capable of translation into money as a common base. The difficulty is rather with complex changes in the valuation of capitals over time, dependent in part on different subjective expectations by entrepreneurs as to the expected contribution of capital to the future stock of output. Since decisions have to be made about the deployment of capitals *before* their contributions to output are known, and since such decisions involve comparisons of alternative uses, it is hard to aggregate capitals into definite future output flows (Kirzner 1976: 139–40). From this kind of Austrian position, moreover, it would be possible to diagnose the problem of fetishism in all types of macroeconomics, Marxist political economy included. Here one might speak of the fetishizing of capital as an impersonal but ineluctable aggregated social force beyond individual control.

Weber's methodological individualism involved a similar scepticism towards socio-economic aggregates. He was particularly adamant on the impossibility of aggregated measures of welfare, due to the incommensurable subjective values given by individuals to their utilities. When using terms like 'capital' or 'labour', Weber did so, not in terms of homogeneous aggregates, but rather in terms of the relational properties of action and institutions. The sole aggregate he was prepared to take seriously was that of total state revenue as raised by taxation, since this was a directly measurable sum, to which government officials and private actors could orientate their activities.

A third general area of shared ground between Weber and Austrian economics involves the acceptance of a generic conception of economic life as a species of action theory. Weber followed the neo-classical approach to the definition of economic action very closely. Having defined economic action in terms of orientation towards 'the satisfaction of desire for utilities' (Weber 1978: 63), he went on to elaborate that the essence of the problem was 'the prudent choice between ends . . . oriented to the scarcity of the means which are available or could be procured for these various ends' (ibid., 65). In this definition it is important to note that the economy is not limited to narrow technical questions of the 'correct' means to realize a given 'end', leaving ends or values external to economic life. Rather, economic life includes choice between 'proximate' ends themselves, and thus embraces a value-orientation to the kind of prudent choice-making procedures, whose historic emergence Weber associated with the emergence of the Protestant ethic. At this very general level, therefore, we might say that Weber's notion of economic life is both 'instrumental' and 'normative'. The economic rationality depicted by marginalism is taken to be the archetypal form of occidental rationality itself. What is lacking in this definition is concern for the problem of necessarily imperfect knowledge which Hayek was later to include in his more recent notion of economic action as 'How to secure the best use of resources known to any members of society, for ends whose relative importance only these individuals know'. Had Weber devoted as much attention to the problem of action under conditions of uncertainty as Hayek or Schutz were later to do, it is conceivable that his entirely instrumentalized picture of bureaucratic domination symbolized in the iron cage metaphor would have been less compelling. For the Hayek definition, unlike that of Weber, stresses the prime difficulty in pursuing rational economic co-ordination of utility-satisfaction without reference to the particular knowledge of 'ends' and 'means' held by individuals.

Even without the added emphasis on imperfect and uncertain information, the neo-classical scarcity conception of economics had, in the hands of Weber and of von Mises, been used to point out certain economic problems inherent in the project of socialist planning. If the setting of scarce means to meet ends was at the heart of the economic problem, such challenges would apply equally to socialist societies as to any others. Certainly, if socialism is regarded as a modern form of social organization, rather than a small-scale decentralized anarcho-syndicalistic affair on the model of a peasant commune, then at least two problems would arise.

The first is the difficulty of making calculations and planning the use of resources without the use of *money*. The function of money as a means of exchange bearing message about 'wants' itself depended on a significant area of *market* organization, most notably in allowing the possibility of capital accounting. Weber's first message was that socialist economies could not get very far beyond assertions of absolute value ideals simply by planning in *kind*. A second problem raised would be the need to place checks on the moral imperatives of socialist forms of substantive rationality if formally rational calculation was to take place. If this were not done, then the danger is that substantive decisions would be severed from all direct relationships with costs and consequences. This is precisely the criticism that certain contemporary critics have made of the redistributive politics of modern welfare states.

While there are certain striking convergencies between Weber and the Austrian economists, there are equally a number of fundamental differences between them. These can be most usefully identified by considering the conceptual repertoire within which Weber analysed relations between economy and society.

As is well known, Weber's ideal-typical conceptualization of the different types of social action treats purposeful or instrumental rationality as one of four possible action orientations — the others being value-rational, affectual action, and traditional action. From this perspective the concepts and laws of

> pure economic theory . . . state what course a given type of human action would take if it were strictly rational [that is, instrumentally rational] unaffected by errors or emotional factors, and if, furthermore it were completely and unequivocally directed to a single end, the maximisation of economic advantage. In reality, action takes exactly this course only in unusual cases. [my parenthesis]

> (Weber 1978: 9)

Weber does not object in principle to the level of formal abstraction involved in economic theory. Indeed, his strong case for the heuristic value of ideal-types — built largely upon the example of economics — depended on the one-sided, abstract accentuation of 'certain elements derived from reality'. Nor does he object to the economists' substantive emphasis on instrumental rationality since this is clearly a crucial element in modern occidental culture.

What Weber does object to is the economists' assumption that economic life is a self-subsistent realm whose operation can be theoretically grasped in an exhaustive manner by means of the postulate of instrumental rationality. There are two issues at stake here. The first matter concerns the status of the rationality postulate, in particular whether it necessarily involves a naturalistic view of the economy or capitalist social relations. The second is the place of the rationality postulate within a more exhaustive account of relations between economy and society.

As far as the first issue is concerned, Weber regards the postulate of instrumental rationality as relevant to a particular analytical interest in utility-maximization under conditions of scarcity. It does not describe an objectively discrete segment of society. Thus

> The quality of an event as a 'socio-economic' event is not something it possesses objectively. It is rather conditioned by the orientation of our cognitive interest, as it arises from the specific cultural significance which we attribute to the particular event . . . a phenomenon is 'economic' only insofar as and only as long as our interest is exclusively focused on its constitutive significance in the material struggle for existence.
>
> (Weber, 1949b: 64)

While Weber accepts the basic neo-classical conception of the 'economy', it is quite misleading to charge him with a naturalistic account of the capitalist economy (Clarke 1982). The flaw in Clarke's position is the belief that Weber's neo-classical conception of the economy necessarily commits him to the proposition that 'capitalist social relations of production' are somehow 'natural' and therefore legitimate. This connection might hold if it would be assumed

1 that utility-maximization through rational choice is synonymous with capitalist social relations of production, and
2 that Weber's epistemology regarded neo-classical economic propositions as representations of some kind of objective reality.

Unfortunately neither assumption holds. In the first place it is clear that utility-maximization through rational choice may as well be a feature of socialist as capitalist social relations. Second, it is equally clear that Weber regards the economists' view of the economy as one more or less useful analytic orientation among many. It is certainly not a natural economic fact of life. Since Weber is a value relativist, there is no absolutist epistemology available to him that could ground such an assertion.

It is even questionable whether all economists give the postulates of instrumental rationality a naturalistic standing. Amatya Sen has recently pointed to massive internal divisions as to the logical status of the rationality postulate. 'If today you were to poll economists of different schools', he writes, 'you would almost certainly find the coexistence of beliefs

1 that the rational behaviour theory is unfalsifiable,
2 that it is falsifiable and so far unfalsified, and
3 that it is falsifiable and indeed patently false' (Sen 1976: 325).

These divisions may also be found among Austrian and libertarian economists. On the one side stands von Mises, who regards the assumption of rational purposefulness as an a-priori truth about human action, as distinct from physiological behaviour. This clearly challenges Weber's belief that purposeful rationality is a construct which expresses the logic of one type of social action that is historically and culturally specific. On the other side lies Murray Rothbard, who regards the rationality assumption as an empirically verifiable truth about economic life itself.

It is evident therefore that commitment to a naturalistic conception of 'capitalist social relations of production' is neither fundamental to Weber nor a clear-cut line of divergence between Weber and economic theory. A clearer distinction between Weber and the main-stream of Austrian economists is evident when we consider the place of the rationality postulate within general accounts of the relations between economy and society. The economists in the main treated economic life as more or less self-subsistent, such that morality or state-sponsored economic measures are regarded as 'interventions' or 'interference' coming, as it were, from 'outside' to disrupt an ongoing entity. Weber, by contrast saw a complex inter-penetration of economic and non-economic influences at work, in the economy itself as well as in the wider society. The fourfold typology of social action-orientations applies to a greater or lesser extent to all areas of social life. This means that forms of rationality, other than instrumental rationality, can be detected within economic life, while instrumental rationality may be located outside the economy.

To be more specific, value-rational orientations involving religious or ethical norms may be found on occasion to be central to the pursuit of economic activity, while instrumental rationality may be found on occasion within institutions outside the market-place, such as the medieval church or the modern bureaucracy. Weber took care to distinguish between 'directly economic phenomena' — whose significance lies primarily in the seeking of utility-maximization under conditions of scarcity — 'economically-relevant phenomena' — whose character is extra-economic (for example, religions), but which none the less exerts a causal influence on economic life — and 'economically-conditioned phenomena' — whose character is extra-economic and which is itself causally influenced by economic phenomena. The profound anti-reductionism here is dramatised in Weber's comment that 'A banking history of a nation which addresses only economic motives for explanatory purposes is naturally just as unacceptable as an explanation of the Sistine Madonna as a consequence of the socio-economic basis of the culture of the epoch in which it was created' (Weber 1949b: 71).

While certain members of the Austrian School, such as Schumpeter, held similar views as to the complex inter-penetration of economic and non-economic influences upon events, most Austrians appear committed to the proposition that purposive rationality can provide an exhaustive understanding of economic events. This is not to deny the significance of surrounding institutions such as legal protection of private property rights and contract to the possibility of economic life. Yet such institutions could be regarded as 'givens' for the purpose of working out the logic of rational choice within economic exchanges. It was left to Weber and other social economists who dissented from this view to show that extra-economic influences impacted continually on the economy, and to indicate what were the typical limits that such influences placed upon the operation of economically purposive rationality. This line of criticism did not depend on the complex findings of naïve induction, as practised by some of the historical school, but rather on the twofold claim that the abstract schema of purposive choice was neither analytically self-subsistent nor universally appropriate in explaining causal relations. In this way Weber found no place for economic a-priorism. 'Whether we are dealing simply with a conceptual game', he wrote, 'or with a scientifically fruitful method of conceptualisation and theory construction can never be decided a priori. Here too, there is only one criterion, namely, that of success in revealing concrete cultural phenomena in their interdependence, their causal conditions and their significance' (Weber 1949b: 92).

One of the corollaries of this position is that there can be no general theory of the relationship between economy and society, in the sense of a set of core axioms from which explanations of particular events could be deduced. Weber's disposition to operate on the basis of a multi-dimensional theory of causal inter-penetration could of course be viewed as a 'weak' version of a general theory, entailing a general orientation to the multi-dimensionality of empirical explanation. It would not, however, fall into the category of 'strong' general theories deriving from axiomatic and/or a-priori propositions. Weber's position, by contrast, is founded on the historical and comparative analysis of particular events and processes, exhibiting singular if complex configurations of causal interdependence.

This attempt to resolve the *Methodenstreit* by combining abstract ideal-typical and historical elements did not convince either the Austrian School or many subsequent sociologists. Von Mises, in a scathing attack on Weber's epistemology, accused him of blurring a vital distinction between historical and theoretical analysis (von Mises 1960). Economic life, in so far as it involved rational choice under conditions of scarcity, could only be conducted theoretically, since it flowed from premises that were necessarily true. An alternative position, which rendered the economists' position complacent and one-dimensional, was later to be outlined by Parsons. He upheld the importance of generic analytical constructs, as distinct from Weber's genetic ideal-types, but argued that the economy represented only one of four analytical dimensions generic to the operation of social action and action-systems. Before we consider these responses to Weber, it is useful to complete discussion of the substantive scope of his social economics.

The methodology of Weber's social economics involves the application of a multi-dimensional framework of analysis to historical 'particulars'. This rules out any unitary analytical schema such as the a-priorist rational choice perspective. While Weber conceives of the generic character of economic life in terms of the struggle to realize utilities in the face of scarcity, he inflects the notions of 'utility' and the struggle to realize 'ends' with a far richer and more complex account of causal processes than the neo-classical economists were to do.

Weber's sociological extension of the logical categories of utilitarian economics is founded on the distinction, already noted, between technical action and economic action. Whereas technical questions involve the problem of choosing an appropriate means to reach a given end, economic action 'is primarily oriented to the problem of choosing the *end* to which a thing shall be applied' (Weber 1978: 67). This conceptual distinction allows Weber to re-define the struggle to realize utility, from the economists' typical concern with individual consumer choices made to satisfy given 'tastes' — that is, technical action — to a broader concern with the choices of both producers and consumers as to the allocation of resources between a variety of ends. Within this conception of economic action, Weber tries to integrate power relations into the highly voluntaristic framework of neo-classical action theory. For Weber, the struggle to realize utilities is not necessarily conducted by sovereign individuals. For it also involves 'power of control and disposal' (Weber 1978: 67) over labour and the other means of production, as exercised by producers.

Weber's intention here is to overcome a fundamental Marxist objection to neo-classical utility theory, namely that producers' search for profit-maximization represents a very different orientation to action than the mere drive to maximize personal utilities for con-sumption (Clarke 1982). For Weber, by contrast, utilities are very broadly defined as 'the specific and concrete, real or imagined advant-ages or opportunities for present or future use, as they are estimated and made an object of specific provision by one or more economically acting individuals' (ibid., 68). In this sense utilities are not defined simply in terms of commodities available for consumption. Weber follows Eugen von Böhm-Bawerk in formulating a broader concep-tion of utilities defined as 'The specific ways that physical goods or human services can be put to use — in the present or future — to meet "ends". Such "ends" may comprise the satisfaction of con-sumer wants or alternatively profit-making, which is "action oriented to opportunities for seeking new powers of control over goods on a single occasion, repeatedly or continuously" ' (ibid., 90). In this respect Weber brings a 'time' element into the consideration of utility-maximization, rather than defining utility simply in terms of discrete acts of want-satisfaction by consumers.

Weber's account of the power element in economic life focuses on the struggle between different interests, whether individual or corporate. Such struggles occur within the market-place, and also within more regulated forms of economic activity. Within the market-place Weber's well-known discussion of the distribution of power focuses on the relative advantages that accrue to both the owners of capital and to those who possess marketable skill (ibid., ch. 9). Such advantages limit the operation of the marginal utility principle, by constraining certain actors in their capacity to exercise rational choices.

Neo-classical economic theory assumes that the consumer is sovereign, such that 'it is the marginal consumer who determines the course of production'. Weber, by contrast, argues that this is true to a limited extent only, since there exist considerable inequalities of power between producers and consumers: 'even though the consumer has to be in a position to buy, his wants are "awakened" and "directed" by the entrepreneur' (ibid., p. 92). Weber's claim, in anticipation of Frankfurt School critical theory, is that 'capitalist enterprises through their aggressive advertising policies, exercise an important influence on the demand functions of consumers'.

Weber's awareness of such power differentials and the challenge they pose to neo-classical economics does not however compromise his methodological individualism, or his account of the purposive rationality of market capitalism. Each of his major economic concepts, such as 'utility' or 'profit-making', depends on the interpretation and meaning that individuals give to their actions. Like the Austrian economists, Weber links action within the marketplace to expectations about the future, expectations which can be translated into the technical rationality of accounting and opportunity costs. Unlike the Austrians he seeks a more developed sociological account of the relational and institutional premises which sustain and reproduce the calculative character of formal rationality. Whereas economists typically restrict their accounts of choice to the relative marginal utilities of goods under present and future control, the sociologist needs to know within what social relations the differential valuation of goods is instituted, enabling formal calculations to take place. For Weber the very possibility of formal calculation of cost and benefit oriented to profit-making (or the expectation of a minimum rate of return on capital) depends on an unequal power distribution between producer and consumer. This in turn depends on private property in the means of production and in goods themselves. In other words, formal rationality requires certain substantive supports if it is to be successfully institutionalized and developed.

The relations between formal rationality and substantive rationality (or what is regarded as rational judged from substantive viewpoints and value orientations) are, however, very complex. In the first place, Weber claims that the practice of formal rationality is no guide at all to the problem of whether the substantive wants of a population are being satisfied. This problem cannot be addressed until the distribution of income is also known (Weber 1978: 109). Second, the possibility of formal and substantive rationality coinciding can never be more than contingent. What counts as substantively rational within a group or culture cannot be reduced to a consideration of the formal rationality of the process of want-satisfaction. Hence the conflict between optimal economic rationality and the substantive rationality of protesting classes or disprivileged status groups striving for justice, is regarded as endemic.

One powerful implication of this position is that the conflict between formal and substantive rationality cannot be resolved in principle by a transition from capitalism to socialism. Socialist planning, however substantively rational when assessed against values of justice, would still be faced with problems of formal rational calculation, if the maximum volume of measurable resources is to be made available for want-satisfaction. Weber also believed that socialism would require an even higher degree of formal bureaucratization than capitalism to compensate for the loss of private economic initiative. In this way he foreshadowed the massive difficulties that twentieth-century socialist planning strategies have experienced in instituting a stable type of formal rationality. The reconciliation of formal and substantive rationality under 'actually-existing socialism' has indeed proved to be fundamentally intractable (Konrad and Szelenyi 1979).

Weber's relentless methodological individualism, coupled with his account of the advantages of formal rationality to individual want-satisfaction, produces a similar critique of socialist planning to that offered by the Austrian School. Yet there are a number of major differences in the route by which he arrives at such conclusions. The Austrian economists rule out socialism largely by denying its compatibility with the exercise of rational choices by individual actors, but in the process fail to provide any adequate account of the power relations and institutional structures that impede individual choice in modern capitalist societies. This leaves us with a choice between a caricature of socialism as 'serfdom', and an unreconstructed liberal nostalgia for a seventeenth-century world of sovereign producers.

Weber, by contrast, reaches his own critique of socialism through a critique of capitalism conducted in sociological and historical terms. This analysis sets the achievement of the neo-classicists in explicating certain characteristics of the logic of choice within formally rational action schema, against a far broader framework of cultural and institutional analysis. Weber uses this broader framework to enunciate certain trans-contextual dilemmas in social life, such as the conflict between formal and substantive rationality. These affect capitalist, socialist, and other types of social organization.

Whereas the Austrians produce a defence of liberalism that is ultimately nostalgic, Weber's social economics offers a more ironic appreciation of the strengths and weaknesses that already characterize capitalism, and the problems that socialism is likely to bring in its turn. Weber's liberal vantage-point is secured in his conception of the scientific profession as an individual vocation based upon an ethic of responsibility. Yet this is to restrict the provenance of liberalism to that of a virtuoso ethic. If there is a nostalgic element in Weber's sociology it is not to be found in a rehearsal of the ideals of *laissez-faire* capitalism and the free producer nor in the reassertion of the *Gemeinschaft* credentials of socialism. Weber's nostalgia is rather for the demise of the morally sovereign actor in the face of the onward march of rationalization within the market-place and within government. This is nowhere more evident than in the *Protestant Ethic* essays. Here the normative account of economic life and individual responsibility associated with the Protestant role in the transition to modern capitalism is overtaken by the bleak instrumental imagery of the iron cage (Weber 1930: 181–3). Weber retreats, in other words, to the position of a 'liberal in despair'.

Weber's pessimism concerning the future of liberalism is quite clearly dependent on the pervasive character of his theory of rationalization. Whether his pessimism is justified depends in large measure on the plausibility of the iron cage scenario, in which the modern world subsists without normative foundations undermining individual moral responsibility. Against this powerful vision there stand a number of strands of contemporary sociological thought which reaffirm the presence of normative elements in the constitution of modern society. The normative patterns that may be detected have been conceptualized in diverse ways around entities such as the democratic polity, professional or service ethics, and communicative rationality.

The reasons for Weber's neglect of such themes are complex. A good deal can be explained by the social context of early twentieth-century Germany in which the potential of a democratic political system, or of professional associations free from state control, was not easy to perceive. Yet there are in addition important intellectual components of the problem. One concerns Weber's inadequate discussion of inter-subjectivity, which left normative order a matter of purely individual assertions of moral will. Another concerns Weber's hostility to organicism, which produced a methodology founded on analysis by means of genetic ideal-type. This involved a refusal to countenance any kind of system theory, and the consequent inability to conceive of generic analytical properties of social action. One major cost of this position was the inability to mount a decisive theoretical critique of neo-classical economics.

WEBER'S SOCIAL ECONOMICS: A CRITICAL APPRAISAL

One of the foremost difficulties with Weber's entire discussion of social action and rationality is the problem of inter-subjectivity. This problem may be formulated in the following way. Given the subjectivism inherent in liberalistic theory, and the consequent objective incommensurability of values posited both by Weber and the marginal utility theorists, how is it possible for inter-subjectivity and inter-communication to take place between actors? Put another way, how is it possible for society to be anything other than a Hobbesian war of subjective wills?

The problem of inter-subjectivity has continued to beset all social theories whose assumptions about social action rest on some version of the theory of the unilateral individual will. One symptom of this difficulty within both economic theory and political philosophy is the increasing recourse to game theory — that is, to interactions of two or more actors, where individual means–end strategies cannot be formulated without regard for the strategies of others. Such celebrated games as the prisoner's dilemma or the assurance game are designed precisely with problems of inter-subjectivity in mind. One of the outstanding difficulties with game theory, however, is the continuing recourse to assumptions of perfect knowledge in transactions between individuals.

This assumption had already come under challenge in the inter-war period, in the work of the later Austrian economists, like von Mises and Hayek. It was also to be a major feature of the work of

Alfred Schutz. His phenomenological sociology sought to address the outstanding problem of inter-subjectivity left unresolved by Weber, through a synthesis of Husserl's philosophical phenomenology, Weber's sociology, and Austrian economics (Schutz 1953, 1954, 1967a). Schutz's intention was in a sense to extend and complete Weber's economic sociology rather than to transcend his work. Schutz was, moreover, trained explicitly within Austrian economics, being a student of both von Mises and von Wiese, and a member of the von Mises seminar. Like Menger and von Mises, he was concerned to provide a unified social science which embraced sociology and economic theory (Prendergast 1986).

Much of Schutz's project involved clarification of how inter-subjectivity was possible. Whereas the Austrian economists derived a picture of market-place interaction through indirect exchange with only minimal inter-subjective norms embodied in legal procedures, Schutz moved in a different direction. His approach set out from an analysis of the commonsense constructs by which inter-subjectivity was made possible within everyday life. Emphasis was placed not only on the single actor's meaning and purposes, but also on a set of actors' experiences of one another, and the means by which the meanings of others' actions were grasped. This centred on the process of typification.

Schutz's attempted solution to the problem of inter-subjectivity was that perfect certainty in communication was impossible, since individual experiences could not be directly replicated. However, communication was made possible through the identification of stable features and patterns in the flow of inter-subjective intercourse. This allowed the possibility of a significant but not certain process of communication, while personal values and personal stores of knowledge remained heterogeneous.

More recent theorists such as Habermas have sought to extend this approach to the problem of inter-subjectivity left unresolved by Weber. Habermas argues that inter-subjectivity need not be limited to accounts of everyday, commonsense understandings of actors' meanings. Taking up Schutz's suggestive comment that '*Verstehen* is by no means a private affair of the observer which cannot be controlled by the experiences of other observers' (Schutz 1967b: 56), Habermas emphasizes the central importance of consensual procedures for adjudicating validity claims. Thus 'Processes of reaching understanding are aimed at a consensus that depends on the inter-subjective recognition of validity claims; and these can be reciprocally raised and fundamentally criticized by participants in communication' (Habermas 1984: 136). The problem with Weber's account of subjectivity is that it is limited to a monologic theory of consciousness, and does not embrace a dialogic element of inter-subjective normative consensus. One implication is that Weber did not find a contemporary version of the normative order characteristic of the seventeenth-century Protestant ethic because he was operating with an abbreviated and inadequate conception of what a normative order might look like. His research was limited to heroic expressions of individual moral responsibility, and did not take sufficient account of social practices based on inter-subjective, reciprocally negotiated norms.

Habermas' argument engages, as we can see, with the familiar theoretical debate concerning the relations between individual and society. Drawing on the work of Mead, Durkheim, and Parsons, his aim is to transcend the individual/society antinomy or dualism. Conventionally, within both liberal utilitarianism and romantic thought, this dualism is portrayed in terms of an opposition between the free will and rational choices of autonomous individuals, on the one side, and the deterministic effect of over-arching structural or systemic forces on the other. Weber's liberalism, like that of the Austrian economists, partakes of this dualism to the extent that methodological individualism is sharply counterposed to various holistic, organicist accounts of social life. However much the starkness of such options is mollified by Weber's accounts of the normative frameworks within which individual actions are institutionalized, it remains the case that his accounts of individual rationality are inflected with a strong sense of individual sovereignty of the will, such that 'ends' or 'values' are in some sense extra-social and thus beyond inter-subjective tests of validity.

Habermas and other contemporary theorists, by contrast, operate within an intellectual context in which the individual/society and agency/structure dualisms have been largely superseded by advances in socialization theory. The premise here is that individual autonomy is a product of socialization, in which the role of individual is actively learnt rather than passively absorbed through structural determination. Individuals make themselves as much as they are made. It follows that concern for the cultural meaning that individuals give to their actions need not be incompatible with an account of the general systemic or structural properties of social life. Action theory and systems theory need not be incompatible since accounts of structures or systems need not resort to organicist or holistic metaphors of the kind Weber found so objectionable. Nor need system theory treat individuals as puppets of structural forces. This is perhaps easier to appreciate if we speak of action-systems theory rather than system theory *per se*.

Weber's resistance to a general theory of society clearly stemmed in large measure from his liberalistic objections to organicism and holism. Within the German context, Weber sided methodologically with the Austrian economists against the historical economists, since the historical economists practised a form of romantic idealism which inflated the cultural integrity of entities such as the German *Volk* into holistic social realities. Ironically, however, Weber's methodological individualism itself partook of romanticism through the influence of Nietzsche, in its emphasis on the sovereignty of the individual will. This did not prevent a recognition of the reality of 'cultures', 'world religions', and 'civilizations', but it did foreclose on any general theory of society, of which these entities were central component parts. Weber's emphasis on the shifting influence of ideal and material interests, and the effect of unintended consequences on actions, renders the search for a general theory fruitless.

Weber's resistance to system theory was also a product of his methodological views on the functions of abstractions in social science, and his particular commitment to a genetic notion of ideal-type constructs. Weber's account of the ideal-type concept is sometimes treated as an end-point to the *Methodenstreit*, reconciling the economists' use of abstraction with the historians' concern with particular historical configurations and uniqueness. This impression is, however, erroneous, since Weber's methodological contribution resolved very little. Fritz Machlup (1978: 236–55) has provided a useful summary of the intensive German and Austrian debates on ideal-typification which occurred throughout the twenties, thirties and forties. When Parsons entered the debate in *The Structure of Social Action*, published in 1937, he entered a controversy that had already generated a number of major criticisms of Weber's position.

One of the main charges made against Weber was that he underemphasized the importance of generic analytical concepts within social analysis. As is well known, Weber's ideal-type was intended as a genetic rather than generic form of abstraction. Genetic concepts were synthetically derived out of the chaotic flux of historically contingent social processes. Their function is heuristic rather than descriptive. The abstract one-sidedness of such constructs is intended to serve historical analysis, that is, the analysis of historically unique configurations or their individual components.

Weber claimed that this type of genetic conceptual abstraction underlay both historical practice and economic theory. Both such claims were highly challenging to the methodological self-understanding of the two disciplines, but for different reasons. In the case of history, Weber challenged the naïve empiricism which assumed that historical analysis could produce explanations, without recourse to abstract conceptualization of an explicit or implicit kind. In the case of economic theory, Weber challenged the view that central concepts such as 'economic exchange' or 'marginal utility' could stand as unproblematic generic concepts, typical of economic activity under all conditions. It is important to scrutinize this argument in more detail, since it helps to explain Weber's resistance to theoretical system-building.

Weber's discussion of the logical status of concepts in the social sciences presents us with two options. On the one hand, there are generic concepts. These describe the typical or invariant character of empirical phenomena. On the other hand, there are genetic concepts which offer abstract, one-sided constructions of historically unique configurations. Social scientific discourse is none the less complicated because concepts have both generic and genetic elements. Weber makes this point in order to overcome the objection that without a generic element, one would be left with an incommensurable set of distinct ideal-typical constructs. In other words, we need some generic sense of city to link together ideal-typical constructs of the western city, Islamic city, medieval city, and so on.

On close scrutiny, however, Weber proves extremely elusive when we try to pin down the generic elements in his sociology. In the particular example of the 'city', for example, we are left with the sense that all existing attempts to derive an adequate generic definition have proved highly fragile. On a more general level, we might note the major interpretative debate as to whether there is a generic core in Weber's sociology around such notions as the rationalization thesis (see, for example, Tenbruck 1975; Roth and Schluchter 1975), or whether he really does succeed in practising his self-proclaimed methodology of particularistic explanation of historical configurations by means of genetic ideal-types.

At many times Weber appears caught in a dilemma. On the one hand, his neo-Kantian epistemology commits him to a relativism which denies cultural or evolutionary universals. On the other hand, his work projects — sometimes overtly, sometimes tacitly — a strong sense of cultural universals which appear as virtual generic features of social life. Typical examples include the idea of rationalization, or, more subtly, the recurrent clash between formal and substantive rationality.

There are two possible ways out of this apparent dilemma. One is to subsume the idea of cultural universals to a specific cultural view-point, such as that which Weber sees as characteristic of occidental civilization. In this way cultural universals may represent generic features of social life as it is experienced and constructed within western thought. In the author's introduction which Weber wrote in 1920 as a preface to the reprinted version of *The Protestant Ethic and the Spirit of Capitalism*, Weber expressly points to belief in the uniqueness of certain western cultural phenomena 'which (as we like to think) lie in a line of development having universal significance and value' (Weber 1930: 13).

The alternative route out of the dilemma is to claim a distinction between the generic properties of social life, considered in abstraction, as compared with the empirical complexities of particular social processes. Weber himself did not explore this possibility very far in his analysis of the role of abstraction in social science. Indeed, his formulation of the ideal-type concept as an essentially genetic form of abstraction ruled it out. One major consequence of this conceptual decision was the effective blocking of a route towards a general theory of society constructed around generic properties of social action.

The most important criticisms of Weber's ideal-type methodology proposed that two or more discrete types of conceptual abstraction had been conflated together within the notion of ideal-type. There is not complete unanimity among Weber's critics on this point (Machlup 1978: 239–55). One major thrust of the discussion was to differentiate between ideal-types of concrete types of action (individualizing concepts) and ideal-types of necessarily hypothetical types of action (generalizing concepts). Weber's ideal-types, such as 'medieval town economy', or 'occidental city', really amount to concepts of the first sort whose logical status is designed with a view to understanding the historical and developmental uniqueness of the

west. Where Weber is at fault is in his failure to distinguish such individualizing concepts from generalizing concepts about hypothetical
entities such as the Robinson Crusoe economy of the contemporary
neo-classical theorists. This latter set of concepts represents a discrete
category of conceptual abstraction which is neither merely applicable
to particular historical situations, nor a mere common trait or
statistical average (Parsons 1937: 605–6). What von Mises (1960) and
Parsons both identified in Weber was a restricted identification of the
functions of abstract conceptualization with historical analysis as such.
This had the effect, as they both saw it, of denying the possibility of a
general theory of social action and of society itself, constructed on the
basis of generic analytical properties of action.

Von Mises praised Weber for clarifying 'the logical structure of
history and historical investigation' and for demonstrating 'the
inapplicability of the concepts and procedures of physics to history'
(von Mises 1960: 74–5). Weber's hostility to deductive theory was,
however, directed at the search for law-like regularities within social
life, akin to Newtonianism. He failed to consider the possibility that
the deductive perspective could be applied to human action, as a
means of understanding the logic of individually meaningful choices
irrespective of the contingencies of time and place. Although von
Mises gives due weight to the insightfulness of Weber's typology of
genetic orientations within social action, his argument is that Weber's
sociology is incomplete in that it neglects synchronic features of social
life, that may be conceptualized by means of generic properties of
action. Within this generic framework, von Mises singles out
purposeful action made under constraints of scarcity, as an a-priori
property of human action which entails certain deductive consequences, such as the laws of diminishing returns and marginal utility.

Von Mises' intransigent version of an a-priorist framework is not
shared by all Austrian and libertarian economists, nor was it common
to all Weber's methodological critics. Alfred Schutz, for example,
made the point that the correct logical status of the concepts of social
sciences was not a matter that could be resolved simply by recourse to
epistemological arguments, rather it depended on the explanatory
question under scrutiny (Schutz 1967a; 1967b). Schutz sees a kind of
continuum at work in processes of ideal-typification. This ranges
from the personal types that constitute the private world of the 'man
in the street', involving a close relation to personal experience, to the
far more anonymous material or 'course of action' types constructed

as pure constructs within the work of social theorists. Each must offer plausible insights into intended meanings and possible causes of action. Unlike von Mises' intransigent a-priorism or Weber's cultural and historical relativism, then, Schutz treats the logical status of the scientific concept as 'an objective meaning-complex about subjective meaning-complexes'. Here the 'objectivity' of the theorist involves specification of the typical and invariant courses of action of hypothetical actors acting according to certain ideal-typical postulates. Prendergast (1986: 17) has expressed the variable character of social science constructs in Schutz's continuum, whereby 'the more generalising the science the fewer the predicates and differences embodied in the definitions of the formal model, the more concrete or historical the discipline, the greater the number of predicates and differences, leading to greater specificity'.

A third conceptual strategy, distinct from von Mises' a-priorism and Schutz's compromise between von Mises and Weber, is offered by Talcott Parsons. His own commentaries on the logical status of economic theory (Parsons 1931, 1934) and upon Weber's methodology (Parsons 1937: 601–39) led him to formulate the basis for a general theory of society which eluded Weber. This set out from a distinction between the 'analytical' and 'empirical' elements in social action. Parsons' argument is that Weber's methodology, defined in a polemic with idealist historicism, stopped short 'at the type of general concept which was nearest an empirically descriptive one, namely the hypothetically concrete type of action on relationship' (ibid, p. 610). This, however, led to an abbreviated account of the status of concepts and abstraction in social theory. Parsons points to the distinction between an 'ideal-type universal' applicable genetically to the constitutive elements of particular concrete cases, and an analytical-element universal, which functions as a generic property of action-systems. In the latter case, certain analytical elements are postulated as necessary in any type of action, though their particular empirical importance will vary in each case. Analytical-element universals do not represent ideal-typifications of a class of empirically possible entities. Their status is rather more abstract than that, in that they represent analytical elements that are postulated as necessary systemic features of any type of social interaction. Analytical element universals are, in other words, generic properties of action-systems composed of a plurality of units of action, rather than properties of each unit.

By this means Parsons seeks to remove the Weberian blockage on further logical extension of the account of concept formation within the social sciences. Parsons' argument is that Weber's restriction of conceptual discussion to ideal-typification (backed up by unproblematic generic class concepts) is likely to result in 'type' — or 'methodological-atomism' (ibid., p. 607). Here 'each type of concept would be a unit of analysis by itself' (p. 618), and concrete analysis would tend to produce a 'mosaic' approach to history. The problem with this is its failure to investigate the systematic interrelation of the units of analysis. Without such an investigation it would not be possible to explain variations in the internal components of units brought into focus through the heuristic use of ideal-type constructs. Explanation by means of ideal-types cannot explain how it is that the 'values of the general elements' in particular entities are not always combined in the specific manner that any discrete ideal-type construct depicts (ibid.). Parsons also makes the point that Weber's methodology would not even permit a systematic classification of ideal-types, without at least implicit recognition of criteria stemming from a more general theoretical system.

Parsons' methodological critique indicates the manner in which Weber's anti-organicism and methodological individualism stood in the way of a logical extension of the account of concept formation, and retarded any move toward a general theory of action, or general theory of society. Whereas Weber's position was forged in debate with the powerful traditions of German romanticism and organicist idealism, Parsons' reconstruction of system theory now proceeded by rejecting a *Gemeinschaft* metaphor and replacing it, so to speak, with a *Gesellschaft* approach to the systemic qualities of modern society. Following Durkheim, Parsons emphasized the shift from an all-embracing collective conscience to the far weaker integrative ties of an individuated society. Although Parsons speaks of 'systems' inviting Weberian criticism as a new theorist of organicism, he is essentially speaking of action-systems, in which individuals make themselves, as much as they are made. The socialization process is, in other words, reflexive rather than ordained by imperative system-needs. Nor is Parsons' 'system' necessarily holistic, in the sense that it represents a theory of totalities on the model of German idealism. Rather, Parsons maintained a neo-Kantian epistemology and liberal political philosophy in which the systems metaphor was deployed as a value-relevant analytical component of social theorizing (Münch

1981; Alexander 1984: 44–5). The concept 'system' is not deployed in the organicist manner of the German historical school of economics. Rather, it was designed to focus attention on the normative conditions of order within differentiated societies. Here the problem of linking differentiated individuals to the social order was refracted through a set of differentiated sub-systems. The system metaphor, although deployed at this abstract level, was essentially linked to action-systems and thus to problems of choice and commitment within structural environments. Parsons' systems considered at this abstract level are not naïve descriptions of actual societies, yet they can still be given empirical reference.

We can develop this argument further by arguing that Parsons offered a more thoroughgoing Kantianism than Weber. Parsons did this by extending the discussion of synthetic a-priori logic in social science from a genetic historical to a generic theoretical (or perhaps meta-theoretical) basis. This subsequently became elaborated, as is well known, in the four-function AGIL paradigm of social action-systems, in which (A) stands for adaptation, (G) for goal-attainment, (I) for integration, and (L) for latent pattern-maintenance.

Parsons' critique of Weber also allows specific insights to be developed in theorizing the relations between economy and society. Weber's ideal-typical method had allowed neo-classicism and Austrian economics to coexist with social economics or economic sociology as two discrete bodies of theoretical wisdom, lacking theoretical integration. Weber's four-fold typology of rational action may be seen as a possible way of subsuming economic theory into sociology, through elaboration of the category of purposive rationality. Yet this 'integrating' mechanism remains a typology of ideal-types and no more than that. Once more we are left with type atomism and an essentially historical framework of analysis allowing the tracing of 'deviations' from ideal-typical formulations, and the search for historical explanations of historical particularities.

Parsons, by contrast, is able, through the distinction between 'analytic' and 'empirically possible types', to address economic theory on its own terms, namely as an ostensible a-priori generic element in social thought. By this means, Parsons answers von Mises' criticism of Weber, in which he complained of the failure to extend the science of human action from the economic problem of scarcity dealt with in Austrian praxeology, to a wider sociological framework. Parsons (together with associates like Neil Smelser) was to locate the provenance of economic theory within the adaptive (A) sub-system of the social system. Its provenance did not extend to the other three sub-systems dealing with goal-attainment (G), integration (I), and latent pattern-maintenance (L) (Parsons and Smelser 1956; for a further discussion, see Holton in Holton and Turner 1986).

The net effect of Parsons' argument is the claim that economic theory is a special case of a more general theory of social action and action-systems. This conclusion is worth emphasizing because it stands in such contrast to the contemporary attempts by economists to argue the reverse, namely that sociological theory or political science represent special cases of a general economic theory.

CONCLUDING REMARKS

Weber did not succeed in resolving the methodological problem of the relations between economics and social theory. He did, however, advance the solution of this problem by offering important methodological and substantive insights, to which following generations of theorists have found it necessary to return. Weber's engagement with Austrian neo-classicism has a broader significance too, for contemporary debates around the new liberal revival and the emergence of the New Right.

The New Right is a misleading notion in so far as it conflates authoritarian moral conservatism with economic liberalism and liberal moral philosophy (Levitas 1986). The connection between these two currents is politically contingent rather than intellectually necessary. Weber's affinities with Austrian economics testify to a shared libertarian emphasis on individual moral responsibility within a rational–legal institutional framework of citizenship rights, as contrasted with the populist *Gemeinschaft* of the 'moral majority'.

The existence of this common ground should not, of course, obscure the distinction between the classical liberal defence of a minimal state, and the twentieth-century re-definition of liberalism to embrace private capitalism, state infrastructural planning, and public provision. Weber's relationship to this distinction is not, however, clear-cut. On the one hand he recognized the formal technical advantages accruing to private entrepreneurial initiative over bureaucratic domination. In this respect he opposed moves for workers' control associated with the German factory council movement of 1917–20, claiming 'we are in need of entrepreneurs' (comments cited in

Mommsen 1985). On the other hand, he rejected any view that market relations within a capitalist society were or could be 'free', in the sense that they dispensed with unequal power relations. He also rejected any possibility of a return to a minimal *laissez-faire* state watching over an economy guided by a hidden hand. Weber by contrast supported a strong German nation-state. This was not, however, the result of commitment to some kind of anticipation of the corporatist Keynesian welfare state. It stemmed, rather, from a profoundly nationalist liberalism designed to uphold German material and ideal interests within an epoch of imperialist competition between the European powers. The critical edge to Weber's analysis of capitalism and the historical particularities of the epoch in which he was writing indicate quite clearly his distance from the current New Right.

While there remains scope for debate as to the precise location of Weber's intellectual and political standpoint within European liberalism, it is clear that the general liberal heritage to social theory which he drew upon left some major residual problems unresolved. One of the most important of these was the excessively monological character of the individual will that was seen as underlying rational choice and moral responsibility. This conception has foundered on the problem of inter-subjectivity. Equally problematic are the liberal solutions to the problem of social order which rely either on social contract theory or on notions of spontaneous order arising from the unintended consequences of action.

Yet for all this, it would be premature to speak of a post-liberal age in contemporary western thought. It is true that modern theorists now speak of the socialization of the individual will through inter-subjective processes such as communicative rationality. Many now also emphasize the system-driven character of modern society in which collective interest groups compete for distributive advantage, leaving individuals a marginal place in the 'life world' (Offe 1985). These developments have not, however, displaced core notions such as the integrity of the individual, individual rights, and individual moral responsibility. These continue to flourish in the discourses of citizenship, legal contract, and professional ethics. In such respects the autonomous individual of liberal theory is neither a mere philosophical abstraction, nor a nostalgic dream of a smaller-scale face-to-face world of inter-personal interaction. On the contrary, it remains an irreducible building block of a *Gesellschaft* society. Western culture is still dominated by liberal action theory. While Weber's spectre of the iron cage has proved timely, his posture of a liberal in despair may yet prove to be premature.

Chapter Three

MODERNISM, POST-MODERNISM, AND WORLD RELIGIONS: SOME ISSUES IN MAX WEBER'S SOCIOLOGY OF RELIGION

INTRODUCTION — MAX WEBER'S CENTRAL QUESTIONS

Within conventional sociology, particularly within the English-speaking tradition, Max Weber's sociology as a whole has often been interpreted as an account of the rise of rational capitalism within the occidental world. The core of the debate between Marxist and Weberian sociology was, for example, dominated in the 1960s and 1970s by the dispute over Weber's causal analysis of the origins of capitalist accumulation (Marshall 1982). It is now clear that this characterization of Weber's primary sociological concerns is too narrow to provide an adequate and theoretically sophisticated perspective upon Weber's sociological corpus. The earlier Protestant ethic thesis debate has shifted towards a broader conceptualization of the notion of rationalization as Weber's primary interest (Brubaker 1984; Schluchter 1981). The rationalization perspective has been important in enlarging the sociological understanding of Weber's interest in the general features of an industrial civilization; rationalization is in fact a process made up of a variety of processes such as secularization, intellectualization, and the systematization of the everyday world. Rationalization created the conditions for a stable administrative system, a systematic framework of legal relations, the dominance of natural science within the intellectual understanding of reality, and the spread of a variety of systems of human control and regularization. It can be argued that this very broad conception of rationalization means that it is possible to subsume Marxist theories of alienation and more general theories of civilization within the one sociological umbrella of the rationalization process (Turner 1985).

The focus of rationalization has had the useful effect of shifting the general character of the Marx–Weber debate away from its limited, narrow, and conventional 1960s framework (Wiley 1987). The Protestant ethic dispute was essentially an historian's problematic; the rationalization thesis is more genuinely an issue of sociological importance, although it clearly embraces disputes in, for example, literary studies, musicology, and cultural history.

Today it is clear that the nature of Weber's central interest is, in fact, a contested and ambiguous issue. While the rationalization thesis is clearly central to Weber's sociology, there are a variety of issues involved in the analysis of the core of Weberian sociology (Hennis 1988). In this chapter, I wish to suggest that a more appropriate approach to Weber's sociology may be located in the problems of modernization and modernity, and that we should regard rationalization as the process which produced modernism. Weber once said that the task of sociology is to understand the characteristic uniqueness of the time in which we live; in this chapter, it is argued that modernism represents the characteristic uniqueness of capitalism. It is important, therefore, to distinguish between the emergence of industrial society and the development of a capitalist mode of production, but it is equally important to distinguish between industrial capitalism and the existence of modern culture. By a modern culture, I mean a socio-cultural system which is the product of the process of rationalization which brings about a social world dominated by the ethic of world mastery, which in turn is best expressed in terms of the dominance of rational calculative norms in the everyday world. Modernism is a social habitus structured by the processes of secularization, rationalization, and intellectualism. It represents the breakdown of traditional forms of hierarchy, self-conception, and cultural processes. It is, in principle, possible to have capitalist societies which are not modern, because the legacy of feudalism or tradition is never fully broken by the emergence of capitalism. It would also be, in principle, possible to have an industrial civilization which was not essentially modern because various forms of traditional culture can survive the technical process of industrial production. In defining modernism in this way, as the end product of the project of rationalism, I wish to suggest that Weber's task was no less than to study and understand the total complex of modern cultural existence.

Within this framework, therefore, I regard the understanding of capitalism and industrialism as sub-themes within the broader problematic of what it is to be modern. The main point here is to emphasize the important differences between the processes of capitalist intensification, industrialization, and modernization as distinctive processes within the broader historical unfolding of rationalization. To present the problem of modernity in this way is also to suggest the possibility of conflicts and contradictions between these separate processes. Indeed, it may be the important disjunction between modernization and capitalism which is one of the most interesting features of western society.

It is also for this reason that Daniel Bell's account of the contemporary contradictions between social structure and modern culture becomes of particular importance for our argument (Bell 1976). Bell has argued in his notion of the 'disjunction of realms' that the contemporary social system is characterized by a number of basic contradictions. For example, while the 'axial structure' of the technical economic system is based upon specialization, hierarchy, and bureaucratic control, the political realm requires the axial principle of human equality, and the cultural realm is based upon various forms of hedonistic self-expression, self-development, and personal gratification. These contradictory principles set up a number of tensions, particularly between the cultural norms of asceticism and hedonism within the economic and the cultural arenas. It is also important to note that these different realms may have different temporal sequences and therefore it is possible to conceptualize modern society as a system of jarring relationships. Indeed, it was on this basis that Bell came to criticize both Marxism and functionalism for maintaining the basic assumption of an integrated social system, whereas in modern society this basis of structural and cultural integration is missing. Bell (1986) has rejected the concept of totality in Marxism and the Frankfurt School, along with the concept of system in contemporary sociology because these concepts necessarily presuppose an holistic perspective on social relations, which Bell believes are in fact inevitably fragmented and conflictual in modern societies.

We can see that to argue for a distinction between capitalism and modernism is to engage in a critique certainly of Marxism, but also of aspects of classical sociology. Furthermore, to recognize the general character of Weber's theory of rationalization is to present a position in which Marxist concepts of alienation and reification are less general than the conceptual apparatus which we find in Weber. In short, to note a distinction between the problems of modernization as such and the specific issues of capitalism is to present an important criticism of the Marxist legacy. Some contemporary radical theorists have recognized this issue and have made an attempt to re-embrace the problems of the modern world without the entire economic baggage of the classical Marxist social theory (Berman 1982).

It is also important to see Weber within the general context of German social and philosophical thought in the second half of the nineteenth century. Weber's perception of the rational character of modern capitalism and his anxieties about the impact of bureaucratic capitalism on the individual were the product of a romantic German critique of the legacy of Bismarck's state-dominated industrial revolution. Weber's anxiety about the individual within the bureaucratic structure of a modern society was parallel to the more general anxieties embraced by Tönnies' distinction between *Gemeinschaft* and *Gesellschaft*. Simmel's fascination for the anonymity of the urban way of life was also a product of this philosophical reflection upon the problems of a money economy, the capitalist production of commodities, the expansion of consumer demand, and the proliferation of state functions and interventions. Simmel, Weber, and Tönnies were, therefore, figures within a critical but anxious perspective on the modernization process in Germany. This anxious inspection of modern cultures also gave rise to questions about the origins of this process.

My argument is that nineteenth-century German social philosophy was primarily a reflection on the problem of the origins of modern culture and on the likely consequences of an uninterrupted process of modernization. In the nineteenth century, the most common answer within German social philosophy to the question of the origins of the modern world was to identify classical culture as the ultimate root of modernity. Within German elite culture, the classical heritage, through the influence of Italy, dominated standards of excellence and perfection in art, culture, and philosophy. For example, Goethe's Italian journey enjoyed a peculiar dominance within the cultural tradition of the German elite; his interpretation of Italian and classical culture set the bench-mark for cultural excellence. The importance of this classical tradition as mediated through the work of Goethe has not received adequate attention in the history of sociological theory, particularly in regard to the development of Weber's concepts of personality, love, and responsibility (Kent 1985; Lepenies 1985). The Hellenic world presented a picture of order, stability, and

71

cultivation within which the personality could develop as an integrated, holistic entity. The classical world presented an image of wholeness, completeness, and integration within which the human spirit could evolve and achieve a harmonious maturity without any problematic conflict between the private and the public domains. By contrast, the world of industrial capitalism, bureaucratic state regulation, and modern values opened up the possibility of fragmentation, standardization, and ultimately disenchantment, whereby the individual was unable to achieve any personal coherence or any harmonious relationship to the social whole. We can see the work of Hegel and Marx as reflections upon this loss of classical coherence, in which both writers assumed that some solution to the loss of community could be achieved through the dialectic of historical development. By contrast, life-philosophers such as Schopenhauer were far more pessimistic about the outcome of the modernization process and saw little real solution to the dangers of a bureaucratic, highly rationalistic social system dominated either by the state or by the masses.

Much of the anxiety implicit or explicit within the contemporary analysis of modernity and modernization finds its origins in the life-philosophy of Friedrich Nietzsche (Hennis 1988; Collins 1986; Stauth and Turner 1986). Nietzsche is important because he attacked the norms of the classical heritage, attempted to show that the most pure values of the German enlightenment were in fact disguises for more dangerous and violent undercurrents, and relativized absolute standards by arguing that God was dead and that therefore we live in a world which is one merely of perspectives. Nietzsche's attack on the classical legacy was originally formulated in *The Birth of Tragedy*, where he showed that the principles of beauty and truth in the classical heritage were, in fact, the outcomes of a conflict between Dionysus and Apollo representing the forces of sexual violence and artistic form (Stauth and Turner 1988). Greek culture and the classical world, rather than resting upon stable values of order, beauty and truth, was the outcome of violent and deep emotions of hatred, conflict, jealousy, and aggression. Nietzsche opened up the unconscious (or rather sub-conscious) world of hatred behind the pure values of classical culture. In his writings on the anti-Christ in *The Twilight of the Idols*, Nietzsche went on to attack, in particular, the Christian tradition as a disguised form of resentment in which the values of love and perfection again masked an underlying conflict in which the pure natural emotions of sex and hatred were transformed and transcribed on to an imaginary plane of ethical standards. In *Thus Spake Zarathustra*, Nietzsche argued that in the modern world general, communal, or absolute values have collapsed, and he expressed this idea in the notion that God is dead.

It is now recognized that Nietzsche's account of the problem of perspectivism, the relationship between power and knowledge, and the relationship between truth and moral values fundamentally shaped Weber's views on epistemology, historical change, and philosophy of science. While an earlier generation of writers thought that the Nietzsche legacy was mainly confined to Weber's notions about charisma, it is now more generally held that the fundamental assumptions of Weberian sociology are, to some extent, a debate with Nietzsche rather than a debate with Marx (Hennis 1988; Mommsen and Osterhammel 1987; Stauth and Turner 1986). For example, Weber's lectures on science as a vocation and politics as a vocation were not only shot through with Nietzsche's imagery and language, but also embraced much of Nietzsche's analysis of the perspectivism and fragmentation of modern cultures.

My argument in this chapter is that Weber, following Nietzsche, saw the origins of modern culture paradoxically in certain irrational forces, and noted that the consequence of modernization was not necessarily an entirely rational world, since it becomes very difficult to find legitimizing principles for action in a world of perspectivism. Whereas Nietzsche saw the irrational origins of modern culture in the violent competitions of the classical world, Weber identified the origins of modernity in religion, and specifically in the irrational quest for salvation. Weber sought to study the historical evolution of modernity by a series of macro-sociological comparisons of world religions in which ultimately he identified the irrational quest for salvation in the Calvinistic ethic as the most prominent and pervasive source of contemporary rational standards and rational values. The paradox of history is the unintended consequence of an irrational drive becoming a rational machine-like culture. The importance of Weber's sociology of religion, therefore, is its central place within the broader account of the global origins of rational systems. Whereas many contemporary interpretations of Weber's historical sociology put a special emphasis on the rational conditions for modern growth (such as a rational legal system, the separation of the home and the work-place, rational financial management, and the emergence of a

73

rational system of administration), it is more appropriate to see the origins of these rational systems within the paradoxes, problems, and contradictions of an irrational religious quest for meaning and personal authenticity. Having outlined in a very general way Weber's concerns with the relationship between irrationality and modernity, I shall now turn more specifically to his general account of the character, origins, and development of modern social relations and cultures. While I wish to present Weber's historical sociology from the basis of his abstract set of concepts in *Economy and Society*, the purpose of this account is not specifically exegetical, but rather an attempt to establish a substantive view of historical development within the framework of a study of contrasting religious systems.

FROM STATUS TO CONTRACT

In the introductory sections of *Economy and Society*, Weber attempted to outline a variety of general concepts for the analysis of social relations. In particular, he provided a categorization of social relationships in terms of either their open or closed quality, and in terms of their communal or associational characteristics. The distinction between communal and associational relations clearly follows the *Gemeinschaft/Gesellschaft* dichotomy of Tönnies. Weber defined social relationships as communal when they were based upon the subjective feelings of the social interactants, where these subjective feelings were either affectual or traditional. An associational relationship involves a rational orientation of social interaction in terms of interests, rather than in terms of subjective feelings. Social relations are closed where various strategies of social closure preclude the entrance of outsiders into the monopolistic privileges of an insider group; by contrast, open social relations do not involve the exclusion of outsiders in the interests of the monopolistic privileges of an insider group. When we combine these two dichotomous contrasts, we can provide a useful heuristic device for the analysis, not only of social relations, but of more general cultural connections. My argument is that, while Weber developed this typology initially and exclusively for the analysis of social relations, we can develop the typology to provide not only an account of cultural phenomena, but also to provide a dynamic, rather than static model of socio-cultural change (Figure 3.1).

It is plausible to argue that Weber, like many other nineteenth-century social theorists, saw the development of European history in

Figure 3.1 From status to contract

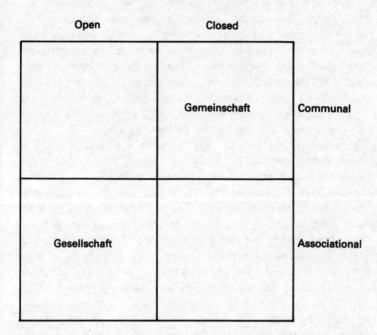

terms of a transition from a system of estates based on legal immunity and feudal privilege to an open market situation characterized by social classes and market relations. In the work of writers like Sir Henry Maine in *Ancient Law*, western history was seen in terms of the evolution of a set of juridical principles, namely from personal status to abstract contract. Since Weber was, himself, a jurisprudential theorist, it was natural for him to think of human history as a legal process from a system of personal status relationships involving the total person to a system of formal abstract market relationships involving, as it were, segments of the juridical personality (Kronman 1983). In Figure 3.1, we can see the transition from status to contract in terms of transition from closed, communal to open, associational relationships. This transition involves a switch from communal relations, involving substantive values and habitual reciprocity, to a society characterized by value pluralism, the indifference of market relationships, the individuation of the autonomous personality, and the evolution of a secular environment, relatively free from the constraining impact of traditional norms. While it would be possible in Weber's terms to think of alternative historical trajectories, Weber, rather like most late nineteenth-century social theorists, did in fact see the history of western societies as an evolution from traditional, closed, communal groups towards open, associational, secular, and rational relationships. We can, in a nutshell, conceptualize this relationship, or rather this transition, in terms of the emergence of a cash nexus between autonomous selfish individuals within the capitalist market-place — namely, a transition from fixed status positions to open contractual relationships.

I wish to superimpose upon this traditional sociological model an alternative but compatible perspective which attempts to locate religious systems in terms of the four boxes within Figure 3.1. That is, within Weber's schema, we should be able to identify those religions which most easily fit within the traditional non-revolutionary situation and those religious systems which either promote secular social change towards modernity or at least are compatible with such modernizing processes. This type of analysis, to some extent, conforms to the position presented by Ernst Troeltsch in his study of *The Social Teaching of the Christian Churches* (Troeltsch 1912). While this analysis in certain respects reflects and corresponds to the sect–church typology of Troeltsch, my aim is to present Weber's world religious typology within the framework of an analysis of the historic impact of open, associational relationships.

Following Parsons' introduction to Weber's famous *The Sociology of Religion*, we can start our account by noting the obvious fact that Weber regarded the Protestant sects as a collection of religious groups which provided the cultural motor which launched modernism (given a variety of suitable and conducive structural conditions). For Weber, the Protestant sects embodied the Protestant ethic, which was the most dynamic form of cultural relationship within the Christian tradition. As evangelical and missionary groups, the Protestant sects were open to the conversion of outsiders, and they were the religious groups which were the most compatible with the individualism of the economic market-place (Abercrombie, Hill, and Turner 1986). It is obvious that the Protestant sects represented a sharp contrast to the world of Hinduism, traditional forms of religiosity, pre-intellectualized forms of magic, and other religious systems which are expressive of undifferentiated village life.

Considering this schema within an historical or evolutionary perspective, Weber argued that the original religious impulse was essentially empirical, practical, and this-worldly, being concerned mainly with questions of health and personal security. The development of religious systems depends crucially upon the emergence of an intellectual class of priests who develop the religious systems into a theoretical perspective on the self and the world. With the development of religious dogmatics, the relationship between religious practice and the everyday world becomes distant, remote, and ambiguous. It was this conflict between the religious perspective and the world — that is, between the sacred and the profane — which provided the main driving force towards intellectualization and the systematization of religious into dogmatic structures. The implication of Weber's argument is that the greater the tension between the sacred and the profane, the greater the possibility of social transformation and cultural dynamism. There are, therefore, three important dimensions from Weber's point of view in religious systems. The first is the character of the devaluation or rejection of the world as a corrupt system. Second, there is the question of the openness of the religious system to outsiders, which is in turn closely related to the problem of missions and evangelical response to outsiders; this is the whole question, therefore, of conversion. Finally, there is the character of the sociological organization of the religious congregation into either a communal *Gemeinschaft* group or into an associational *Gesellschaft* relationship. Having developed these dimensions to his sociology of religion, Weber could then categorize and rank religions according to their relationship to these three characteristics.

Within Weber's schema, Hinduism assumes a particularly pre-modern characteristic, being, in Weber's terms, not committed to evangelical propagation of belief, being largely local or national in character, and assuming a predominantly *Gemeinschaft* structure. Hinduism did little to shake or undermine the Indian social structure, being by contrast a religious system largely accommodated to its social environment. In a similar fashion, Weber argued that Confucianism was a religious code primarily of court officials, providing them with a suitable gentlemanly, ethical outlook. Confucianism was the least critical and radical of the so-called world religions. Similarly, Weber argued that Buddhism was a religious system not particularly interested in the evangelical conversion of the world, offering instead a doctrine of personal resignation and comfort to mendicant monks. Buddhism adopted an hierarchical organization, being less concerned with this-worldly problems and more in the development of a special technique of contemplation and withdrawal. In general terms, therefore, these 'Asiatic religions' contributed little to the transformation of social reality.

This argument, however, left Weber with a problem which was to distinguish between the so-called Abrahamic religions, namely Christianity, Islam, and Judaism. At one level, these religions enjoy very similar sociological and theological characteristics. They are monotheistic, literate, ascetic, congregational, and, at least in principle, committed to some form of evangelical activity. In particular, these three religions, which in many respects can be regarded as three variations on a common theme, were ethical systems which profoundly devalued the world, regarding this world as a place of evil forces and destructive capacities.

In *Ancient Judaism*, Weber drew attention to the important role of the prophet in Old Testament religion, which gave Judaism a profoundly radical role in traditional societies. The prophet and ethical prophecy laid the basis for a social critique of the social order which was a corrupt world; it was regarded as a profound departure from the social contract between God and his people. Prophecy called the people back to their social relationship with God and thereby devalued and criticized this world as a falling away or departure from the original code of morality which was the basis, not simply of the Jewish tribal confederacy, but of the world as such. While Weber recognized this radical character of Jewish prophecy, he argued that with the Diaspora, Judaism became a narrow, particularistic, inward-looking religion of an exclusive community. The rite of circumcision was, in particular, a manifest demonstration in Weber's view of the social closure and isolationism of the Jewish community. In fact, Weber came to regard Diaspora Judaism as the pariah religion of a subordinative people whose ethical system was based upon a form of resentment. In this respect, Weber in part followed a number of arguments originally developed by Nietzsche in the theory of resentment. However, while Nietzsche had argued that Christian morality was the expression of resentment, Weber redirected some elements of the Nietzsche theory on to Judaism. Finally, Weber noted that the dietary practices of Judaism were yet another instance of its social closure against outsiders. The Diaspora transformed the inner search for salvation into an exterior practice of ritualistic behaviour such as diet and circumcision, with the result that Judaism ceased to be an ethical prophetic religion with a missionary task to convert the world to a new religious order. Judaism had, therefore, ceased to be a significant religion of social transformation.

Weber adopted a very similar position in his unfinished and incomplete analysis of Islam and Islamic history (Turner 1978). Again, from a casual examination of Islam, it is self-evident that Islam contained many of the rational, radical, and transformative features which Weber associated with inner-worldly asceticism. Islam was clearly a prophetic religion, with a decisive emphasis on literature and holy scripture, with an ethical code which condemned this world as a place of human evil, and with a clear conception of the importance of mastery over this world in order to achieve human salvation. In many respects, the rational character of Islamic law and of Islamic theology was strikingly relevant to the whole issue of rational modernization. On the face of it, one would expect Islam to be more radical in its relationship to 'the world' than was the case for Protestantism. However, Weber argued that Islam had been blocked in its development by the fact that it became primarily the religion of a warrior group, and that this militarization of Islam had converted the quest for personal salvation into a quest for land and wealth. For Weber, Islam had all the characteristics of a feudal religion of warriors, because of its emphasis on military success in this world. The division in Islam between the household of faith and the household of war characterized this feudal development within Islam, transforming the radical, ethical prophecy of the pristine religion of the Prophet into merely the pursuit of wealth in land. We can see, therefore, that Weber attempted to resolve the problem of the Abrahamic faiths by arguing that only Christianity emerged as the religion with the maximum capacity for bringing about modernization. Judaism failed because it became an inward-looking, particularistic religion of a pariah people, whereas Islam failed by becoming the religion of a dominant and dominating class of warriors. Both religions became, therefore, traditional in their orientation, and the original tension between the salvational drive and this world was lost.

Weber was unable to complete his projected sociology of Christianity, which would have complemented his other studies of ancient Judaism and the ancient religions of Asia. It has often been noted that Weber's view of Roman Catholicism was somewhat stunted and underdeveloped, since his commentaries on Catholicism were almost wholly concerned with pre-Reformation Catholic culture within

European feudalism. Weber failed to analyse or to consider the social and historical implications of the counter-Reformation and the modernization of Catholicism in Europe. It is also well known that at the end of *The Protestant Ethic and the Spirit of Capitalism*, Weber noted that his friend and colleague Ernst Troeltsch was undertaking a complex and extensive study of the historical development of Christendom in terms of the now famous church–sect typology. Although Weber did not, therefore, extend and complete his view of Christianity within the world religions, he did provide an important sketch of the sociological characteristics of the Protestant sects within the sociology of religion, *The Protestant Ethic and the Spirit of Capitalism*, and in his essays on religion in North America.

The dynamic and historically important feature of the Calvinistic sects was their sharp and profound devaluation of the world, creating an unbridgeable gap between the sacred and the profane. The Calvinist was isolated and alone in the world, confronted by the terrible majesty of his God, unable to employ the resources of the sacraments, Christian rituals, and the priesthood in order to contact his God. The Calvinist was alone and connected to God mainly by the revelation of truth in the New Testament. Weber, of course, thought that the Calvinist was confronted by a profound salvation anxiety, since there were no clear signs or indicators of inner personal value in terms of salvation. Since the Calvinist could not escape from the world into mysticism, he was forced into self-mastery and the control of the world through an ethic of inner-worldly asceticism. Weber differentiated the pure doctrine of Calvinism from the other sectarian movements within the Reformation which, in some way or other, modified or softened the stark and terrible message of religious isolation. For example, the Methodists and other pietist groups took personal emotional salvation as an indicator of God's favour and mercy. Within these sectarian groups, the emotional experience of conversion provided some index of the person's status before the awe-inspiring majesty of this absent God. The social consequences of the Calvinist doctrine within Weber's sociological account are well known. In terms of Weber's schema (Figure 3.1), the Calvinistic ethic provided part of the leverage in cultural and psychological terms for the transformation of western societies from closed, communal relations to open, associational relations. The freedom of the Calvinist believer in relation to his God was, so to speak, an analogy of the freedom of the worker in the market-place to form contracts and other social obligations. More importantly, the rationality of the Calvinist position favoured the development of natural sciences, since the believer had a religious conviction that the study of nature was compatible — indeed, demanded by — the religious ethic of world mastery. The cold rationality of Calvinism was perfectly compatible with the modernist project — that is, the imposition of rational forms of behaviour and perspectives on the natural world, on social relations, and on the personality. The this-worldly asceticism of Calvinism was, therefore, not simply compatible with capitalist production, but, widely and more importantly, with the rational project of modernity as a whole as manifested in science, culture, and economics. Whereas the other-worldly religions were compatible with existing social relations, the profoundly disturbing message of Calvin drove the Calvinist believer into the world not in a spirit of accommodation, but in a spirit of mastery and challenge. The concept of the calling in the salvational system of Calvinism provided the model from which other notions of calling or vocation in science, medicine, and law were ultimately developed. The concept of a calling in science embraced the ethic of enquiry, mastery, regulation, and control, giving the scientific calling in the world a religious underpinning (Turner 1981).

WEBER AND LIBERAL THEOLOGY

In his writing on the philosophy of social science, Weber had attempted to establish some guidelines for the analysis of the role of interpretations and values in social science. It is well known that Weber attempted to draw some demarcation between neutral accounts or explanations of social relations as factual connections, value-relevant interpretations, and value-judgements. In his sociology of religion, clearly Weber attempted to provide a value-neutral account of the main characteristics of religious institutions, beliefs, and practices. However, his historical and sociological account of the character of the world religions necessarily entailed a theological judgement or theological interpretation of the relationships between religious groups and traditions. The point here is to draw attention to the (as I will argue) privileged position of Calvinistic Protestantism within Weber's account of the world religions. More specifically, by taking a position on the historical role of Protestantism, Weber was also inevitably drawn into theological discussion involving a religious viewpoint of the character — for example, of Calvinistic Protestantism in relation to rational Islam.

We know from historical, biographical, and anecdotal evidence that Weber was indeed impressed by the world-view of liberal Protestantism and admired the heroic tradition of religious calling within these sects. Although his own intellectual development eventually ruled out any personal commitment to faith, Weber retained a strong admiration for the principles of liberal Protestantism with respect to personal behaviour, moral authority, and family relations. We know, for example, that Weber's mother and the young Max Weber were both influenced by the theological and moral views of the American preacher W. E. Channing (Fugen 1985). Weber also embraced much of the religio-moral teaching of writers like Goethe and the letters of William Penn, especially on the moral themes of marital love (Kent 1985). We also know, for example, that Weber was, at one period of his life, closely involved in the work of the Evangelical-Social Congress (Mommsen and Osterhammel 1987).

However, my argument does not rest only on biographical details, since I want to assert a closer relationship at the analytical level to Weber's sociological theories and certain theological assumptions. In part, this account of Max Weber's sociological perspective follows the interesting discussion of Weber's epistemology in Anthony T. Kronman's *Max Weber* (1983). Kronman makes the important and interesting observation that Weber's own theory of personality (that is, a system of rational, ethical regulation involving a life-project) reflected his ethical outlook, which was in turn compatible with a broader Protestant viewpoint. Kronman notes that the development of the concept of a transcendental God had two very important sociological or cultural consequences. First, the world has no meaning apart from the meaning which God imparts to the world; this notion of the meaning of the world being given to it by God follows from the doctrine of transcendentalism. The second consequence is that the norms which human beings follow are ethical commandments rather than fixed laws of God or nature. The consequence of this theological position is to locate the problem of meaning in the central issues of epistemology and sociology. Kronman argues that Weber's methodological views follow from this argument or from this theological perspective. Weber's methodology, according to Kronman, has two very important central arguments. The first is a distinction between facts and values (the famous is – ought distinction), and second, that the

apparent facticity of the world is meaningless without cultural interpretation. Just as the Calvinist finds the world meaningless without
the intervention of God, so the sociologist is necessarily involved in
interpretation — that is, the imposition of meaning upon the world.
Kronman goes on to argue more generally that 'one may fairly
describe Weber's theory of value as a secular form of Christianity —
Christianity without God' (Kronman 1983: 153). One could argue,
by contrast, that this problem of the relationship between language
and facts or between values and things was also a legacy from
Nietzsche. The important problem for Weber was that, given the
death of God, we necessarily live in a world of conflicting interpretations as a consequence of perspectivism and that sociology has an
acute problem of finding a secure, reliable, or effective perspective
from which to view other perspectives.

We can also argue that Weber's theory of personality as a rational
plan for life to dominate the habitus was also part of an ethic of world
mastery, and that Weber adhered to a theory of hierarchical personality in which the full blossoming of personality depended upon the
rejection of affectual, traditional, and instinctual elements. If we
consider Weber's theory of social action which involved a differentiation of types of action into affectual, traditional, value-rationality,
and means–end rationality, then we can see that he placed
personality at the end of a continuum from nature to society.
Personality in Weber's schema must involve the inner-worldly ascetic
norm of personal regulation in order to achieve not only self-mastery
but also world-mastery.

I have in this section attempted to make three observations. The
first is that Weber's personal life was, at various times, shaped by
many concerns which came from the liberal Protestant tradition.
Second, following Kronman, I have noted that certain theological
views about the nature of the meaningfulness of the world influenced
his epistemological writings, and finally, I have drawn attention to
the possible relationship between Weber's notion of personality and
the idea of salvation in ascetic Calvinism. In the final section of this
part of my argument, I wish to draw attention to some parallels
between Weber's implicit history of world religions in the sociology of
religion and the political relationships between world religions,
involving ideological conflict over religious priority and authority.

Following Weber, we can note that the Abrahamic faiths are highly
intellectual and, in certain respects, rational religions because they

have, in rather different ways, certain classes of intellectuals who develop their doctrines into coherent systems of theology. These theologies involve, for example, certain theodicies which explain God's action in the world and God's relationship to religions in the world. The development of a priestly or intellectual class brings into the foreground questions about God's own thoughts about or relationship towards religions which exist in the world. Since, for the Abrahamic faiths, there is only one God but many religions, this raises the issue of which religion is, so to speak, God's preferred religious identity. World religions, by and large, claim that the God they worship has a special relationship to them through a binding contract. For example, Yaweh had a special relationship to the tribes of Israel, since He was involved in a social contract (the Covenant) with this people, in fact with His people. By contrast, it must be clear that Christ had no intention of forming a special religion called 'Christianity' and that in large measure Christianity is the product of Pauline preaching and practice as eventually institutionalized in the primitive church. Islam, in this respect, is probably somewhat special, since in the Quran, Allah declares that 'His' religion is named 'Islam', which is the universal religion of all of those who submit to the one God.

These theological and ideological conflicts between religious faiths which, in some sense, belong to the same cluster, gave rise to theories of the relationship between the Abrahamic traditions. For example, it is quite common for certain Jewish theologians or writers to note that Christianity is a sectarian association related to a particular Jewish prophet, namely the prophet Jesus. From the perspective of Judaism, Christianity appears as a somewhat peculiar offshoot, departing from the genuine culture of the Jewish tradition. By contrast, Christianity must regard Judaism as an unreformed and recalcitrant branch of the genuine reformed 'Judaism' of Christianity. It is only in relatively recent times, for example, that the Roman Catholic church has publicly announced that Christ was crucified, not by the Jews, but by humankind as such. The failure of Jews to convert to Christianity is now taken to be a general indicator of the wickedness of man as such. Again, we can note that Christianity regards the development of Islam as a departure from Christianity, traditionally treating Islam as a mere sect which, at some future date, will return to the fold. In Dante's epic *The Divine Comedy*, Islam is presented as a schism within the Christian church to be eternally punished by God's wrath.

Finally, Islam regards both Christianity and Judaism as defective forms of monotheism. Islam sees itself as the summation and transformation of the monotheistic traditions of Christianity and Judaism.

Borrowing the language of Marxism, we can argue that world religions attempt to establish the legitimacy of their religious claims by positing the existence of certain epistemological ruptures which separate the incomplete truth of previous religions from the expanded or complete truth of the contemporary faith. These epistemological ruptures are well developed, highly complicated arguments within existing theological traditions. Within the social sciences, these theological positions often reappear under new titles. We can regard orientalism as a western tradition of enquiry which took over the Christian legacy, such that traditionally both Islam and Judaism are regarded as lesser or defective or incomplete traditions in comparison with Christianity (and its secular offshoots). The orientalist tradition has historically regarded Christianity as more rational, more individualistic, more developed, less prone to magic and other deviations, and more in tune with the requirements of a democratic individualistic and rational culture. Neither Judaism nor Islam provided a culture within which natural science could flourish; neither Judaism nor Islam developed a political culture within which dissent and opposition could develop; and finally, neither Judaism nor Islam therefore provided the social infrastructure whereby rational capitalist practices could emerge. The whole tradition of orientalist writing both in history and sociology has produced a hierarchy of religious systems in terms of their relationship to the rationalist project of modernity, and this hierarchy is closely related to the theological view of Christianity with respect to other religious traditions.

INDIVIDUALISM

Clearly, individualism played an important part in Weber's evaluation of the significance of Protestantism as a transformative culture, and Weber's liberalistic ethical position also gave the individual a central location within the debate about the ethical character of modern societies (Turner 1988a). As a legal theorist, Weber would have been familiar with the history of the emergence of the concept of legal personality in the development of corporations in Italian commerce. Weber was also aware, as we have seen, of the gradual development of the concept of a legal contract, binding together two legal entities with the specific purpose of economic activity; modern contracts, therefore, were unlike the magical bonds which united individuals in pre-modern society. However, the importance of Protestantism was its emphasis on the isolation of the individual, the subjective experience of guilt, and the rational organization of life to transform the individual into an ethical personality. Individualistic Calvinism emphasized the self-motivated activity of the autonomous and separate individual, whose life was organized by a detailed scheme or calling and who adopted a highly calculative and rational attitude towards the environment. Individuals who were trained or brought up in this doctrine were, in a sense, perfectly matched to the needs of a modern capitalist culture.

Within the comparative framework of his sociology of religion, it is important to recognize that Weber did not deny that the Asiatic religions had a concept of the individual. However, Weber saw the individual in Asian cultures as a personality oriented to the world in terms of contemplation and inner knowledge as the main channel for salvation. The Asiatic self is a cognitive agent seeking immersion in divinity through ecstatic possession of gnosis. By contrast, the western self is an entity in which will and action are placed at the centre of activities, and therefore the western self seeks autonomy through a series of active technologies of the self. Whereas in Asiatic religions the self seeks repose and quietness through the contemplation of truth, the western self in the Weberian schema is seen to be a willing, choosing, and active agent.

Weber's view of individualism has, to some extent, been supported in recent years by the comparative work of Louis Dumont (1983; 1986). For Dumont, the western self stands outside the world attempting to control it through cognitive and willing activities; the Asiatic self is immersed in the world through the contemplation of truth. For Dumont, this gives a clear set of dimensions which he called 'the individualistic configuration' in order to define what it is to be modern. This configuration includes

individualism (as opposed to holism), primacy of the relations of men to things (as against the relations between men), absolute distinction between subject and object (as opposed to a merely relative, fluctuating distinction), segregation of values and facts and ideas (opposed to the indistinction or close association), distribution of knowledge into independent, homologous and homogeneous planes or disciplines.

(Dumont 1986: 27)

It is interesting to locate these discussions of individualism within the more traditional nineteenth-century life-philosophies of Schopenhauer and Nietzsche who, in one respect, analysed the same issues. Whereas Schopenhauer saw the solution to contemporary problems in terms of a pessimistic surrender to reality on the basis of a Buddhist system of contemplation and meditation, Nietzsche argued that it was only through a revaluation of values that one could mobilize the will to power in a creative fashion. Clearly, Weber appears to reject Schopenhauer's mystical orientation to the world in favour of activism, rationalism, and individualism.

In summary, Weber argued that the radical character of Christianity derived from the presence of a transcendent personal God whose actions in the world were based upon a division between the sacred and the profane, such that the world we live in is, in a sense, devalued and devoid of meaning. The meaningfulness of the world depends upon action whereby interpretations and theodicies are imposed upon reality. The solution to these problems is to be found in the development of ethical personality through an ascetic ethic of world mastery. Whereas both Judaism and Islam laid some foundations for such a world-view, for the reasons we have considered these two religions did not provide the modernizing, rationalizing drive which Weber thought was essential for the emergence of modern systematic cultures. Weber adopted this position despite many analytic problems (such as the fact that at one level Islam would have to be regarded as a more appropriate religion for the modernizing process). For example, God in Islam is more abstract, less figurative, and less encumbered by personal attributes. The development of Islamic calligraphy is one consequence of this highly rational conception of a God without human attributes.

FROM MODERNISM TO POST-MODERNISM

I have so far given an account of Weber's master conception of the rationalization process which produces a world dominated by modern conditions, values, and institutions. We may regard this as Weber's version of the project of modern rationalization which, for Weber, pointed in the direction of a society dominated by bureaucracy, regulation, and calculation, producing a totally stable but stultifying environment. This somewhat bleak picture of the modern condition was, in some respects, Weber's answer to the Marxist tradition, since he wanted to suggest that any future socialist society dominated by economic planning would be simply a more profound example of the processes of rationalization and secularization which had transformed capitalism in the European and North American contexts. It can be suggested that Weber had two versions of the modernization project, one producing a world of stable calculations and another pointing in the direction of an incoherent, unstable, and meaningless world of polytheistic values and nihilism.

The first — in a sense, a positive view — version of modernization linked Weber's sociology to the Enlightenment tradition of Kant, while the second — the pessimistic — version of modernization connected Weber to the tradition of Kierkegaard, Schopenhauer, and Nietzsche: In this pessimistic version of the rationalization project, the instability of values and the absence of absolute guides (with the death of God) produce a world of endless perspectives in which reason becomes aware of its own limits. The problem of the modern world is that, although we have the means to achieve certain ends or goals, it is often extremely difficult to produce convincing general arguments of a consensual nature to justify or legitimize any particular end. This can be regarded as part of the Nietzsche legacy, since it was Nietzsche who argued that any rational view of the world must ultimately perceive the limits of its own capacities and authorities, because it would necessarily recognize ultimately the arbitrary character of its own stance. Therefore, Nietzsche concluded that most forms of rational enquiry must result in either pessimism or nostalgia, since a rational justification for rationality is difficult to sustain, particularly in a world of competing perspectives (Turner 1988b). This is one way of saying that social reality is socially constructed and, once the constructed character of the world is recognized, it becomes somewhat difficult to sustain what have been called 'grand narratives' which disguise the arbitrariness of narrative as such.

In short, Nietzsche identified the problem of thought in the metaphoricality of thinking itself. In Weber's methodology, as we have seen, this view leads to the position that it is not possible to have a general theory and that at best we might aim for general concepts. Because the world is a chaos of conflicting meanings, it is difficult to find a basis or principle of legitimacy which will carry general rather than particular respect.

Finally, to this rather negative picture of the world, Weber added a view of the negative consequences of bureaucracy; namely, that it would result in a collection of human beings who were merely cogs within the grand machine. This can be regarded as Weber's version of the contemporary debate regarding the death of the subject.

Although Weber never employed these particular concepts, I am suggesting that there is another side of Weber's modernization theory — namely, an antithetical view of modernism which, using contemporary terminology, we may call Weber's version of the post-modernist debate. Although there has been much confused and confusing discussion over the notions of modernism and post-modernism, there is some virtue in these concepts as representing rather different visions or commentaries upon the modernization project. It turns out that the notion of 'modern' is, in fact, an ancient term with very early precursors in theological and philosophical reasoning (Kaufmann 1986). There are strong historical reasons for regarding seventeenth-century baroque society as the first genuinely modern epoch which regarded itself as modern (Maravell 1986). Although the term 'post-modernism' was first employed in terms of architectural and artistic criticism, it has become more widely used in literature and, more recently, in social theory. It has been suggested that post-modernism is the outcome of a mass consumer society in which, given the explosion of literary forms, the maintenance of the grand epic novel became less and less possible. Post-modernism appears to be also associated with the growth of computers and electronic devices which have made accessible to the total population the previously elite culture of the minority, forcing the avant-garde to use outrageous forms of expression in order to achieve distinction (Jameson 1985). As modernist works of art were widely accepted by museums, art galleries, and universities, it became important for new forms of art to reject the modernistic programme in culture by developing post-modernist artefacts which are not acceptable to establishment institutions.

In sociology, the emergence of a post-modernist world was, perhaps, first identified clearly by Daniel Bell in *The Coming of Post-Industrial Society* (1973). For Bell, the post-industrial world depends increasingly on knowledge production rather than on the capitalist production of commodities, relies increasingly on intellectual rather than on manual power, and therefore generates increasing leisure time, since it is no longer necessary to exploit manpower in terms of the conventional Marxist scheme. Bell went on to elaborate this argument by identifying certain tensions or contradictions between the political, social, and economic realms, noting the increasing contradictions between hedonism and asceticism. More importantly, Bell recognized a new form of the self emerging out of these social relations — a self increasingly anxious, isolated, and neurotic. These trends in democratic, consumer societies brought about the end of art (especially representational art), the loss of the self in modern drama, and the emergence of what Bell called the Dionysiac pack in which, ultimately, reason was undermined by the new sensibilities of a culture committed to mere enjoyment. Bell noted the interesting paradox in socialism arising from the new post-modernist mood:

> The rebellious impulses of cultural modernism now run smack up against a paradox. The radicalism of the non-western world — that of China, Algeria, or Cuba — is a puritanical one, while the Marxism of the Soviet Union is culturally repressive. Cultural modernism, though it still calls itself subversive, finds a home largely in bourgeois, capitalist society.
>
> (Bell 1976: 147)

This post-industrial society, therefore, has many connections with the world predicted by Weber in the classic metaphors of the iron cage and the machine, in which the democratization of society must, through a process of oligarchy, lead to a standardized cultural world of sameness. In this pessimistic scenario of bureaucratic domination, we can once more see the legacy of Nietzsche. Nietzsche, influenced by the work of Alexis de Tocqueville, had argued that the growing dominance of the doctrine of equality would produce a political herd or, in Nietzsche's terms, result in the animalization of man in modern bureaucratic democracies. Rather than producing a new form of individual liberty, the iron cage of bureaucratic society, with its levelling trend of equality, would result in the destruction of the autonomous and sensitive individual. The more a state attempts to achieve egalitarian citizenship, the more it will use the modern systems of bureaucratic surveillance and dominance. While obviously neither Nietzsche nor Weber predicted the outcome of a post-modernist period, there are elements in their social philosophy which, at least, anticipated the paradox of reason discovering its own un-reasonableness.

SOLUTIONS TO POST-MODERNITY

There now appear to be a number of solutions available to the problems raised by modernity and post-modernity. In this chapter, I am arguing that post-modernity is a conceptual position derived from the paradoxes of rationality, which we first clearly recognized in the works of Nietzsche and Weber. The artistic solution to post-modernity can be found in Nietzsche's arguments concerning the creative and positive nature of art as a pure activity, not dominated by resentment. For Nietzsche, music and art represented a realm in which thinking and feeling were reunited. This particular tradition has given rise to the notion that Nietzsche proposed an aestheticization of reality as a solution to nihilism. In this solution to the instabilities of the polytheistic world, ethics are translated into aesthetics. Whereas there is a strong emphasis in Nietzsche's theory of tragedy on the importance of art as a therapeutic and creative activity, Weber's sociology largely rejected the idea of an aesthetic vocation in the world. As Lepenies (1985: 299) has argued, Weber did not succumb to either an aesthetic or a religious interpretation of the problem of knowledge in contemporary society, but sought rather to develop an ascetic vocation in sociology as the only secure basis of understanding and interpretation. This laid the basis for an ethic of responsibility as the only possible orientation to reality in the absence of absolute values and common certainties.

As we have argued elsewhere (Holton and Turner 1986), Parsons was largely free of the nostalgic quest for the securities and certainties of a previous age which largely dominated much of late nineteenth- and early twentieth-century sociology in Germany and elsewhere. It is clearly the case that Weber did not share the liberal certainty and optimism which characterized Parsons' sociology. It is interesting in this respect to compare Weber and Parsons on the historical contribution of Protestantism to the modern world. Whereas Parsons thought that the evolution of the Protestant plural value system was perfectly compatible with the needs of a democratic and largely secular polity, Weber's sociology is always riddled with tensions, uncertainties, and ambiguities about the future outcome of both religious evolution and democracy. Parsons' view of religion was largely shared by the more optimistic branches of Protestantism which flourished in the United States of America. While Weber argued that, in a sense, Protestantism had created modern culture, modern rational culture no longer required religion. Indeed, modernity would destroy religion, but for Weber there was no going back. While Weber did not, therefore, embrace a totally nostalgic vision, there was a profound sense of cultural and moral crisis in his sociology which, as I have suggested, led to the quest for an ethic of individual responsibility as the antidote to the problem of perspectivism and nihilism.

In this range of problems within Weber's sociological theory and methodology, the question of religion remained prominent. I have argued that Weber inherited a number of issues from Nietzsche's philosophy. These aspects of Weber's legacy from Nietzsche included the debate about secularization, the pluralism of world-views, and the perspectivism which infected the debate about morality. Weber, however, sought to reject Nietzsche's argument that the highest values of Christianity were an expression of resentment, and in his ethic of responsibility we can discover a form of secularized Christian response to the world through an individualistic, liberal theology. However, for Weber religion remained problematic, although he recognized that for some it was always possible to fly back into the arms of the church. Many of these issues have, in contemporary sociology, been taken up forcefully by writers like Daniel Bell in *The Cultural Contradictions of Capitalism*. Anticipating many current debates, Bell has noted that with the emergence of a modernist problematic, there is a transition from the ethical to the aesthetic. For Bell, the problem of modernity has, in cultural terms, been approached in terms of the aesthetic justification of life:

> For the modern, cosmopolitan man, culture has replaced both religion and work as a means of self-fulfilment or as a justification — an aesthetic justification — of life. But behind this change, essentially from religion to culture, lies the extraordinary crossover in consciousness, particularly in the meanings of expressive conduct in human society.

> (Bell 1976: 156)

Yet the oddity is that, as the theological foundations of the modernist project collapse, and as the church as an institutional order is forced into retreat, new cults emerge to fill, as it were, the gap left over by the erosion of traditional faith. These new cults, however, are again expressions of intense subjectivity and sensitivity, giving expression to hedonistic surrender and personalized self-fulfilment. Again, these discussions in Bell remind one of Weber's observations that, given the crisis of modernity, it was likely that, particularly young people, would flee to the new cults of intensive personal brotherhood, hedonism, and self-experience, away from what Weber regarded as the serious tasks of politics and science.

THE SECULARIZATION DEBATE

Weber shared a theory of secularization with the majority of late nineteenth-century thinkers in Germany and France who had come to the conclusion that modern rational society would not provide an environment in which traditional religious belief and practice could flourish or survive. In the German context, of course, there had been an extensive debate both in theology and early Marxism over the erosion of religious belief and over the incompatibility between the church and capitalist society. Following David Strauss and Ludwig Feuerbach, both Marx and Engels had argued that capitalism would be the death of traditional Christian institutions and culture. While Hegel had anticipated a future form of religion which would be highly rational and abstract, conforming to the abstract citizen, Marx and Engels saw the spread of socialism as a necessary condition for the erosion of religion, as the material bases of religion were eroded.

Although Weber also shared a similar conception of religion, his views were more closely tied to those presented by Troeltsch in *The Social Teaching of the Christian Churches*. Troeltsch had argued that the history of Christendom could be seen as the perpetual and endless conflict between the church and the sect. The church represented the universalistic message of Christianity as controlled and managed through the church, as a collection of sacraments regulated by priests to the exclusion of lay participation. The sect, by contrast, stressed the direct and immediate relationship between man and God unmediated by sacraments, liturgies, and priests, giving a special emphasis to experience and brotherly love as the basis of communal life. To some extent, the church–sect typology was a further version of the *Gemeinschaft–Gesellschaft* distinction. Interestingly, Troeltsch argued that, with the collapse of the universal church, the historic confrontation and contradiction between church and sect had disappeared, giving rise to a new form of personalized religion, which he called 'mysticism' and which he felt would dominate modern societies. Weber adopted this view to some extent in his sociology of religion, noting that the modern world would be characterized by the predominance of subjective emotionalism, small groups based upon brotherly love, and a new form of religion as personal gratification and satisfaction.

Although there is ample evidence of the institutional decline of the organized church throughout Europe and North America, there is no clear evidence either that we live in an entirely secular society or that secularization and the development of industrial capitalism are inevitably linked together. In some capitalist cultures, religion has shown a remarkable resilience and persistence. In the American context, it appears to be the case that Christianity has functioned as an important feature of popular culture, giving expression to the strong individualism of the American tradition — a feature of American society first systematically commented on by de Tocqueville. Another illustration would be the Netherlands, which has had one of the longest experiences of commercial capitalism in Europe, but has also retained a strong religious tradition, and indeed it can be argued that the Netherlands has never been secularized in any significant fashion, although the old system of religious pillars appears to have weakened (Bagley 1973). In other societies, such as Italy, Spain, and Ireland, religious differences continue to play a fundamental part in the political structure of modern life. In the late 1970s and 1980s, however, an entirely new range of problems has emerged for the conventional sociology of religion and for debates about modernism — namely, the rapid and dynamic explosion of fundamentalist movements within the Abrahamic religions.

In Israel, in the United States of America, and in many parts of the Islamic world, there have been strong undercurrents of fundamentalist revival which have shaken many of the conventional assumptions of the sociology of religion, but more importantly have begun to change the political map of the modern world. To some extent, we can see the revival of fundamentalist religion, not as disconfirmation of the existence of post-modernism, but precisely as a response to the pluralization of the life-world in a culture dominated by the problems of perspectivism and relativism which, in turn, we may see as an outcome of the impact of modern forms of consumerism on contemporary societies. The final argument of my commentary on Weber's sociology of religion is that the threat to religion comes not from the rational, modernist project, but from the diversity of the life-world of individuals brought about by the impact of the market and modern consumerism on different religious cultures. In order to illustrate this argument, I shall turn to the recent history of Islam in order to present some criticisms of Weber, but also a modest defence.

TWO PHASES OF ISLAMIC HISTORY

Three separate but related processes profoundly changed the Islamic regions in the nineteenth century. First, the Ottoman empire was carved up into relatively separate nation-states under the impact of European colonialism. Second, the economies of the old Islamic world were incorporated into the world capitalist system as highly dependent units. And, third, there was a significant cultural response to these changes through various reform movements. We can regard these three developments as processes of cultural and structural differentiation. These economic and social changes brought about a certain secularization of Islamic societies. A new intelligentsia was created in association with an imperial structure. The failure of this class of intellectuals to achieve full integration into the western system produced eventually an intellectual leadership for nationalism and anti-colonialism. The result was an intense ambiguity as to the relationship between nationalism and westernization.

In certain contexts, very deliberate programmes of secularization were adopted (as in Kemalist Turkey). Traditional and popular Islam became in these developments closely associated with the historic decay and decline of Islamic culture in the face of modernizing and rationalistic western societies. These programmes of secularization involved the creation of new legal systems which typically limited the social role of Islamic holy law, so that the Shariah was relegated to the status of personal law. The introduction of French codes of legal arrangements in North Africa and English administration in Egypt profoundly changed the traditional role of the religious courts. There was also a significant separation of religious and secular institutions of education. At a more mundane but highly expressive level, there was also a modernization of dress and custom as in the so-called Turkish hat law of 1925 which implied a significant change in values and practices, especially between men and women.

This institutional revolution, which involved a differentiation of social structures, was broadly legitimized by modernist ideology. A central theme of modernism was that, once Islam was liberated from its folk traditions and foreign accretions, it could flourish, providing the culture appropriate to a modern, rational, dynamic social system. Modernism was legitimized by an appeal to pre-modern Islamic primitivism, since it was held that early Islam was rational and uncontaminated by later populist accretions. The return to the Quran in practice brought about profound changes. The leading figures in these developments were Rashid Rida (1865–1935), Jamal Al-Din Al-Afghani (1838–97), Muhammad Abduh (1849–1905), and Ahmad Lutfi al-Sayyid (1872–1963). These movements for social reform had a number of features in common. They required a return to the purity of the Islamic tradition in order to achieve social change and political progress; they involved a critique of popular religion, and they required the development of new educational institutions to promote an Islamization of society. These reformist movements were largely anti-western, but not anti-modernist, and they were based upon the assumption that a reform of Islam would create a new social dynamism. To summarize these features:

> Islamic modernism implanted an outlook or attitude towards the past as well as the future. Pride in an Islamic past and the achievements of Islamic civilization provided Muslims with a renewed sense of identity and purpose. This countered the sense of weakness and religio-cultural backwardness fostered by the reality of subjugation to the west and by the preaching of many Christian missionaries. At the same time, emphasis on the dynamic, progressive, and rational character of Islam enabled new generations of Muslims to more confidently embrace modern civilization.
>
> (Esposito 1984: 55)

The return to Islamic origins either brought about or legitimized very radical changes in attitude and values. These changes were particularly interesting in terms of political approaches to Sufism, saintship, and folk religiosity (Gellner 1969).

We can identify different stages of this historical process. The early waves of liberal reinterpretation of Islam gave way eventually to more nationalistic and then socialist interpretations of Islamic history. The first development of conservative puritanism was the Wahhabi movement in the eighteenth century which, through the leadership of Muhammad ibn Abd al-Wahhab, brought about a religio-political change in the region of Mecca and Medina. This movement laid the basis for a unified Muslim community embracing the holy cities and enforcing a new order of religious activity under the radical mono-theism of Islamic revivalism. The Wahhabi movement attacked local Sufism, destroying shrines and tombs in the name of purified Islam. By contrast, the Salafiyyah movement of Rashid Rida assumed a more moderate and liberal form, suggesting certain changes in Islamic constitutions to bring about a westernized form of democracy. In a later period, there was a greater emphasis on nationalism and anti-colonialism, especially during the Nasserite period in Egypt. In Egypt, Syria, and Iraq, the liberal reformism was replaced by more radical nationalistic groups, often with a socialist ideology. In Egypt, Nasserism, and the Baath Party in Syria and Iraq, adopted the view that neither western capitalism nor state-socialist communism could provide the solutions required for Islamic reform and proposed their own version of Arab socialism. These national movements also mobilized Islamic symbols, values, and practices to justify political reform. This Islamic legitimacy involved not a return to the classic Islamic polity, but a new centralized Arab socialism in which the state was to control religion in the interests of national unity. It was in this period that the Muslim Brotherhood also developed a radical interpretation of Islam, but largely outside of government institutions. The Muslim Brotherhood sought to Islamize populations by deepening their commitment to Islam and by protecting them from foreign contamination (Esposito 1983).

It can be argued that these changes to Islamic society and culture, involving rather definite and distinctive patterns in different countries, illustrate various themes in Weber's sociology of religion (Turner 1974; 1978). Islamic reform, although often anti-western, adopted much of the internal logic of the Protestant ethic thesis: the emphasis on ascetic discipline, the rejection of magic and popular cults, the critique of saints and local religious hierarchies, the separation of religious and secular law, the purification of Islam from foreign accretions, and the emphasis on primitivism as the most rational form of ethical prophecy. My argument is, therefore, that the reformist period in Islam in the late nineteenth and first half of the twentieth century can be regarded as illustrative of Weber's account of the modernist rational project. In the more recent period, however, there has been a resurgence of Islam with somewhat new features. Whereas the nationalist governments of Egypt and Syria attempted to mobilize Islam in order to bring about social control with the aim of modernizing the society, the fundamentalist resurgence of the contemporary period often appears to be anti-rational and anti-modernist. In various parts of the Islamic world, the nationalist modernizing governments have been challenged or overthrown by more fundamentalist, puritanical forms of Islam which have rejected or opposed modernization, whether western, Islamic, or socialist. The most spectacular illustration is the fall of the government of the Shah of Iran, but in Pakistan the fall of Ali Bhutto was also associated with a return to puritan Islam. The governments of Khomeini and the late Zia ul-Haq legitimize their control in the name of Islam, often against the secularizing tendencies of their predecessors.

Various explanations of these changes have been attempted, but John L. Esposito (1983: 11) provides a useful summary of these developments:

(1) An identity crisis precipitated by sense of utter impotence, disillusionment and loss of self-esteem; (2) disillusionment with the west and the failure of many governments to respond adequately to the political and socio-economic needs of their societies; and (3) the new found sense of pride and power which resulted from military (Arab–Israeli war) and economic (oil embargo) success in 1973.

Although the modernizing project of the post-war period in Islam brought about many important and valuable changes in society, there were also many systematic negative consequences of rapid modernization, including demographic imbalances, migration problems, the transformation of traditional family life, and the erosion of traditional forms of spirituality.

The new fundamentalism is characterized by its critique of the failure of traditional Marxism to reach the masses through a popular discourse, thereby remaining merely an ideology of the western-trained elite. There is also frequently a criticism of Islamic absolutism — that is, the authoritarian Islam of Saudi Arabia which, in addition, is often seen to have been corrupted by western consumerism. Saudi governments have been criticized for merely using Islam to legitimize tribal rule. Criticism of the Saudi version of Islamic government came to a dramatic conclusion in 1979 when a group of Muslim militants seized the Grand Mosque in Mecca and declared the arrival of a Mahdi, indicting the government as corrupt and embarked upon an illegitimate programme of modernization. The new fundamentalism can, therefore, be seen as a drive for an egalitarian universalism based upon a community, as against the pluralism of associational types of religion which invite diversity and differentiation.

We can, however, see these fundamentalist drives as religious aspects of the cultural response of Islamic traditionalism to the issues raised by a post-modern society. Following Jameson (1985), the growth of consumerism, modern forms of credit, mass travel, expansion of global information systems, and the establishment of a world communication system have resulted in important social, cultural, and personality changes in traditional societies as well as in so-called modern societies. The consequence of these developments is a profound pluralization of life-worlds resulting in a proliferation of lifestyles, values, and institutions. The coherence of the old, closed, communal world has given way to the kaleidoscope of modern pluralism which we can in turn associate with the presence of a world-market system which breeds both tolerance and life-world pluralism. In response to this life-world plurality, religious elites and popular Islamic leaders have adopted a profound anti-modernist position in order to shore up religious belief. The same arguments also apply to the new radicalism of the ultra-orthodox sections of modern Israel, which seek (often violently) major changes in Israeli values and institutions.

My argument is that much of Islam was, in fact, compatible with capitalist development or, more broadly, with the rational modernization of society, involving new emphases on asceticism, literary skills, and rational active values. To take the now famous Protestant ethic thesis, Islamic reformism involved a celebration of the Protestant work ethic, particularly in the writing of reformists like Afghani and Abduh. These writers, in their reformist discourse, redirected Islamic values in a way which was compatible with Weber's argument: 'Hard work and social responsibility, abstention from alcohol, and the discipline of the Ramadan fast were re-emphasized. Islamic values and morality were an integral part of Islamic reform' (Esposito 1984: 76). Most modernizing Islamic writers drew attention to conflicts between Islam and westernization, but this was a retrospective critique. Whereas monotheistic Islam, in its modernizing phase, was perfectly compatible with a modernist rational culture, I have put more emphasis on the conflict between post-modernism and *all* religious value systems. From the post-modern perspective, the theologies of the Abrahamic religions are simply 'grand narratives', and spirituality becomes simply one technology of the self. Religions must not only respond to the nihilism behind such theological deconstructions, but they must also address themselves to the social forces that lie behind these conceptual, stylistic, and philosophical developments. The changes which provide the base for such rethinking are, in fact, related to new economic and social forces giving rise to global consumerism and urban life-styles associated with mass cultures.

I have, more by implication than direct criticism, suggested that Weber's sociological account of modernity had to give a privileged position to Protestantism, which Weber achieved by noting certain 'flaws' in the other monotheistic traditions. However, the problem of post-modernism is a global issue, not specific to any particular religious tradition. We can, to some extent, identify some aspects of a post-modern criticism even in sociology. For example, Robert Bellah's *Habits of the Heart* (1985) laments the passing of a more authentic, moral, and communal culture in America, arguing that in the post-modern world looking good and feeling good have replaced, or become more important than, being good and doing good. In this perspective, post-modernism appears to be associated with the emergence of a new middle class whose interests and attachments are global and who have no roots or location within the national culture.

CONCLUSION:
WEBER'S VERSION OF POST-MODERNISM

We have argued that Weber was, in a theological sense, liberal in his evaluation of religious history and in his implicit, but necessary, identification with Protestantism. Although Weber could no longer accept the religious basis of faith, he was both emotionally and intellectually identified with the German Protestant tradition. Weber's analysis of the process of modernization was, therefore, shot through with ambiguity and uncertainty, since for Weber the modern world must become essentially disenchanted. Weber attempted to regulate this ambiguity and uncertainty through the advocacy of an ethic of responsibility. I have, therefore, suggested that Weber has two versions of the modernization process. The first was more optimistic in calmly accepting the inevitability of rationalization, secularization, and the spread of bureaucratic management with the increasing democratization of culture and politics. The second version was far more pessimistic and ambiguous, noting in certain respects the modernization process would be self-defeating, because all rational systems must inevitably recognize the limits of reason and the arbitrariness of rational thought. This second version of modernization was the legacy of Nietzsche, who had argued that knowledge was necessarily metaphorical and that reason must tragically recognize its own limitations.

We have attempted to explore these themes through Weber's account of world religions, drawing specific attention to certain important changes in the modern world such as the revival of fundamentalism as a critique of the pluralism of the post-modern world. We have interpreted these fundamentalist movements as attempts to de-differentiate the social structure (Lechner 1985a), and as attempts to limit the explosion of life-styles and meanings by establishing normative boundaries around consumerism. The consumerist implications for religious orthodoxy are particularly potent in the Middle Eastern, or more generally Islamic, world (Stauth and Zubaida 1987).

With the increasing intensity of modern forms of communication, it is paradoxical that the religious message of reformism is more effectively carried by modern media which, at the same time, also deliver a secular, pluralized, and simulative reality. It is this dense world of pluralistic meanings that threatens to call a halt to the modernizing project, leaving behind a post-modern world of symbolic simulation (Baudrillard 1983). This global world of post-modernism was, I have argued, anticipated in Weber's pessimistic vision of social change. Weber's notion of the polytheism of values anticipated a supra-abundant world of endless meanings which do not constitute *a* meaning. Weber's self-directing personality has become the supra-subjective self of narcissism. Finally, Weber's quest for a world of ethical autonomy has become a world of aesthetic simulations. Many of these developments were glimpsed by Weber in his notion that in the modern world religiosity would have to become personalized, subjective, and pianissimo in its inner quality. However, given the current strength in political and cultural terms of modern fundamentalism as a reactive movement within the world religions, we may expect a re-Islamization of Muslim culture which may have the effect of limiting the processes of secularization and pluralism. In so far as fundamentalism is successful, we may more generally experience a re-sacralization of the world (reality) — much against the expectations, not only of Weber, but of most classical sociologists. Alternatively, we may anticipate a global system which, through the processes of differentiation, is able to encapsulate simultaneously powerful forces of rationalization and sacralization.

Chapter Four

ON LAW, MORALITY, AND MODERN SOCIETY: THE RATIONALIZATION PROCESS

IDEOLOGY AND LAW

The problem of law in relation to the social structure can be seen as a specific case of the general question of ideology and society, or even more broadly as an issue in the sociology of knowledge. It is difficult to conceptualize a *general* theory of law, because it is at present problematic to achieve any consensus about a *general* theory of ideology. There are of course also many unresolved conceptual problems relating to the very notion of 'ideology' (Turner 1987). At present, there is little scope for theoretical or empirical confidence in the ability of either Marxists or Marxist sociologists to specify the precise content of ideology in capitalist society, the interests served by such an ideology, or its functions in relation to social classes or modes of production. The problems of specifying *the* ideology of capitalism and its necessary or contingent relations to capitalist production are well known (Abercrombie, Hill, and Turner 1980). Although there are willing exponents of the theory of 'hegemony' in industrial society, the empirical grounding for this viewpoint is often limited, if not largely absent (Hoffman 1984).

The drift of much recent debate over ideology is to argue that ideology stands in a contingent relationship to capitalist socio-economic arrangements (Abercrombie, Hill, and Turner 1983). However, in the language of conventional Marxism, it is difficult to show that certain ideological practices are a 'condition of existence' of a mode of production or that specific ideologies can be 'read off' from given classes. It can be argued that the theory of ideology must move from determination to indetermination, because the ideological character of any society is simply the indeterminate effect of a

103

ceaseless, competitive struggle between classes, strata, and social groups; the content and function of ideologies appear to have highly variable relationships to the precise nature of these societal conflicts. This perspective can be seen as an application of Weber's view that sociology is forced, in the absence of a general theory of social relations, to aim at the explication of general concepts.

The theoretical development of contemporary sociology of law appears to have taken a trajectory (Hirst 1979; Hunt 1978; O'Malley 1983) which is parallel to the sociology of knowledge. From a Marxist perspective, law has been traditionally regarded as having certain crucial functions: to constitute and interpellate the legal subject as an abstract unity (Therborn 1980); to guarantee property relations, private property, and exchange (Poulantzas 1978); and to control the working class through the agency of the criminal law (Pashukanis 1978). In general, juridical legitimacy is thought to replace religion as the social cement of capitalism under the controlling gaze of the state. These essential propositions of Marxist legal theory are in fact difficult to sustain.

With the growth of corporate structures, there is no longer any necessary correspondence between the person, the legal subject, and the economic subject (Abercrombie, Hill, and Turner 1986). In contemporary capitalism, the state intervenes frequently against the overt interests of private capital and legislates to limit absolute rights over private property (Brittain 1978; Atkinson 1975) by, for example, regulating the inheritance of wealth. Although the dominant class has historically been in possession of, or had access to, a repressive legal apparatus, in practice law has not been used systematically or continuously against subordinate classes or minority groups. The common law is in principle common to all citizens, and it has to some extent protected the common rights of the people (Hay *et al.* 1975; Macfarlane 1981). The English legal system also offered various forms of pardon, sanctuary, and leniency to offenders (Hepworth and Turner 1982; Rolph 1978). In general, the legal systems of capitalist society do not always take the form of an 'axiomatic system, comprising a set of abstract, general, formal and strictly regulated norms' (Poulantzas 1978: 86). Britain, the United States, Canada, Australia, and New Zealand are 'case law' nations but also capitalist, and they do not exhibit the formal rational stability which Weber associated with modern capitalism (Turner 1981). While the legal systems of modern societies may have been subject to similar processes (such as secularization), it is difficult to show precisely how these changes relate to the economic requirements of capitalism as such.

To employ a metaphor which is itself now subject to considerable critical revision, there is at present major instability in the theory of the superstructure of late capitalist society. The assertion that 'The totality of these relations of production constitutes the economic structure of society, the real foundation, on which arises a legal and political superstructure and to which correspond definite forms of social consciousness' (Marx 1971: 20) is now pock-marked with revisions and reservations. There is no uniform relationship between base and superstructure. There are also major problems in defining 'base' and 'superstructure'. Law not only regulates the base, but actually constitutes an element of the relations of production. Law is thus not so much a reflection of, but a requirement for, social relations of production. The concept of the 'ownership' of the means of production clearly refers to law and therefore to the ideological superstructure.

The uncertainty and lack of theoretical consensus about ideology/ law are consequently products of a far deeper problem in the analysis of capitalist society; this deeper problem is the collapse, particularly in Marxism, of any coherent theory of social class (Cohen 1982). The contours of this theoretical problem can be briefly stated here since this issue is fully explored elsewhere in this study. For Marx, it is social being that determines consciousness, and the key feature of 'social being' is one's relationship to the means of production. It is class position that determines social being, and it is social being which constitutes social consciousness. One difficulty in specifying the role of law in capitalist society within a Marxist framework is a theoretic effect of the difficulty of specifying 'social class'. A strong version of materialism would be that class determines both the contents and the function of law (in supporting property rights, controlling the working class, or forming the ideological cement of capitalist relations). But what is 'class'?

For Marx, class refers to a structure of positions in terms of relationships to the means of economic production (Elster 1985). Despite references in classical and contemporary Marxism to indeterminate class positions such as 'middle class', 'service class', or 'lumpenproletariat', there are essentially two major classes — the dominant class which owns the means of production, buys labour power to produce commodities, and realizes an economic surplus as profits; and the working class, which is forced to sell labour power as a commodity in order to labour productively in an exploited relationship to the dominant class. The elementary forms of the class structure are complicated in late capitalism by the fact that the state intervenes directly in the productive process, property is partly 'depersonalized' by the growth of corporate ownership, and large sections of the working class are permanently unemployed (but do not starve) as a consequence of de-skilling, restructuring, and de-industrialization (Braverman 1974; Hill 1981; Scott 1979). The state enjoys a relative autonomy from the capitalist economic base, developing interests of its own and giving rise to a new 'service class' which is separate from both capitalist and working classes (Abercrombie and Urry 1983; Gershuny and Miles 1983). There are major theoretical problems with a Marxist theory of class. Furthermore, it is possible to develop a Weberian theory of economic classes (in terms of the labour, credit, and commodity markets) which is far more powerful than the classical Marxist version (Wiley 1967). These issues are well known and have been regularly rehearsed.

More importantly, the contemporary problems of capitalism produce a major shrinkage in the size and social importance of the working class. The decline of the traditional working class is a consequence of the decline of traditional industries: the productive, wage-earning, labouring class is slowly contracting with the disappearance of labour-intensive, traditional forms of permanent employment (Browning and Singelmann 1978; Lash and Urry 1987; Gorz 1982). At the same time, changes in the structure of corporate industrial ownership are also reducing the size and coherence of the dominant class. There is of course massive evidence of persistent social inequality and prominent forms of inequality in power, prestige, and wealth. However, the traditional 'ruling class' is also experiencing a transformation (Rubinstein 1980). Institutional investment — the state, banks, pension funds, and stock market — is now largely responsible for industrial growth and conforms to the demise of family capitalism. This process is very well documented (Bell 1961; Prais 1981; Scott 1979; Utton 1979; Zeitlin 1974). The result is that capitalism has developed in such a manner as to bring about a quantitative contraction of both major classes, at least in their traditional form — a situation which requires a major re-direction in the social analysis of class structures. For example, one difficulty with traditional Marxist analysis was that it assumed that the working class, once formed as a class-for-itself, remained constituted as a class on a permanent basis. In contemporary capitalism, the working class is experiencing a process of rapid de-formation (Przeworski 1977; 1985). Professions and quasi-professions within the service class as agents and clients of the state now form the pivot of the class system (Johnson 1982). The result is that Weber's analysis of status groups, status consciousness, and social closure is now more relevant than traditional Marxism as a theoretical framework for an understanding of the social structure of late capitalism, an issue which is dealt with separately in this study.

WEBER AND THE SOCIOLOGY OF LAW

My argument is that the major issues in contemporary sociology of law were all pre-figured in the unresolved difficulties of Weber's attempt to specify the relationship between law and capitalism. It has been argued with some credibility that Weber's sociology of law is the core of Weberian sociology (Parsons 1971; Kronman 1983). Weber's sociology of law was in part a critique of the romanticism of the German historical school of law and stood in opposition to the notion that law is an organic expression of the community of Folk Mind (Brand 1982). Weber was also critical of what is now known as an instrumentalist view of law as an expression of class interest, but he was also hostile to the idealism of Stammler (Weber 1977). It is, how-ever, possible to state the central aspects of Weber's theory in a number of basic propositions. The content and form of law cannot be wholly explained by reference to the class interest of the dominant class, because law, especially formal-rational law, has an immanent logic. The nature of law is partly determined by the form of the pro-fessional training of lawyers, who may develop interests of their own as a professional group which do not entirely coincide with those of capitalists. A system of formal-rational law is the most appropriate system for rational capitalism, which requires predictability and stability, especially in the administrative infrastructure and in the regulation of economic contracts. However, it is also recognized that historically capitalism can operate under a variety of systems of law.

It is well known that Weber's account of rational law in relation to the development of capitalist society is difficult to reconcile with the form and development of English case-law. This has been referred to as the famous 'England problem' (Trubek 1972). It is also important

107

to keep in mind Weber's argument that in England the legal process was more controlled by the class interest of judges than in any other society (Corrigan and Sayer 1985: 153ff). There may also be a parallel 'Scotland problem', in that Scots law was influenced by the Roman law tradition, and thus in Weber's perspective more compatible with capitalist economic development. The economic backwardness of Scotland may be regarded, as a consequence, as something of an empirical challenge to Weber's thesis. Of course, the Scottish case as a whole is of special relevance to Weber's Protestant ethic thesis, given the early and intensive development of the Calvinistic reformation in Scotland, leaving England more predominantly Anglican at its religio-cultural core (Corrigan and Sayer 1985; Marshall 1980). It can be argued that England achieved capitalist development despite rather than because of its legal system, which approximated the irrationality of *qadi*-justice in terms of an arbitrary system of case-law.

There appear to be three conventional solutions in the sociological literature to the so-called 'England problem'. It is possible to suggest that English law was suitable for capitalist conditions, because there was an important identity of interests, particularly class interests, between common-law judges and the English bourgeois class. Alternatively, it can be suggested that, although English case-law was not wholly rational, it was sufficiently stable to promote capitalist development, or at least not to impede that development. The third theoretical solution is to admit that the English case remains deviant from the point of view of Weber's general argument. However, a more radical solution is to argue that capitalists can operate under a variety of legal forms, provided there is some minimal legal stability for exchange relations. There are two aspects to this position. First, it appears to be empirically the case that existing capitalist societies have, or exhibit, a variety of legal systems and forms of jurisprudence. Second, there are theoretical arguments for believing that capitalism has a basic legal requirement which is the legal enforcement of contracts. The nature of legal contracts was particularly important for Weber's general view of legal history, since he, rather like Sir Henry Maine, saw legal development as a process from personal obligation to impersonal contract (or 'purposive contracts') (Kronman 1983: 100). Once the basis for economic contracts is secured, the precise legal requirements of capitalism as an *economic* system may be quite limited. This final solution suggests that there is no determinate or enduring relationship between the legal superstructure and the economic base, and that law is shaped by a variety of historically contingent features: legal traditions, legal training, the nature of legal professionalization, the class relations between professionals and clients, the connections between the profession and the state, and the location of the state within the world economy.

THE PROBLEM OF LEGITIMACY

In sociology, the normal interpretation of Weber suggests that the issue of legitimate authority provides an important feature of Weberian sociology (Parsons 1937). In particular, law may be seen as the crux of legal-rational authority and as the basis of social cohesion in a capitalist society. In this view, law not only provides the anchorage for capitalist relations of property and exchange; it is also the final arbiter of those common values which are the cohesive factor not only of capitalism, but of any social system. There are a number of problems with such an interpretation of Weber.

Like Nietzsche, Weber thought that secularization had undermined religion as a public system of values and institutions to such an extent that there was no ultimate prop for general social values. In short, Weber built Nietzsche's perspectivism into his sociology of values in capitalism. The social world had been fundamentally relativized, and one consequence was that natural law no longer offered a basis for common values. The result was that social stability required, not so much shared values, but the normative coercion of citizens to a system of obedience. Rational law as a formal system of legal deduction could not handle substantive claims to justice by subordinate classes, and the conflict of classes resulted in two irreconcilable principles: law as social regulation versus law as a fountain of social rights. These legal conflicts reflect the profound conflict within capitalism between the economic inequalities relating to class relations and the principle of democratic equality within the political system (Turner 1986a; 1986b).

Like Nietzsche, Weber saw the social world of capitalism as constituted by competitive struggles for wealth, power, and prestige. Law and bureaucratic regulation provided a necessary but minimal and fragile institutional framework which placed some limit on the extent and impact of these competitive conflicts. We must also keep in mind that Weber developed his sociology of law within a society which was dominated by the legacy of Bismarckian bureaucracy. Such a secular and bureaucratic society does not have, however, any grounding in general values, let alone absolute standards. It is impossible to predict with any precision the contours of such a social system: Weber's methodology ruled out teleology. However, for Weber, the long-term consequences of capitalism did involve the rationalization of social relationships, intellectualism, secularization, the collapse of individual autonomy, and the iron cage of capitalist relations (Hennis 1988). There is, as a result, a tension in Weber's view of history. Although history has no purpose, end, or meaning, Weber felt compelled to accept the pessimistic prediction that what lies in front of us is the polar night of icy darkness. There is increasing rationalization, but this takes the form of meaninglessness and the dominance of means over ends. There was therefore a tension between the teleological implications of the rationalization thesis and Weber's methodological views on the inappropriateness of 'general laws' in the social sciences.

ABSTRACT SOCIAL RELATIONS

It is impossible to understand Weber's sociology without understanding the theme of 'the tragedy of culture' in the sociology of Georg Simmel, particularly in his study of the growth of exchange and money where he provided a model of the development of social abstraction. In an indirect fashion, Weber's view of legal abstraction can be seen as a particular application of Simmel's account of the growing abstraction of money as the symbol and effect of abstract social relations.

For Simmel, the use of paper money is the measure of the growth of abstract, formal, social relations which are increasingly subject to calculation, and indeed produced by universalistic exchange relations (Simmel 1978; Turner 1986c). The history of money as a medium of exchange is the history of its divorce from any immediate, tangible value. Direct barter gave way to leather money, leather money gave way to paper money, and paper money was replaced by the bank card. The growth of cheques, credit notes, and bank cards represents the growing indifference of social exchange to the particular, personal characteristics of economic agents. Confidence in money presupposes the expansion of social relations based on impersonal trust with the backing of the state. The sphere of money is the entire sphere of social relations, or more precisely the sphere of the public, rational domain of social interaction.

While money creates and expresses these social relations of stable exchange, it is also a measure of human alienation. It represents tragically the separation of the content and form of human actions. Money is in Simmel's analysis the reification of the pure association between things as expressed in their economic character. Thus, human individuality and human agency become congealed and fixed in abstract money relations. Money as a reliable measure of value becomes the vehicle for intellectualization, calculation, rationalization, and reification. Money thus comes to represent instrumental reason in a direct form. In particular, money as primarily a means of exchange becomes an end in itself — in fact, *the* end of human actions. With the rise of a positivist science of the economic, moral values and economic activities become in principle, and to a large measure in practice, separated. The extent of that separation must be opened to empirical enquiry rather than outright condemnation (Bell 1976).

Weber's sociology of law can be seen as an adaptation and application of Simmel's sociology of money to the juridical arena. Law is one of the prime manifestations of the growing rationality and intellectuality of social relations, providing a reified shell of calculated stability for economic processes. Law, money, and the market-place become measures both of alienation and of individual freedom from the unpredictable world of primitive exchange. Money and law measure both civilization and alienation. This social stability is therefore bought at a cost; namely, that all substantive questions of justice have to be squeezed into the precise mechanism of formal-rational law. The quest for legal stability is no longer merely a means to achieve comparable legal decision making and instead becomes an end in itself.

ACCIDENTALISM VERSUS STRUCTURALISM

For a variety of reasons — some of which we have just considered — contemporary sociology often displays a withdrawal from any attempt at a general theory of unitary phenomena. The search for determinate linkages between social relations which characterized nineteenth-century sociology, and in particular nineteenth-century evolutionism, has largely collapsed into what may be called 'accidentalism'. There is often a lack of confidence in our ability to make comparative or historical generalizations. In more general terms, Norbert Elias (1987) has defended the crucial importance of a broad historical and comparative perspective in sociological explanation. Another exception in the sociology of law is the social system theory of Niklas Luhmann (1985). It can be argued with some justification, however, that Luhmann considers law as an excuse to develop a particular theoretical position. Furthermore, it is not clear how system differentiation relates to actual historical processes.

This hostility to generalization in modern sociological theory is a manifestation of the criticism of Grand Theory. The result is that the social world is seen to be a sphere of historical contingency and accident. Manifestations of this accidentalism in sociological theory are widespread. One particularly influential development has come from linguistic structuralism and post-structuralism under the influence of Nietzsche. The basic argument here is that the signifier and the signified stand in an arbitrary relationship, or, in Foucault's formulation, the rationalist assumption that there is a necessary relationship between the order of words and the order of things is metaphysical (Cousins and Hussain 1984; Foucault 1970). This position, which is now influential in social science, results in a radical relativism. Our knowledge of the world is the effect of classificatory schemes, but these classifications are arbitrary and there is no way of choosing between them. It is further argued that rationalism is based upon a series of hidden metaphors. Foucault's position depends heavily on Nietzsche, and results in the argument that history has no logic and that causal reasoning gives a primacy to the rationalist episteme which cannot be justified. Within the post-modernist framework, history thus becomes both unfamiliar and contingent. For Lyotard (1984), any type of 'grand narrative' in any discourse is no longer possible in a post-modern epoch.

In Marxism, antipathy to Althusserianism has resulted in a renewed emphasis on the causal importance of class struggle as the motor of history as against what was held to be the functionalism of Althusser. There is in Marxism a general tension between mode-of-production analysis which lends itself to formalism and determinism, and class-struggle analysis which is reductionist and accidentalist. There is also associated with anti-teleological positions a rejection of unitary concepts in social science. There are a number of positions which thus converge around what I have called accidentalism, and which involve accepting the view that there are no general theories, no strictly causal arguments, no unitary concepts, and ultimately no determinate relationship between 'words' and 'things'. To assume that historical change has any consistent direction or process is to employ unfounded rationalist metaphors. Generalizations are forms of rational knowledge which disguise forms of power.

THE LIMITS TO ACCIDENTS

The new emphasis on the metaphoricality of language produces a powerful epistemology which is difficult to criticize (Rorty 1982). Objections to an accidentalist view of history are easily dismissed as teleological, or worse. There are, however, at least two objections to these arguments which are worth consideration, and the outcome of my objections is a limited argument in favour of 'classical sociology', namely in favour of the possibility of general theories. The first objection is that in practice Foucauldian analysis does embrace a view of historical development. It is possible to interpret the early Foucault in the following manner. The demographic revolution in the eighteenth and nineteenth centuries gave rise to new requirements of urban social control. New types of discipline emerged to organize 'populations', which Foucault describes under the general category of Panopticism. There were corresponding forms of knowledge which controlled these new urban populations: penology, criminology, sociology, clinical medicine, and demography. Society under Panopticism becomes increasingly regulated and administered by rational practices which are informed by a rationalist episteme. While Foucault denies teleology, his view of Panoptic rationalization and the mental division of labour is not unlike the arguments of both Durkheim and Weber. Like Durkheim, the pressure for social change is exogenous population increase, and Foucault's account of the changing forms of punishment is parallel to Durkheim's notion that criminal law changes from repressive to restitutive with the transition from mechanical to organic solidarity. Like Weber, Foucault has an implicit teleology — namely, that western society has come increasingly under the controls of discipline and bureaucracy. The argument here is that, while modern social theory has been typically anti-evolutionary and anti-teleological, there is generally an implicit and covert theory of social change which has developmental assumptions.

113

In any case, there are in principle only four types of social change theory, which may be combined in various forms:

Exogenous	Endogenous	
A External crisis (Malthus)	B Class struggle (Marx)	*contingent*
D Evolutionism and Darwinism (Spencer)	C Differentiation (Parsons)	*teleological*

Nineteenth-century social change theories were located primarily in cells D and C. There was an emphasis on macro-social change involving conflicts between societies or groups within them, and involving various adjustments to the natural environment. Evolution and differentiation bring about systemic adjustments and developments within social systems. There has been a definite shift in contemporary thought to A and B, because few modern theorists have embraced Grand Theory. However, I have claimed that few social theorists are able to maintain radical accidentalism (cell B), because in practice social theorists make assumptions about social development involving systemic changes.

In addition, it is theoretically problematic to take a position in which everything is contingent. We have already noted that there is an inclination to reject the notion that capitalism requires a *special* type of law (which is systematic, gapless, deductive, and formal-rational) on the grounds that different capitalist societies have different forms of law. However, even on a commonsense basis, it would be difficult to assume that capitalism could develop and continue on *any* legal basis. One would expect some limits to accidentalism, and these limits would be ultimately imposed by the conditions of existence of the mode of production, or in Parsonian terms on the functional requirements of social systems, or in Weber's terms by the limiting requirement of legal stability in relation to economic contracts. Within those limits, variations would be determined by contingent class struggles, inter-state conflicts, and global economic struggles. The nature of law would thus be determined by complex relationships between the functional requirements of the social system, the form of legal training, social conflicts, and the immanent logic of law-making. As a result of this discussion, I want to put forward a modest defence of a non-contingent view of the relationship between law and modern society from a developmentalist perspective.

LAW AND SOCIAL CHANGE

The conclusion of this discussion of the theoretical problems of the sociology of law involves an attempt to marry certain sociological traditions from classical sociology in order to present at the outset a general description of legal changes in the transition from traditional to modern societies. This description can be rendered in the form of a typology.

Typology of changes in legal institutions

	Traditional	Transitional	Modern
1	Non-systematic law	legal unification	professionalization
2	Customary possession	legal individualism	private v. corporate
3	Repressive criminal code	criminology	medicalization
4	Feudal immunity	citizenship by property	universalism
5	Natural law	individualism	statism
6	Socio-drama	penology	rehabilitation

The typology is based primarily on Weber's argument that law-making develops from charismatic, prophetic law through traditional or customary law, to law which is legal-rational or formal-rational. Formal law has stability and continuity which are necessary conditions of economic calculation and prediction. Local, customary laws are gradually replaced by laws which apply to the nation-state. These changes are also the effect of an expansion of formal citizenship rights, in which the legal subject (the citizen) becomes increasingly abstract and universal. For example, anti-discrimination laws promote the value that in the public arena particularistic criteria (such as gender and race) are incompatible with the formal democratic process. These changes are also accompanied by professionalization — namely, the emergence of the legal expert. The social and theoretical background to Weber's particular account of this process was the debate with the organic analogy of the Historical School of Law which related to the emergence of the modern nation-state out of *Gemeinschaft*. In particular, these changes were associated with developments in the concept of property.

Whereas early capitalism required legal notions of possessive individualism, contemporary society is characterized by certain conflicts between rights to *personal* private property and corporatism. An examination of rows 2 and 4 suggests that the growing abstraction of formal law means that notions of 'property' and 'person' became detached. There is a separation of the 'legal personality' and the economic agent-as-person with the growth of concepts of corporation and limited liability. This development clearly had an early history with the Italian conceptualization of 'fictive corporations' (Canning 1980), but modern concepts of the corporation have to embrace legal entities which may have global characteristics, and which have highly complex patterns of legal identity and liability. Also, there is an expansion of the rights of citizenship, which become increasingly separated from ownership of personal property. For example, in the twentieth century, legislation on divorce and marriage contracts meant that women retained their legal personality on marriage rather than becoming submerged in the public identity of their husbands. Legislation relating to the treatment of children extends citizenship claims and also confirms the trend away from property ownership as the basis of formal rights because children are no longer simply domestic property. There is a development away from notions of feudal immunity from law to positive claims which expand the idea of citizenship on the basis of universal laws-in-principle (Poggi 1978).

These changes also denote a secularization of law, especially with the collapse of natural law, but this secularization brings with it a problem of value relativism which cannot be easily solved. One might argue that in the period of liberalism, it is the individual which is the source of value, but it is notoriously difficult to reconcile particular and peculiar 'individual' wants with notions of social justice. The ideas of equality of condition and equality of outcome cannot be embodied in legislation and institutions on the basis of the nature of particular individuals. In addition, the notion of the *private* individual is a sociological fiction. The state in modern society is typically regarded as the fountain and focus of values in which individuals or groups appeal to law and the state for the promotion and protection of rights. This argument has to assume some 'relative autonomy' of the state from class interest, and this is admittedly also problematic as a political theory. I have suggested therefore a defence of some aspects of Weber's legal liberalism — namely, that we can see in modern societies a transformation of the individual/property relationship which makes 'individuals' legally abstract.

In the table, rows 3 and 6 attempt to express Durkheim's view of law and social change (Durkheim 1978). In a traditional society organized around the *conscience collective*, law expresses the nature of social solidarity through ritualized socio-dramas and by the public repression of deviance. In the transition to organic solidarity, the punishment of offenders becomes secluded from public inspection, and eventually capital punishment is replaced by Benthamite utilitarian principles which are manifest in classical criminology and penology. For example, with the decline of traditional forms of punishment, Australia emerged as a penal settlement and convict society which was in many respects a Benthamite experiment on a massive scale. The scaffold and the public confession give way to the 'scientific' reform of offenders and the custodial role of the penitentiary (Spierenburg 1984). Finally under restitutive law, questions of compensation for victims rather than retribution against offenders become more important. There are also changes in the conceptualization of crime as certain types of crime and deviance become redefined as 'diseases', whereby social control is transferred from priests and the church to the medical profession which, with the backing of the state, becomes the custodian of 'normal' behaviour. The result is a 'medicalization' of the population via an extension of medical categories (Zola 1972).

The typology may suggest a certain commitment to an evolutionary view of legal changes as the result of an unfolding of rationality as an essential feature of western capitalism. By recognizing that legal and social change are modified by various forms of social conflict, the model does not have to assume an inevitable evolutionary development. In America, the introduction of 'voluntary' execution for prisoners with life sentences might appear as counter-evidence. In Britain, the dominant slogan of 'law and order' in the 1980s made the reformist approach to the 'treatment' of crime appear somewhat out of date (Bean and Whynes 1986). The return of fundamentalist attitudes in puritan Islamic regimes would also be a counter-instance, and there are also strong fundamentalist pressures in contemporary Christianity which seek a return to traditional forms of punishment. The balance between the repressive and restitutive features of law is clearly a case in point, but these are essentially empirical, not theoretical, problems. There is also the theoretical argument that de-modernization of societies involves a process of de-differentiation (Lechner 1985a). While these legal changes may be reversed and transformed by various forms of contingent class struggle, by social movements, or de-differentiation, or by changes in professional organization, as a general description the typology has merit as a summary of socio-legal developments in the transition from traditional to modern society.

LAW, RELIGION, MEDICINE

The argument so far may appear to embrace a rather simplistic view of secularization. Although capitalism does not necessarily require religion, religious belief in the form of 'civil religions' may still offer some legitimation of the system. It can also be argued that religion does not disappear so much as undergo a reallocation to the medical sphere, which now defines appropriate behaviour and conduct, especially with respect to sexuality and the family. The existing typology can be re-expressed to incorporate this argument concerning law, religion, and medicine.

The historical argument is that, in a society dominated by an all-powerful conscience collective, there is a solid core of the society which is regarded as sacred. The perimeter of such a society is guarded by rituals of inclusion and exclusion which, in conjunction with repressive law, control membership and reinforce common values. The notion of 'citizenship' is underdeveloped, while concepts of 'the people' are dominant, because relations expressing *Gemeinschaft* organize public space. The crucial aspect of such a socio-cultural system is that there is little normative and conceptual separation between sin, crime, and disease, with the result that religion, law, and medicine are not differentiated as separate professions, because knowledge of deviance is not wholly specialized (Kristeller 1978). We can thus imagine the boundary of such a society as defined by undifferentiated threats from plagues, crimes, disease, heresy, sin, and madness, but these are simultaneously medical, theological, and legal categories. For example, leprosy was thought to be caused by sexual promiscuity, but it was also a punishment by God. Leprosy was in addition hedged about by legal restrictions. For example, there were quasi-juridical limitations on marriage, inheritance, and residence for those designated as lepers, and there was also a religious service which pronounced lepers to be 'dead'. Similar arguments can be put forward with respect to venereal disease, epilepsy, and insanity (Turner 1983). In such a system, the state, professions, and penal institutions are all underdeveloped, partly because the society depends on the absence of individualism and the prominence of a sacred core. Because market relations are weak, traditional values associated with status rather than with class are in full force.

In the transition to a modern society, religion, medicine, and law begin to develop as separate and distinctive institutions which also correspond to category distinctions between sin, crime, and disease. There begins to emerge a professional specialization of competence to deal with these 'threats' to social order. This specialization eventually involves competitive struggles between groups claiming special knowledge and distinctive objects of study. The competition between doctors, barbers, surgeons, apothecaries, and others over the body (or parts of the body) is characteristic of emerging specialization in the arena of the management of human problems. This competition follows the usual course of conflict for privilege as outlined in Weber's notion of 'social closure'. Because the conscience collective becomes weaker and 'thinner', the main threat to established social classes is represented by the undisciplined working class, whose urban hovels are centres of disease and disorder. These 'dangerous classes' emerged at different times and with variable impact in European societies, but by the second half of the nineteenth century they constituted the major organized threat to bourgeois order. Various forms of 'policing' were developed in response to the social dislocation associated with urban life (Donzelot 1979).

In capitalism, religion contracts and addresses itself to certain residual phenomena left over from state welfare, psychiatry, medicine, and law. The competence of the clergy to deal with the phenomenon of deviance is challenged successfully by the law and medicine. Although large sections of the population claim formal denominational affiliation, theological commitment lacks real content (Martin 1978; Wilson 1982). It is medicine, not law, which replaces religion as the guardian of moral norms. The medical regimen implies a moral way of life: monogamy, fitness, diet, heterosexuality. The new threats to this moral order are diseases of old age, affluence, and sexual deviation. Medicine expands to embrace categories which were previously legal or religious: political disaffection, deviance, and stress are converted into diseases which have remedies with a strong moralistic content, but the differentiation of deviance into specialist categories remains an essential element of modern society.

A GENERAL THEORY

This account so far is a general description of socio-legal changes and not a theory. The sketch which I have outlined in this chapter attempts to provide a concrete analysis of legal change which would establish a sociological perspective very different from the logical conditions of social differentiation in Luhmann's theory (1982). To conclude, therefore, the argument attempts to specify certain changes in the nature of the social system which could explain the general features of these legal changes. In feudalism and early capitalism, property in land has to be conserved by a system of primogeniture, and thus it is important to have moral, religious ideologies to discipline family members, especially wives and eldest sons. Departures from patriarchal forms of primogeniture produce a weak and divided ruling class, and the stability of feudal land tenure is called into question. It is equally necessary to have laws of strict settlement, because in feudalism and early capitalism, households were patriarchal. Patriarchy and gerontocracy were effects of the property requirements. These conditions were necessary for the continuity of household wealth and the concentration of wealth in a few hands. However, the reproduction of family wealth required specific institutions for the reproduction of people: moral regulations on sexuality, celibacy, and marriage by arrangement. Law in this context was simply one aspect of a coercive normative system.

In England, the necessary relationships between the family, the household and private property began to break down in the late nineteenth century in a process which may be called the 'depersonalization' of wealth. The Joint Stock Companies Act (1844) and changes in banking arrangements to facilitate long-term investment meant that property owners were less dependent on their kin for capital accumulation. Long-term investment sources came from outside the family. It was no longer necessary to subordinate wives by legal means to guarantee family fortunes. The expansion of citizenship rights, the growth of legal universalism, and the separation of personal rights from property correspond to this shift in forms of economic production from the family firm to the corporation. The result was that capitalism could 'tolerate' sexual permissiveness in the private sphere, provided the worker was disciplined on the factory floor and in the labour market. The control over labour was secured by economic compulsion (such as unemployment), the separation of the worker from the means of production, and, to some extent, by evangelical Christianity. There is, for example, the well-known argument that Methodism was crucial in the development of the English working class (Thompson 1963). The urban environment was made safe by prisons, police, asylums, sewerage, and professional medicine.

Late capitalism has the following features: the concentration of productive wealth in a small number of global corporations; the emergence of global production and a global division of labour; the regulation of the economy by the state, especially through corporatism; the disappearance of the traditional working class with the decline of traditional, labour-intensive production systems; the relative decline of the nuclear family household; and the transformation of traditional patriarchy based upon the nuclear family.

These features suggest somewhat contradictory developments. There is an expansion of citizenship under notions of individual rights and universalism. In particular, women, deviants, and minority groups seek to achieve legal guarantees of rights to equal treatment. Pressure groups which seek equality of treatment for homosexuals, legalization of prostitution, abortion, pederasty, euthanasia, or drug reform may bring about changes which are not incompatible with the economic requirements of late capitalism. Given the economic separation between the family and the company, legal changes relating to sexual preferences within the private sphere do not necessarily have any significant impact on the economic organization of capitalism. Such changes in rights within civil society may be perceived, however, as incompatible with the 'moral order' by moral pressure groups — despite the fact that any such 'moral order' is often residual and problematic. Sociologists of deviance have suggested that public morality is periodically reinforced by 'moral panic' (Cohen 1972). A more powerful argument is that the moral boundaries of modern societies are defined by the medical profession. Contemporary panics about AIDS, herpes, VD, and cervical cancer point to a medical regimen based on monogamy, heterosexuality, celibacy, and a set of recommendations which constitute a 'government of the body' (Turner 1984). Although prostitution, homosexuality, and soft drugs have been legalized in many societies, medical wisdom indicates

121

the negative effects of 'casual sexuality' both to the individual and to the community. This medical view of the equation (the good life = monogamy) is often advocated by the medical profession in societies where the traditional family has often become a statistical minority; for example, in Australia approximately one-quarter of all households are nuclear and one-third of the population is defined as 'single'. The modern state is thus caught in cross-pressures between claims for the liberalization of personal activities under the doctrine of individualism and appeals for a return to conventional morality on the part of the 'moral majority'. It is difficult to see how these contradictory claims about substantive moral issues could be resolved under the umbrella of formal-rational legality, which is abstract and formal.

The institutional characteristics of late capitalism produce a further instability for the state and law. As a number of writers have noted recently, it is difficult for the nation-state to exercise legal control over multi-national corporations by statutes which were formulated under the conditions of early capitalism. There are a number of problems. Multi-nationals often have more economic power than small states, and it is difficult to decide legally where responsibility and liability is to be located in such global organizations. These companies can afford to employ large legal firms and the best legal advice to secure favourable legal decisions. At the other end of the social scale, the working class has been exposed to massive economic and political change during the recession of the 1970s and 1980s. Given high levels of unemployment and inflation, subordinate classes have been unable to provide any successful opposition to wage-freeze, de-industrialization, and redundancy. The implication of this situation is not revolutionary politics, but an upsurge in sabotage, street violence, vandalism, theft, and sporadic civil disturbance. In the arena of conventional politics, there are strong movements towards a new form of status politics where political life is organized as a series of negotiations between the state apparatus and distinctive status blocs within the community. It follows that state intervention via the criminal law and police in the control of civil society may well increase, but in a situation where the state finds it increasingly difficult to legitimate such intervention in the absence of a dominant ideology, common values, and moral consensus.

These developments suggest some rather paradoxical combinations. There is an expansion of personal rights with respect to the private domain under an individualistic ideology and an expansion of citizenship rights under universalistic criteria (such as equality of treatment), but there is an erosion of individuality as a result of state regulation. There is the disappearance of overt punishment by repressive law as a socio-drama, but the growth of repressive measures of the state under criminal law is also apparent. The growth of specialist units within the police force to deal with civil disorder would be one illustration. There are periodic expressions of moral panic via the medical profession, but there is also the weakening of the notion of 'criminal intent' through the conversion of deviance into disease. The impact of criminology, and more generally sociology, on jurisprudence is to bring into question the whole legal tradition which underpins the concept of *mens rea*. Finally, there is the separation of 'legal personality' from property in a situation of competitive struggles between local and international capital.

Capitalism does not, in summary, require particularistic categorization of persons. This development was the basis of Weber's liberal fears for the future. Indeed capitalism, by bringing the world-system within the network of exchange relations, undermines particularism at least in principle: kinship, patriarchy, gender, and race are archaic criteria from the perspective of legal universalism. As a matter of empirical fact, we do of course find racism, sexism, and ageism in capitalist societies, but these are not requirements of the capitalist economy, and these forms of particularism are constantly challenged by social groups which appeal to abstract legalism to secure rights. It is for this reason that Marxism in its classical form always regarded capitalism as a system which brought about modernization through the destruction of traditional culture. Of course, these struggles are not always successful and most of them carry contradictory implications for capitalist civil society. Hegel, Marx, and Weber were correct in believing that capitalism contains within it certain potentialities for abstract universalism, although in this study of Weber and liberalism we have suggested that it is the market rather than capitalism which historically brought about a growth of social rights. Religious universalism in doctrines of salvation fostered economic universalism, which in turn was expressed through forms of legal universalism. Following Weber, we can argue that there is an immanent logic of rationality in western law that becomes conjoined with an immanent universalism in market relations which are indifferent to the particularities of personhood.

DE-DIFFERENTIATION AND LEGAL STATUS

Although there is still much disagreement as to the core themes of Weber's sociology, it is generally recognized that the rationalization process was a central aspect of his historical sociology. For Weber, law has evolved away from magical, charismatic law-making (by prophecy) towards systematic, public legal codes (such as the constitutional laws of modern states). As a result, law has become less *ad hoc* and more stable. Weber argued that such legal stability was important for capitalist exchange relations. The systematic character of legal thought in modern legal systems is an essential aspect of this stability; the consequence is an interaction between the needs of a capitalist economy and legal rationality. In this chapter, I have suggested that this rationalization process can also be observed in criminal law and penology where the public rituals of the scaffold have been replaced by the scientific management of the criminal.

The purpose of this presentation has been to offer a modest defence of Weber's sociology of law as a general theory of legal change (with special reference to capitalist development). In the process of making that defence, I have also made a deliberate attempt to defend eclecticism as a theoretical virtue. First, Foucault's analysis of the emergence of Panopticism as a principle of surveillance can be regarded as simply an example of the rationalization of penological management. Second, in so far as secularization is a dimension of rationalization, the decline of the sacred in legal thought was an important feature of Durkheim's treatment of the transition from mechanical to organic solidarity. For Durkheim, the disappearance of retribution as the purpose of law and the emerging emphasis on restitution and reciprocity as a feature or consequence of the division of labour provided criteria for establishing the process of secularization in modern societies. The erosion of the sacred as the organizing principle of traditional cultures was also associated with a growing specialization of knowledge which made it possible to distinguish or rather to generate differences between crime, deviance, disease, and moral failing. The rise of legal utilitarianism implied that it was possible to measure crime and punishment with scientific objectivity and precision. This process of differentiation was an essential feature of legal rationalization. Finally, we might notice certain points of convergence between the rationalization theme in Weber's sociology and Parsons' analysis of structural differentiation as the crucial aspect of social modernization. Legal differentiation has involved an intellectual division of labour between law, criminology, penology, and sociology, which has been a reflection of institutional divisions between various agencies of social control. The professionalization of legal practice is particularly important for the development of juridical rationality (Luhmann 1982).

One criticism of conventional social change theories (evolutionism and functionalism, for example) is that they cannot explain reverse process. In the case of Weber's rationalization process, it recognizes the possibility of charismatic revival in opposition to rationalization, but no systematic explanation of a return to charisma is offered. The same argument has been raised against Parsons' theory of structural differentiation. Parsons has been criticized for his uni-dimensional approach to the problem of order (to the exclusion of an analysis of conflict and disorder) and for his evolutionary perspective on social differentiation (to the exclusion of a study of change involving de-differentiation). Although many of these conventional criticisms have proved to be invalid (Holton and Turner 1986), neo-functionalism promises to develop Parsonian sociology in a productive and innovative direction (Alexander 1985).

Frank Lechner (1985a: 160–1) has provided the convincing argument that differentiation 'produces multiple sources of tension and raises the problem of the articulation of the spheres with each other'. The sub-systems of the social system at various levels (personality, social, and cultural) become with differentiation more specialized and autonomous, creating new problems of sub-system relationships and 'interpenetration' (Münch 1982). Differentiation makes highly problematic existing values and definitions of social membership. Lechner (1985b) has argued that various fundamentalist movements in America can be interpreted as movements against differentiation (and therefore modernization) which aim to restore and revitalize absolute moral commitment; these movements focus in particular on issues in the Latency and Integration sub-systems. Other social movements against de-differentiation may focus on other sub-systems, bringing into concern problems relating to authority or adaptation in the political and economic institutions.

It would be possible to consider the de-differentiation of legal institutions (or, more generally, control institutions) as a process which is likely to create new conditions of disorder. In this chapter, it has been argued, following Weber, that there has been a general process of legal rationalization involving both the secularization of law (its separation from religious values) and its specialization (such as the creation of institutions concerned with the policing of populations, the regulation of prisons, the development of legal professionalism, and the emergence of a complex court system for different branches of the law). If neo-functionalist arguments are correct, then we would expect certain disorderly features of this rationalization process to give rise to 'fundamentalist' responses in contemporary societies. Weber was partly aware of this problem.

We have already noted that Weber, following Nietzsche, recognized that secularization had profoundly affected the authority of law by weakening the values that lay behind legal authority. In particular, Weber observed that the Natural Law tradition had been eroded because it was difficult to accept the generalized values which had supported the notion of a 'Natural Law' of God. While these traditional moral supports had been eroded by modernization, Weber noted that oppositional groups in society (especially the German working class) typically appealed to substantive moral values (such as justice) which a formal, rational system of law cannot easily recognize. It is clear from these two illustrations that Weber did not regard rationalization as a smooth, conflict-free social process.

In contemporary law, we can also indicate a number of areas where there are sub-system frictions over legal issues which arise from uneven and contradictory patterns of secularization and rationalization. We would argue that the decline of retribution as an aspect of law is an index of modernization, associated with the erosion of *lex talionis*, the expansion of citizenship rights, and the decline of certain religious doctrines (such as the theory of original sin). The long-term impact of Bentham's philosophy has been a concern for educational correction and rehabilitation. As Foucault noticed in *Discipline and Punish* (1977), the modern prison attempts to create useful, docile bodies rather than imposing the monarch's vengeance. While there is an institutional commitment to rehabilitation, there are also strong moral movements within society for the restoration of physical punishment (including capital punishment) in order to express a sense of collective outrage. As Peter Berger argued in *A Rumour of Angels* (1969), some crimes are so enormous (such as the destruction of the Jewish community by the Nazis) that society does not have available an appropriate judicial and moral response. The sense of moral indignation cannot be placated by the existing principles of restitution. Taking an illustration from outside European societies, Islamic fundamentalism (especially revolutionary Shi'ism in Iran) in rejecting western modernism has restored retributive penal measures against adultery and theft (Lakhdar 1981).

The decline of retributive aspects of law is associated with the problem of legal responsibility in jurisprudence. Punishment can only justly be handed out to an offender who at the time of the crime knowingly and with intent committed an offence. If social science is itself a manifestation of rationalization, then the impact of social science has been to undermine *mens rea* and thereby to undermine doctrines of retribution. While the *mens rea* doctrine is complex, sociologists have typically questioned legal responsibility by their emphasis on the social factors which shape or determine individual actions. The implication of much sociological theory was that society rather than the individual is 'the cause' of crime; therefore, it is society which is 'to blame' for the crime rate. This argument, which was fashionable in the 1970s (among the members of the York Deviancy Symposium in Britain), has less prominence in the 1980s when there is more concern with victimology — with the needs and problems of victims rather than offenders. This shift in attitudes is a reflection of a more conservative period in European society generally and in Britain in particular. In a period of recession and industrial decline, the liberal mood of the 1960s has been replaced by a 'tougher' approach to prison and legal reform. However, at least some pressure for a sterner penal system has come from feminism and the women's movement. There are pressures not only for consistency in the judicial response to rape, for example, but also for retribution against gross sexual offence and a greater appreciation of the problems of the victim (Adler 1987). We would argue that these conflicts are illustrations of integration problems in the social system, which are consequences of the rationalization (differentiation) process.

Another area of empirical enquiry would be the growing conflict between medical technology, state involvement, and the legal aspects of personal status. Medical advances, which represent features of the rational intellectualization of life, have made possible an extensive regulation of life itself — through abortion, artificial insemination, contraception, transplantation, vaccination, and so forth. For Foucault in *The History of Sexuality* (1979), these developments are aspects of the new bio-politics of modern societies, involving a struggle over the production and reproduction of bodies. These developments in medical technology have forced the state to enter into realms which were the traditional sphere of religion; the state is drawn into the social–medical debate as to what constitutes 'life' (Robertson and Chirico 1985). In most of these issues, there is neither a clear political nor a determinate legal solution, because, as Weber so clearly indicated, medicine (which has fully embraced the discourse of positivistic science) can tell us how to cure certain ills, but it cannot provide moral solutions. The outcome of these political movements relating to AIDS, abortion, *in vitro* fertilization, and euthanasia is to involve the state and the legal system in a series of contradictions. In particular, modern medical developments have raised the question as to who or what owns a fertilized human egg, which has been stored in a laboratory in a situation where the original couple that produced this fertilized egg are now dead? It seems evident that the modern state will become the guardian or owner of a considerable amount of human 'material' (plasma, limbs, sperm, and so forth). This problem surrounding the definition of life has equally difficult implications for the legal definition of 'a person'. In turn, the Roman Catholic church appears to have adopted a theological position in which a human egg at the point of inception is a 'person', with citizenship rights.

CONCLUSION

In this chapter I have addressed three issues. The first argument has involved a defence of Weber's analysis of law against Marxist legal theory. Contemporary Marxist theories of law (especially those developed by Poulantzas and Pashukanis) have tended to replicate Weber's position by arguing that law in capitalism becomes abstract, systematic, and formal, because capitalist economic relations require legal stability and precision. Other Marxist arguments about the role of criminal law in the subordination of the working class, the protection of private property, and the interpellation of the legal subject were themes anticipated by and developed in Weber's sociology. Although Weber's sociology of law can be defended against its Marxist critics, there are major problems with Weber's historical sociology of law. For example, there are well-known difficulties with his views on English case-law and Islamic *qadi* justice (Turner 1974; 1981).

128

Second, I have attempted to defend the importance of a general theory of law which is eclectic in drawing upon a variety of intellectual traditions within classical sociology. In particular, this argument has sought to defend a typology of changes in legal institutions which incorporates the perspectives of Weber, Durkheim, and Parsons. These changes include the growth of legal unification with the dominance of professional regulation, the decline of repressive criminal codes and retributive penal practices, the growth of rights of universal citizenship, the secularization of law with the erosion of Natural Law, and, finally, the growth of international legal relations controlling corporate bodies. These changes may be summarized by the notion that there has been a broad trend towards legal rationalization. In general, these changes reflect a transition from *Gemeinschaft* to *Gesellschaft*, from a society dominated by immunities to a society in which market relations create universal categories relating to the legal individual, contracts, freedom of exchange, and tolerance.

Third, in order to avoid the criticism that such a general theory would be necessarily teleological, this chapter has considered recent developments in neo-functionalism which have attempted to develop a functionalist perspective on disorder and conflict as products of de-differentiation. The abstraction of formal rational law does not provide a vehicle for the overt expression of outrage and resentment against gross forms of crime and deviation. In contemporary societies in the west, there are strong moral campaigns to bring back capital punishment and other forms of retributive justice since there is considerable public frustration with what is seen to be the failure of a penal system based on the notions of rehabilitation, re-education, and re-training through public service. There are other moral campaigns regarding social control of homosexuality which express moral fundamentalism. We have suggested that many of these campaigns to restore values are effects of sub-system tensions and conflicts. In short, the quest for a general theory of legal change would not commit us necessarily to teleological functionalism.

It is important to locate Weber's sociology of law within the context of late nineteenth-century Germany. Under Bismarck's leadership, Germany had experienced rapid political (but not necessarily cultural) integration. The creation of a unified legal system was important for both economic and administrative purposes. Weber sought to emphasize the role of law in promoting political and economic stability and certainty, but he rejected the romantic view that law can be based in the folk community, because the assumptions about an integrated community could not be sustained. He also rejected idealistic and historical appeals to Natural Law. For Weber, law was command with the support, if necessary, of state coercion. Because Weber saw Germany surrounded by hostile and competitive forces, law had an important function as social cement. However, the law was heavily implicated in class conflicts, professional squabbles, and jurisprudential disagreements. Thus, Weber argued that law was subject to a rationalization process, but the impact of this process was highly variable.

Chapter Five

STATUS POLITICS IN CONTEMPORARY CAPITALISM

THE DEBATE ABOUT STATUS

The concept of 'status' in Max Weber's sociology has been the centre of considerable debate and controversy; unfortunately, this debate has often produced more misunderstanding than clarification, partly because the issue is overshadowed by certain ideological and political problems. In this chapter I wish to defend some aspects of Weber's use of the notion of 'status', and in particular to draw attention to the idea of 'status politics' as a framework for the analysis of modern capitalism (Turner 1988c). The purpose of this discussion is, therefore, not so much to contribute to exegesis, but rather to develop the concept of 'status politics' in the analysis of modern democratic polities. In particular, this discussion draws attention to the prevalence of status politics in societies which are deeply divided by social criteria involving status attribution and particularity. A minor feature of this argument is the proposition that, empirically, social class, as defined by economic criteria, is declining in importance as the major division in political life. Although the main focus of this argument is on the application of the concept, in order to perform this explanatory function it will be necessary to consider some of the conceptual and exegetical problems associated with Weber's notion of status.

The use of the term 'status' has been confused by an association with at least four major controversies surrounding the epistemological, ideological, and political implications of Weber's treatment of social stratification. Of major importance is the fact that Weber's classical distinction between class, status, and power has been seized by subsequent sociologists as a major alternative to Marx's central concern with the economic characteristics of class divisions in capitalism. The result has been that many of the major approaches to the discussion of social inequality have been organized around the theme of Weber versus Marx (Bendix and Lipset 1953; Dahrendorf 1959; Giddens 1973). It has often been suggested that Weber's schema is more flexible and subtle as a framework for the analysis of different forms of inequality which centre on economic, political, and prestige differences. It is also asserted that Weber's notion of 'status' provides a perspective on precisely those forms of social differentiation which Marx's emphasis on economic differences cannot adequately explain; namely, the problems of racism, gender differences, nationalism, and age groups. In short, Weber's tripartite view of power relations offers a perspective which is capable of analysing class, while also providing analytical insight into the formation of pariah groups, caste differences, and racial orders (Neuwirth 1969; Rex 1986).

Clearly, in his analysis of capitalism and critique of socialism, Weber offered a radical alternative to Marxist positions on the crises of capitalism (Turner 1981). Weber rejected the Marxist conceptual approach to proletarianization and pauperization, by noting that the standard of living of the German working class had actually improved over the nineteenth century, that the working class was increasingly fragmented by the technical division of labour, that a new class (the middle class) had emerged to provide essential service functions for capitalist production, that the state intervened progressively in both the market-place and production systems, and that, finally, capitalism required some feature of state regulation to cope with the business cycle. Finally, Weber had argued that socialism would require rationalization of economic production, leading to increasing dominance by a bureaucratic state and the party machine. Socialism, rather than being an alternative to capitalism, was simply an extension and elaboration of the more fundamental process of economic rationalization. Of course, these arguments have been challenged by a variety of writers, who have suggested in particular that Marxist conceptual tools can very adequately cope with the problem of the new middle class, contradictory class locations, and the importance of managerial functions within the work-place (Carchedi 1977; Crompton and Gubbay 1978; Wright 1985). The problem of the new middle class has subsequently given rise to a complex and inconclusive debate on the various merits of Marxist and Weberian approaches (Abercrombie and Urry 1983).

The problem of status as a useful sociological concept has therefore been overlaid by the conflict between Marxist and Weberian perspectives on social stratification, but the concept is also fundamental to certain alleged differences in Marx's and Weber's views of history. Thus, the notion of 'status' further differentiates Weberian and Marxist approaches to sociology, since the contrast between status and class is also indicative of a different theory of historical change. Given the fact that there appears to be relatively little chance of a working-class revolution inside modern capitalist societies, a number of writers have appealed to Weber's notion of 'status group' as a way of analysing the fragmentation of working classes and have drawn attention to the growing predominance of status differences within modern societies (Parkin 1982). It can be argued:

> nationalism and citizenship, religious beliefs and ethnic loyalties, regional associations and linguistic groups have often proved stronger than proletarian class consciousness. And movements of this kind arise from just that 'fragmentation of interest and rank' which, according to Marx, would be obliterated by 'egotistical calculation and the constraints of factory production'.
>
> (Bendix 1974: 151)

According to Bendix, therefore, Weber's concept of 'status groups' was associated with a different view of historical change.

Weber noted that with the development of capitalism, there has been a growing separation between the work-place and the family, and between economic power and political authority. These differences between Weber and Marx are often put within a much broader canvas, whereby within Weber's view of history we can see a shift from feudal estates to economic classes and to status differences as the primary features of the development of social stratification in European societies. Although Weber used the concept of 'status honour' to discuss the formation of status communities, he also recognized the importance of status as legal immunity within the feudal system of estates. The emergence of a capitalist system of economics destroys this tradition of immunity by creating a social system in which the cash nexus becomes the leading element within the distribution of power and rewards. This notion of legal immunity was fundamental to the distribution of power in feudal systems, creating distinctive estates with their own privileges, life-styles, and honour (Poggi 1978). Within such a society, participation takes place mostly through region- and territory-wide *Staende*: bodies formally constituted for the purpose of voicing the corporate claims of the feudal and (separately) of the town element, and of setting the terms under which both are willing to support the ruler's undertakings. To obtain that support, the ruler is constrained to acknowledge the immunities and prerogatives vested in such bodies and in their constituent social groups.

(Poggi 1983: 97)

By contrast, Marx was generally committed to the view that slavery, feudalism, and capitalism were all social systems based upon economic class differences, although of course he was aware of the issue of legal immunity within the system of feudal estates.

We need to recognize that there are various strands in Marx's analysis of class from the programmatic and elementary statement of class struggle in the *Manifesto* and the more complex, sophisticated and sociological treatment of class interest and class forces in *The Eighteenth Brumaire of Louis Bonaparte* (Cottrell 1984). While there are these variations within Marx, it is difficult to see how Marxism as a theory of history could totally abandon or seriously modify the commitment to the notion that feudal society was a class society (Hindess and Hirst 1975). More generally, class struggle has featured as one of the prime movers of history within the endogenous sources of social change, particularly in the transition from feudalism to capitalism (Holton 1985).

The idea that status as a concept is closely related to different views of history in Marx and Weber eventually became associated with the question of classlessness in contemporary capitalist society, especially within modern American politics. It has been commonly observed that Weber's emphasis (for example) on conflict in the relationship between status groups and the importance of usurpation was transformed and submerged with the development of the Warner School of sociology in America (Gordon 1950; Pfautz and Duncan 1950; Wenger 1980). In the American context, there was a tendency to blur the distinction between the idea of 'social class' and 'social status'. Stratification was seen in terms of a continuous gradation of differences of prestige, income, and wealth with no clear divisions within this gradation of differences. The notions of 'class struggles' and 'class conflicts' were to some extent replaced by the ideas of 'status contradictions' and 'status crystallization'. Research on the possibilities of social mobility replaced the traditional Marxist analysis of the divisive character of class confrontations. In short, the emphasis on status stratification, as a classless continuum of privilege and prestige, gave expression to an individualistic ideology which conceptualized America as an open system of achievement and opportunity (Parkin 1978).

The theory of non-egalitarian classlessness was first outlined systematically by Stanislaw Ossowski (1963); the thesis has three components: '(a) A continuum of persons possessing minutely different amounts of prestige, (b) a series of status groups hierarchically arranged, (c) a vast middle class which includes a large segment of the working class' (Rinehart 1971: 149). The thesis was associated with the structural functionalist theory of stratification (Davis and Moore 1945) and was also developed by writers like Robert Nisbet (1959). The argument that American society is characterized by its classlessness has been challenged by a number of writers; the assumption that the notion of 'classlessness' can be latched on to Weber's concept of 'status group' has also given rise to considerable controversy and dispute (Wenger 1980). Other writers have noticed that

American sociologists have failed to see that the absence of classes may both in ideology and in social fact *more* effectively conceal existing inequalities and a social structure clearly divided into recognisable classes. The invisibility of poverty in the United States, already referred to, suggests such a conclusion, as does the fact that income distribution has become more unequal in the past decade, the very decade of the 'affluent society', which has witnessed so much individual and collective mobility, the mass diffusion of formally restricted status symbols, and the breakdown of long-standing ethnic, religious, and even racial barriers to opportunity.

(Wrong 1977: 130)

The Weberian parentage of this theory of status gradations has also been challenged by a number of writers. In particular, there is an important argument to suggest that we should clearly separate the notion of 'status group' as a community with a common life-style from the idea of estates within a feudal system based upon legal privilege. Estates like caste systems cannot be regarded as historically progressive within a Weberian framework, since this meaning of 'status' involves the attribution of particularistic privileges to groups

135

which monopolize symbols of power and superiority, often through a system of inheritance both material and cultural. Status privilege does not indicate or depend upon open mobility and a system of equality of opportunity, but rather on closure and restriction of opportunities to groups which have achieved a considerable licence to enjoy inherited symbolic and material wealth. The salience and resonance of classlessness in egalitarianism and status gradation in the American context may well have reflected a nostalgic commitment to the principle of small town democracy against both mass society and capitalism which were similarly indifferent to refinement and manners.

Finally, status has also been used to differentiate Marxist and Weberian sociology in terms of a number of conceptual epistemological, and methodological questions. Within the conventional litany, it is typically argued that, whereas Marx's analysis of class was analytical, Weber's use of stratification in terms of class, status, and power was primarily descriptive (Dahrendorf 1959). It is also commonly noted that, whereas Marx was primarily concerned with differences at the level of production and economic relations, Weber characteristically saw class and status as features of consumption and market situations. According to Giddens (1973: 78), the primary difficulty with Weber's conception of status and class is that it implies 'the recognition of an indefinitely extensive number of classes'. These problems are also associated with Weber's methodological use of ideal types and his apparent commitment to methodological individualism in which both status and class are conceptualized in terms of the life chances of an individual with respect to the distribution of privileges and rewards within the market-place and within the arena of prestige and honour (Barbalet 1980).

For Marxists, Weber's approach to stratification is ultimately flawed by a subjectivism which is associated with his individualistic approach to sociological phenomena. In a terminology which is highly misleading, these differences are sometimes conceptualized in terms of Weber's subjective notions of social differences and Marx's objective analysis of the structures of inequality in terms of economic classes. Finally, there is the idea developed by Karl Löwith (1982) that, whereas Weber offered merely a diagnosis, Marx proposed a therapy for the alienation and exploitation of individuals in a class society. Marx's analysis of class was overtly and directly related to a political programme of change, whereas it is implied that the commitment to value neutrality in Weber's sociology ruled out such a direct and open connection between analysis and action. Weber's pessimism led him to concentrate significantly on the continuity of inequality in terms of bureaucratic authority in the transition from capitalism to socialism rather than on the progressive possibilities of political change as such. In conclusion, we might simply note that the notion of 'status' stands at the centre of a number of disparate lines of argument separating Marx and Weber and thereby separating social- ism and sociology as activities. In the process of this confrontation, the concept of 'status' has often been either drained of any significant content or rendered incoherent by being forced to do too many ideo- logical, political, and analytical duties. In order to clarify some of these issues, we should turn next to Weber's formal analysis of status in *Economy and Society* and his use of these notions in his various studies of religion, politics, and social organization.

THE CONCEPT OF STATUS IN WEBER'S SOCIOLOGY OF DOMINATION

In sociology we can distinguish four primary meanings of the term 'status'. First, there is the somewhat trivial notion of status as position in the development of role theory. In this usage, role is con- sidered to be, as it were, the active side of status as simply a position within society. Second, there is the idea of status as personal esteem involving some notion of deference towards an individual. This use of the term is related to Goffman's notion of 'face', involving the social processes of deference and embarrassment (Goffman 1967). Third, there is the notion of 'status' as a system of estates whereby a society is divided by legal and cultural privileges into separate, caste-like groups. Finally, there is the notion of 'status group' or 'status community', signifying a collectivity of persons enjoying a similar life-style, a common moral system, a unifying language or culture, whose separateness within society is bound up with their monopoly of cultural privilege. This aspect of status has been developed by Pierre Bourdieu in the idea of distinction as a system of judgement of taste separating individuals as a consequence of their inheritance and development of different forms of culture (Bourdieu 1984).

Although all four meanings of the concept of 'status' are to be found in the work of Weber, my argument is that the primary meaning of 'status' in his historical and comparative sociology was the idea of status communities and estates as collectivities held together by certain exclusionary privileges. It is for this reason that the idea of status in Weber's sociology is probably best located within his sociology of domination; we should regard status as part of the system of power within a society. Social stratification is about the generation, maintenance, and distribution of power within societies.

In general, the debate about Weber's analysis of status has been conducted with reference to his formal definition of status contrasted with class and political parties. In my brief exposition of Weber's theory of status, I shall draw attention to the use of status and status community in his substantive analyses of social structure, with special reference to China, Israel, and Islam. There are broadly three areas in Weber's sociology where we should examine the discussion of status and status groups. First, there is the brief but instructive formal definition of status and status group in the conceptual exposition which occupies part one of volume one of *Economy and Society*. Second, there is the more extended and elaborate discussion of class status and party in the chapter on political communities in volume two. Third, there are the historical and comparative studies of the formation of status communities and their political role in Weber's sociology of the religion of India, the religion of China, the sociology of religion, and the specific study of the city. The general drift of my position is that probably more is to be learnt from Weber's use of the concept 'status group' than from a review of his formal definitions. However, in order to understand the character of Weber's approach to status, I will start with the more formal exposition of the notions of 'status' and 'status group' which are features of Weber's attempt to provide a general theoretical sociological analysis of the notions of open and closed social relations that are either associative or communal. These formal discussions of relationships then lead into an attempt to build more general concepts of social structure involving the unequal distribution of power.

Status relationships may be seen as part of the authoritative structure of social interactions. Weber defined a social relationship as communal if it was based upon the subjective feelings of the inter-actants where these feelings could be either affectual or traditional. By contrast, he defined a social relationship as associative if the orientation of social action rested upon some form of rationally moti-vated consideration of interests or if it was directed towards some absolute value. This distinction, of course, to some extent reflected that made by Ferdinand Tönnies in the classic distinction between *Gemeinschaft* and *Gesellschaft*. If we combine this discussion of association and community with Weber's notions of open and closed relationships, then clearly we can produce a fourfold table or property-space illustrating four ideal types of relationships. Weber noted that whether or not relationships would be open or closed would be determined by traditional, rational, or affectual criteria. For example, rational criteria of closedness would be based on certain utilitarian principles whereby it is to the advantage of the participants in order to secure rights and duties, to close a relationship to outsiders. These formal distinctions provided Weber with an initial framework for categorizing various forms of social relationships; for example, the market-place in the capitalist mode of production is an open associative relationship, whereas personal, erotic, and familial interactions involve closed communal relationships. From the basis of this elementary notion of closure, we can see how Weber prepared the way for a more general discussion of status and status groups, involving various forms of closedness towards competition for privileged status, attributes, esteem, and honour.

In the chapter on status groups and classes in *Economy and Society*, Weber defined status as the effective claim to social honour or esteem in terms of a set of positive or negative privileges. Status, furthermore, is usually founded on a set of criteria including a specific style of life, a formal education, or the prestige derived from occupational or hereditary positions within a society. In practice, Weber argued that status was expressed through connubium, commensality, the monopolistic enjoyment of certain privileged forms of acquisition, or, alternatively, the abhorrent rejection of certain forms of acquisition, and, finally, upon traditional status conventions. He went on to argue that 'status group' refers to a plurality of social actors who, within the setting of a larger collectivity, successfully claim a special form of social honour and typically certain status monopolies over the enjoyment of privileges. Status groups may emerge as a consequence of their life-style, especially where their life-style is associated with the development of a vocation or a profession, or through the basis of an hereditary charisma (for example, traditional Islamic saints) or through the monopolistic possession of certain political or hierocratic powers (Weber 1978: 305–6). In short, status groups are communal groups which, through various means, enjoy certain forms of privileged access to scarce resources, especially where these scarce resources are of a cultural, moral or symbolic character. These status groups are ranked in terms of negative or positive privilege systems. Furthermore, status groups typically have their origin in some strategy of usurpation; they involve a collective struggle to improve access to esteem through usurpatory strategies. A typical example of this would be from the Indian caste system, whereby the adoption of certain high-caste activities brings about an improvement in status; this process has been referred to as 'sanskritization' (Srinivas 1952; 1966). Srinivas defined the process of sanskritization as one involving the claim of a low-caste tribal or other group to the status and privileges of a high or twice-born caste. As a general rule these changes in status are followed by a claim to a higher niche in the caste system than that conventionally conceded to the claimant group by the local village community. Finally, in this section defining the formal characteristics of status and status groups, Weber argued that, depending on the currently prevailing system of stratification, it is possible to speak of either 'status society' or a 'class society'. Whereas class societies are at least formally characterized by an open competition for economic benefits without reference to traditional or charismatic forms of authority, status societies depend very heavily on the successful imposition of traditional or charismatic forms of authority. Weber, possibly agreeing with Marx's view of the revolutionary character of class relations under capitalism, implied directly or indirectly that class relations based upon economic competition are wholly destructive, or at least corrosive, of existing traditional patterns.

Having outlined some of the basic aspects of status groups in terms of closed social relations, Weber in the chapter on political communities in *Economy and Society* went on to elaborate and substantiate the notion of 'status group' and 'status community' as separate and distinct from social classes in society. The first issue is that by comparison with economic classes, status groups (*Stande*) are usually social groups of a communal nature. The communal character of the status situation is reinforced by the reproduction of a specific form of life-style within the group. By contrast, economic classes are characteristically aggregates of individuals linked together by exchange or productive relations (Weber 1978: 932–9). These communal aspects of status relations have been emphasized by a variety of commentators on Weber; for example, Frank Parkin (1982) has drawn attention to the combative character of status communities as opposed to socio-economic classes. Status groups are organized communally both for the defence and expansion of their entitlements. Status groups aim to achieve legal recognition of their privileges in order to intensify the closedness of their ranks against outsiders. Thus Weber argued that 'the road to legal privilege, positive or negative, is easily travelled as soon as a certain stratification of the social order has in fact been "lived in" and has achieved stability by virtue of a stable distribution of economic power' (Weber 1978: 933).

Where these processes have been fully developed in the direction of a monopolization of privilege, Weber suggested that a status group might evolve finally into a closed caste. Weber noted that various forms of endogamous marriage laws, ritualistic forms of exclusion, and ideologies concerning the purity of interpersonal contact served to reinforce the exclusiveness of the caste. In addition, he developed the idea of the pariah group which is ritualistically and legally excluded from contact with the host society. Weber, implicitly and explicitly reflecting on the views of Friedrich Nietzsche, combined the notions of resentment and pariah groups to generate a powerful theory of ingroup–outgroup relations of conflict and oppression (Sigrist 1971).

Within this relatively formal outline of a theory of status communities, therefore, we can see that Weber was concerned with certain historical and comparative processes which both produce and undermine social relations based upon closure. In particular, he was concerned with the emergence and disintegration of relatively coherent social groups, from occupational communities through to caste systems. Status communities thereby involve collective action to maintain and extend certain kinds of privileges, both material and spiritual, against the intrusions of other social groups. Having outlined this formal theory of status group formation, we can now turn to the more interesting question of Weber's use of these concepts in the comparative analysis of cultures.

Although the issue is controversial, in employing the notion of an Asiatic mode of production for the analysis of oriental societies, Marx argued that the stagnation of these societies was associated with absence of private property in land and therefore in the absence of conflictual social classes as the levers of social change (Turner 1978). To some extent, in his analysis of oriental societies through the use of such concepts as patrimonialism, Weber placed particular emphasis on status communities as closed systems of cultural and material reproduction. For example, in his study of Chinese society Weber gave prominence to the political and cultural role of the literati. He argued:

> for twelve centuries social rank in China has been determined more by qualification for office than by wealth. This qualification, in turn, has been determined by education, and especially by examination. China has made literary education the yardstick of social prestige in the most exclusive fashion, far more exclusively than did Europe during the period of the humanists, or as Germany has done.

(Weber 1951: 107)

These literati were a secular stratum of genteel laymen who came eventually to have total control over the imperial civil service. This stratum came to enjoy considerable privileges and immunities within the Chinese system, being free in particular from manual labour and immune from corporal punishment. In Weber's argument this stratum contributed considerably to the stability and traditionalism of ancient China, because there was a natural affinity between Confucian ethics and the life-style of this stratum of civil servants.

Weber adopted a very similar position in his analysis of the role of caste in the history of Indian social structure, where he suggested that the ritualism of the caste structure inhibited the emergence of rational economic systems based upon competition and open markets. In *The Religion of India*, Weber noted that caste is 'doubtless a closed status group. All the obligations and barriers that membership in a status group entails also exist in a caste, in which they are intensified to the utmost degree' (Weber 1958: 39–40). Although the history of Europe in the feudal period has been dominated by the presence of estates, which Weber regarded also as closed status groups, the feudal estates did not have entirely rigid norms of commensalism and connubium. More importantly, 'as a status group, caste enhances and transposes this social closure into the sphere of religion, rather of magic' (Weber 1958: 43). This rigid system of status orders was finally legitimized by the all-embracing doctrines of karma and samsara, which were general theodicies of social inequality.

Weber sought to contrast these systems of rigid estates in both China and India with the history of occidental societies which, through the combination of the occidental city structure and Christian universalism, permitted the emergence of a political order based upon a universal faith rather than on ritualistic systems of exclusion. The city became the basis of a new social and political order which, over a very long period, gave a special emphasis to the rights of the individual, the organization of politics on the basis of citizenship, and the emergence of economic markets which were indifferent to status or race or religion (Abercrombie, Hill, and Turner 1986). In the west the development of the city as an urban community provided the basis for the eventual destruction of other forms of closed association based upon kinship and family relations. The transformative capacity of the city in western culture gave rise to the whole political philosophy of civil rights associated with the urban political problems of civic status groups in the city structure. By contrast, 'the establishment of the ''city'' in the occidental sense, was restricted in Asia, partly through sib power which continued unbroken, partly through caste alienation' (Weber 1958: 338). In occidental culture, therefore, the importance of universalism and individualism in Christianity contributed to the destruction of clan association, whereas Islam 'remained the religion of a conquering army structured in terms of tribes and clans' (Weber 1966: 100).

It is well known that Weber's sociology of religion raised acute problems in terms of the contributions of Judaism and Islam to the emergence of rational systems of law, religion, and ethics (Turner 1974). In the case of Judaism, Weber argued that the Diaspora had transformed Israel from a political association into an exclusive religious community, whose pariah status was constantly reaffirmed by the enforcement of circumcision, ritual purity, economic separation, and rigid rules of in-group marriage. The consequence was that Judaism became a closed status religion whose very existence depended upon highly particularistic rules of diet and group regulation. In the case of Islam, Weber argued that the conversion of Islam from a charismatic community into a rigid feudal system was brought about by its dominance as a military power in the Middle East. The dominance of this military ethos and this imperial structure meant that cities under Islamic rule retained their character as mere military camps. In addition, Weber argued that Islamic law and religion retained a highly rigid and traditional form, precluding the emergence of individual rights of protest and ruling out the possibility of rational changes in legal content. In Islam, the military stratum came to enjoy the privileges of an exclusive status community based upon a distinctive concept of honour grounded in the ethic of a religion of

143

conquest. Therefore Weber argued that 'concepts like sin, salvation, and religious humility have not only seemed remote from all elite political classes, particularly the warrior nobles, but have indeed appeared reprehensible to its sense of honour' (Weber 1965: 85). Because Islam came to be dominated by this warrior status community in its early years of expansion, Weber argued that the revolutionary impact of inner-worldly asceticism was never fully unleashed on Islamic cultures.

This brief overview of Weber's comparative study of status communities in relation to the emergence of different forms of salvation doctrines has been introduced to suggest that Weber, like Marx, regarded the emergence of capitalism, at least in some respects, as a progressive historical force, since closed status communities prevent the emergence of universalistic norms of religious, legal, and economic conduct. In occidental feudalism, the estate system was not conducive to the development of capitalism and exchange markets, because it depended upon rigid and traditional notions of social conduct. However, in feudalism, there was the possibility of contradictory and conflictual relations between autonomous cities, merchant culture, and urban universities on the one hand, and feudal landlords, priestly orders, and rural traditionalism on the other. It is clear that Weber regarded the autonomous city as an essential corrosive of rural traditionalism legitimized by conventional forms of Catholic belief. In India, the caste system, as we have seen, was a form of closed status community, and Weber emphasized the importance of this caste structure as a condition inhibiting the development of capitalism. In a similar fashion in China, the literati inhibited the growth of rational systems of belief and conduct, giving great stability to traditional Confucian religious beliefs. Similar developments took place, according to Weber, in Islamic and Jewish cultures, where the full impact of religious asceticism and rationalism failed to develop, because of the growth of status exclusiveness among Jewish communities which, in order to survive, were forced to emphasize their particularity and differences. In the case of Islam, it was the merchants of a warrior stratum which precluded the development of urban rationalism and open economic markets based upon the emergence of private property. In Islam, although a transcontinental merchant culture developed, it was to some extent overshadowed by the continuing importance of military ethics based upon the status honour of Islamic warriors.

This account of Weber's use of the notion of 'status community' has been presented in order to situate Weber's formal analysis of status within the wider historical concerns for the emergence of a rational and individualistic culture. The consequence of this overview is to bring about a certain agreement with the position adopted by Morton Wenger (1980), who argued that the concept of 'status' in Weber, far from suggesting progressive social changes, was used (especially in the sense of estate) to suggest rigidity, traditionalism, and the ossification of cultures. It was the emergence of economic classes in the context of capitalist markets rather than the continuity of estates and closed status communities which pointed to the possibilities of social mobility and radical change based upon a cash nexus. Of course, Weber recognized the importance of status exclusiveness in capitalism associated with the emergence of professions and vocations, where educational achievement became an important feature of social closure. However, these professional status communities, utilizing education as a form of social closure and monopolization of privilege, were quite separate from the issue of status societies based upon a rigid form of estate ranking. However, the point of this interpretation of Weber is to assert that status was not simply a formal descriptive concept in Weber's sociology, but part of a dynamic and historical framework for the analysis of modern cultures. It was a fundamental feature of his sociology of domination related to the historical sociology of modern capitalism.

CRITICISM AND DISCUSSION

Weber's views on status, his analysis of rationalization, and his attempt to draw significant contrasts between occidental and oriental cultures have been extensively reviewed and criticized in the literature. In this chapter, I shall not focus on these historical and comparative criticisms of Weber's use of the concepts of 'status', 'status group', and 'status community'. The aim here is to define the major features of status communities and to argue that the concepts of 'status' and 'status group' provide an important insight into certain features of contemporary politics. Against both Marx and Weber, the argument is that status, for reasons which will be explained, becomes more rather than less significant in the development of the political systems of late capitalism. In presenting this view, I shall add to the terminology by attempting to develop the notion of 'status blocs', by which I mean columns of social actors organized in terms of some particularity (such as race, ethnicity, language, age, or gender); it is argued that these status blocs are combative and that they are constituted by the interaction of status with the modern state under conditions of democratic equality.

We can argue that the essential features of status communities and status blocs are concerned with the closedness of social relations. First, it is noted that status blocs are integrated social solidarities or collectivities which are organized around certain interests or values with the goal of maintaining social privileges. While some writers (Stone and Form 1953) have attempted to make a distinction between status groups as integrated, combative, social collectivities and status aggregates, which are diffuse and dispersed groups of people enjoying the same status, in this particular argument I shall argue that status blocs are highly integrated, organized, and solidaristic. It is assumed that status blocs exercise social closure in order to maintain their cultural exclusiveness, whereby the benefits of membership of the bloc are reinforced and reproduced. The maintenance of status bloc politics involves the constant conflict of usurpation and exclusion, whereby different status blocs vie with one another for the monopolization of cultural benefits. In this thesis, status blocs are an essential part of the process of political mobilization, whereby groups, enjoying relative levels of privilege and disprivilege, constantly organize in the interests of maintaining or improving their position within the society.

Although this argument does not deny the existence of social classes in modern societies, Weber's tendency to dichotomize status politics and class politics is rejected. Following Parkin (1982), it is useful to distinguish between status groups which emerge within social classes (and are related therefore to the division of labour and the property system), and those that cut across social classes (and are thereby related to the general distribution of honour and prestige within a society). Using a slightly different terminology, I shall argue that status blocs are columns which cross-cut classes and are organized as political entities which do not necessarily draw their support from class phenomena. That is,

> communal status groups that cut across class lines show no signs of diminishing — rather the reverse. They draw upon sentiments and identities that owe little to the vagaries of the division of labour,

and their impediment to pure class formation and action is likely to be all the more formidable for it.

(Parkin 1982: 99)

In this sense it is clear that status bloc politics are not an alternative to class politics in the sense that they preclude each other. Rather, status bloc politics and class politics appear to exist side by side; however, I wish to argue shortly that status bloc politics have become more significant at least in the political system than class-based politics in contemporary capitalism. As Parkin notes (1982: 100),

in the present depths of industrial gloom and depression the heightened class activities that Weber would have predicted have been accompanied by a resurgence of ethnic group demands that he would not have predicted. Class and status group concerns do not, it seems, simply alternate with changes in the economic climate.

However, following Weber there are reasons to believe that status blocs and status communities are more able to mobilize their members than economic classes, which, in both Marx and Weber's terms, are somewhat anonymous aggregates of individuals sharing the same economic position in society.

Briefly stating my general thesis, it is argued that in contemporary democracies where the principles of equality and citizenship have been established, however inadequately, sectors or blocs of society which experience discrimination and inequality by reference to certain particular criteria (such as race or age) are mobilized to attain privileges under the general slogans of equality of opportunity and equality of condition. In the early stages of capitalism and modern democracy, social groups which adhered to liberal principles promoted the idea of equality of opportunity, but, since this criterion of equality is relatively individualistic, they did not necessarily form political blocs or social movements. However, with the expansion of modern citizenship rights as a universal principle, a wide spectrum of the population experiences various forms of particular inequality, and they thereby organize together to demand changes in social conditions to promote either equality of condition or equality of outcome (Turner 1986a). Because of electoral pressures, governments are forced to respond to such pressure-group demands from sectors of the community which claim to experience disprivilege and prejudice on the grounds of some particular characteristic. In short, the very success of citizenship tends to produce inflationary demands for greater access to both political and social rights (Turner 1986b). The consequence of these political and social movements (in general, the phenomena of new social movements) is to create blocs or columns of status communities held together both by the development of interests with respect to their particular group characteristics and by the response of the state to their political demands. Therefore, status blocs are produced by a political consciousness of privilege and dis-privilege and by the response of the state to its sectional clientele. It is for this reason that I wish to refer to these groups, perhaps somewhat clumsily, as 'administratively determined status blocs' and to refer to modern politics as 'administratively determined status-bloc politics', which we may regard more simply as a modern form of clientelism. My argument is that this perspective on modern politics provides a general theoretical model for the analysis of the organization of demo-cratic politics in terms of the status interests of gender, age, ethnicity, and cultural difference.

In briefly stating the argument, I wish to distinguish my position from that held by writers like Ossowski, Wrong, and Nisbet, who have in various ways argued that contemporary politics is charac-terized by the development of inegalitarian classlessness or by the continuity or existence of inequality without social stratification. Following Wenger's criticism of recent sociological writing on status groups in American sociology (Wenger 1980), my analysis of status bloc politics does not imply an evolutionary development of society from nineteenth-century class society to twentieth-century status society. If anything, the analysis of status politics implies a cyclical relationship between class and status. Furthermore, there are no teleological implications to the argument, since the thesis stresses the importance of contingent relationships between culture, politics, and economics, between which there are no law-like relationships.

At least, the argument does not involve the presence of inevitable relationships between status, politics, and economics. As a result, the analysis of status politics does not imply an optimistic view of political development, since the argument does not involve some notion of a status gradation compatible with a high level of social mobility. The argument involves the idea of relatively rigid status blocs or columns which might be contrasted with the horizontal nature of estates in feudalism. In spatial terms, the notion of status politics in this argument implies the existence of vertical columns of relatively separate political groupings competing directly with one another for the patronage of the state. Therefore the analysis of status particularity and status politics in contemporary society does not necessarily imply some notion of political pluralism as the necessary ingredient of a truly democratic society. As we will see, the argument is in fact relatively pessimistic, since it assumes that status-bloc politics will involve an inflationary situation in economic, political, and cultural terms.

The spread of the notion of equality in democratic systems creates the conditions for an explosion of social expectations, since the claims of one group for social preferment generate expectations in related groups for equal forms of treatment. In the United States the social improvement in the condition of blacks leads to demands from other migrant or ethnic groups who, in terms of equality, feel discriminated against, or are disprivileged given the improvement of the condition of blacks. Status politics involves a form of leap-frogging, where expectations assume an inflationary character.

The argument that the combination of democracy and status-bloc politics produces inflationary demands can be presented within a number of different perspectives. For example, Daniel Bell (1976) has argued that, if we accept the notion that equality is one of the distinctive characteristics of modern society, then we would expect an inflationary impact because the delivery of social entitlements gives rise to an enormous expansion in social services, which in turn implies a considerable tax burden. From an entirely different vantage point, Claus Offe (1985) has noted a variety of causes which give rise to an expansion of the service sector in contemporary capitalism. These causes include the rising expectation for services, the sectional interests of professional groups, the response of the state to public pressure from interest groups, and changes in the nature of wants. The political pressure on status blocs and the response of the state produces an increase in the tax burden and, within an international economic environment, may cause adverse economic processes within the national economy. The consequence is a vicious circle between the demands of the electorate, the response of democratic governments, and the capacity to deliver such services on the basis of an increasing gross national product. While T. H. Marshall noted a contradictory relationship between citizenship and class, in contemporary societies we might observe a contradictory relationship between internal democratic process based upon status politics and external constraints of an international capitalist system in which the value of currencies has been destabilized; the contradiction is now between the internal political process and the global economic constraints of a world capitalist system.

CLASS POLITICS AND STATUS POLITICS

In order to establish the importance of status blocs within contemporary politics, it is not necessary to prove that economic class no longer has significance for political, social, and cultural life. The inequalities which result from differences in possession and access to the means of production are still clearly significant. Indeed, with the current world recession, there is clearly evidence of increasing economic inequality in class terms as represented by wealth and income. However, my argument is that the traditional divisions of politics by class have been transformed with the relative decline of the working class as a unified bloc and by certain changes in the character of the capitalist class. In Europe in particular, class divisions have been transformed by the gradual erosion of traditional heavy industries associated with shipbuilding, the railways, and mining.

Historically speaking, the British working class, as a class in itself and for itself, was dependent upon the growth of labour-intensive, heavy industry in the nineteenth century. As Marx noted, the growth of large factories, the decline of rural occupations, the development of industrial discipline, and the corresponding emergence of trade unions transformed an aggregate of workers into a relatively unified and relatively effective political organization. In the second half of the twentieth century, there has been a profound decline in these traditional industries, resulting not merely in high levels of unemployment, but in the gradual destruction of the working class as the backbone of the English social structure. This relative decline in the size of the working class and the transformation of its political nature are reflected in the decline, at least proportionately, of trade-union membership and the diminution of commitment to the Labour Party as the organ of the working class. In Britain, the emergence of the Social Democratic Party, the relative revival of the Liberal Party and the collapse of the traditional division between Labour and Conservative are the political consequences at least in part of the demise of the traditional, urban, organized working class in Britain (Tracy 1983).

In presenting this argument about the decline of the working class as the principal vehicle for political protest in Europe, I am to a large degree following the argument of André Gorz in *Farewell to the Working Class* (1982). For Gorz, major changes in the character of work in the late twentieth century have transformed the relationship between capital and labour, making the prospect of massive and more or less permanent unemployment a significant feature of contemporary capitalist societies. This transformation of work is brought about by technological and managerial changes, resulting in a widespread de-skilling of labour. This destruction of work is not necessarily a progressive and liberating social change, because it involves a further domination and alienation of the working class by technical, economic, and other social processes over which they have little or no control. Rather than gaining control over their work-place and status situation, the working class has been marginalized from the very process of production itself as a consequence of changes in the character of technology, skill, management, and work-place organization.

We should see this decline of the traditional working class within an industrial, capitalist environment alongside the fragmentation of classes, the de-personalization of property, and the emergence of new middle strata of white-collar employees. Indeed, one might argue that the crucial issue in contemporary society is not the traditional division between capital and labour, but a new set of status differences between the employed and the unemployed. Given these changes in the characteristics of modern capitalism, we may either require a new description of the society or a new framework departing significantly from the conventional Marxist viewpoint.

DISORGANIZED CAPITALISM

The argument presented here may appear to have some relevance to the analysis of contemporary capitalism presented in the works of Claus Offe (1985). For Offe, capitalism may be described as disorganized (in contrast to the notion of organized capitalism as developed by Rudolf Hilferding) because there is a lack of fit between the institutions of political representation within a democracy and the requirements of capitalist profit and reproduction. In more specific terms, Offe's work is organized around the question,

do the procedures, patterns of organisation, and institutional mechanisms that supposedly mediate and maintain a dynamic balance between social power and political authority (i.e. seek to coherently *organize* the socio-political systems of contemporary welfare state capitalism) actually *fail* to perform this function? If so, what are the symptoms, consequences and potential remedies of such failures of the process of mediation?

(Offe 1985: 6)

Offe's general answer is, indeed, that these institutions fail to perform these relevant functions, and therefore we might appropriately describe and define contemporary capitalism as disorganized.

In more detailed terms, Offe perceives an inflationary situation in the political and economic sphere. This is because the 'attribution of public status to interest groups' brings about an inflationary expansion of demands and also a shift from specific concerns to more general debates about the underlying legitimacy of democratic institutions. Offe argues:

The pervasive shift is from conflict over group interest to conflict over ground rules, from the definition of claims to the definition of legitimate claimants, from politics to metapolitics. This shift takes place in the conservative as well as the social democratic camp, even though in different variants. The conservatives propose the restoration of 'order' and call for the abolition of state interventionism; the social democrats understand that reformist interventionism presupposes for its success and continuity new arrangements over orderly cooperation and relatively conflict-free modes of interest representation. Both variants imply changes in the mode of interest representation, new regulations for the conduct of group and class conflict.

(Offe 1985: 231)

These new forms of disorganization between politics and economics are intensified by the inflationary impact of interest group formation and the pursuit of particularistic interests within the framework of a universalistic democratic political order.

There are a number of problems with Offe's formulation of this problem. First, there is strong argument to suggest that there is permanent conflict between the political forms of representation in a democracy and the inequalities of class resulting from the economic organization of capitalism. For example, T. H. Marshall (1977) argued that citizenship had expanded from an elementary system of legal rights towards a wider political representation of the working class, and finally to a social and economic incorporation of working-class opposition within the capitalist industrial system. For Marshall, the conflict between political representation and social inequality was a more or less permanent feature of capitalism from the middle of the nineteenth century. There are good reasons for thinking that this thesis of Marshall is tenable, and that therefore the disorganization of capitalism is not necessarily something specifically modern, but a feature of capitalism dating back to the middle of the nineteenth century. In addition, one might argue that capitalism has been making various adjustments to this contradiction between citizenship and class over a very long period and that therefore the implication of crisis in Offe's theory is not warranted. The contradictions between universalistic claims to equality and the bare facts of economic inequality may be permanent features of an industrial capitalist system rather than an accumulation of crises leading towards a legitimation deficit of catastrophic proportions (Turner 1986b).

Second, although Offe recognizes significant changes in the character of capitalism, he retains a conventional Marxist sociology of capital–labour relations which is incompatible with his economic sociology of labour-market relations. Offe, like E. O. Wright, wants to reject many aspects of conventional Marxism while still retaining many features of the general paradigm. For example, Offe recognizes that the exploitative relationship between capital and labour may no longer apply, given the transformation of the work situation of the working class in capitalism, but he still wishes to trade upon many aspects of the Marxist framework. Against Offe, I wish to suggest that, although capitalism faces a number of serious political issues in the interface between politics and economics, these contradictions and tensions may not lead to a total collapse of the system, but rather a number of ineffectual adjustments to the contradiction between the inflationary claims of political interest groups and the limited system of economic production within a global framework of recession.

The tensions between the political framework of democracy and the economic requirements of an industrial capitalist society have been noted by a number of writers who perceive capitalism in terms of a set of contradictory pressures rather than in terms of disorganization or crisis. Indeed, many of these tensions can be traced back to the framework presented by Alexis de Tocqueville in his *Democracy in America*. As de Tocqueville recognized and subsequent writers have reinforced, the concepts of equality and citizenship are revolutionary and essentially modern. The principle of formal equality produces a general commitment to and concern for the empirical realization of egalitarian norms throughout civil society. Once this principle of formal equality has been established by the institutions of citizenship, then we can expect disprivileged citizens to appeal to this formal norm in order to compensate for some particular feature of their own communities or status blocs (Bell 1976). The result is that

> inequalities between status groups become the object of policy, not the promotion of individual equity . . . liberal democratic orders, like their totalitarian counterparts, do not eliminate the status group as a functioning basis of collective association in the egalitarian political community.
>
> (Prager 1985: 194–5)

While ethnic, racial and religious differences remain strong in democratic orders, Jeffrey Prager (1985) argues that these commitments are superficial and the most salient obligations are still essentially modern ones — namely, those of class or occupational grouping, which he treats as status groups. The equation of class and occupational groupings with status groups is, I have argued in this chapter, not only a terminological confusion, but also a conceptual mistake, since the character and functioning of status blocs in contemporary society are unlike those of economic class. Furthermore, I have claimed that modern politics generates ethnic, racial, and religious status blocs both as a consequence of the existence of formal equality as a principle and as the outcome of the state's response to these groups. In short, the argument follows that presented by Daniel Bell (1976) that conflicts over entitlements are the stuff of modern politics, producing a fiscal crisis which the state cannot manage adequately because the economic demands of status blocs tend to be expansionary and inflated. However, the argument here is that this situation does not necessarily require the notion of 'disorganization', since these tensions appear to be permanent or at least a long-term structural feature of democratic, capitalist, welfare systems.

These tensions within contemporary political systems are particularly well-illustrated by the problem of race relations within an egalitarian framework. In America, blacks were mobilized to redress a social disadvantage of colour under the aegis of democratic equality in a social system, where they had been excluded traditionally at least in the South on the basis of skin colour. While this status bloc of blacks was organized to achieve a universalistic principle of equality, the changes in the law which gave them a civil status have to some extent reinforced colour as a basis of stratification, since there are now paradoxically certain benefits associated with the disprivileged status of race. Comparing the new system of legal relations between blacks and whites with the older system of Southern relations, Nathan Glazer (1983: 318–19) has argued that

> it is a law designed to achieve equality and not to ensure dominance. But it shares one thing with that earlier law: It names groups and because the groups are named, individuals inevitably become beneficiaries or non-beneficiaries of law specifically because of group membership.

This case is a particularly good example of status-bloc politics administered by the state. Another example would be the modern status of the North American Indian, who, while being substantively disprivileged, may enjoy certain privileges from legal compensation for the loss of land under the idea of positive discrimination in order to achieve greater equality of condition. Where social groups have gone beyond the minimal demands for equality of opportunity towards equality of condition and outcome, then the intervention of the state in response to the political pressure of status blocs brings about an inflationary condition which puts pressure upon the economic basis of contemporary democracies. The very success of democracy produces clientelism which requires greater bureaucratic regulation and state intervention, bringing about further social control within the political sphere and also a greater tax burden on the economy.

THE NEW POLITICS OF CLIENTELISM

In this chapter I have attempted to justify the use of the concepts 'state-administered status bloc politics' as a framework for the analysis and explanation of contemporary forms of politics organized around the particularistic criteria of age, ethnicity, language, and gender. It has been further claimed that although class in the classical Marxist sense is still an important feature of industrial societies, empirically class is increasingly less relevant to the organization of modern politics because of profound changes in the economic basis of society. In addition, the argument has been that disorganized, capitalism, far from being a modern crisis of the political and economic system, is in fact a permanent tension within so-called liberal, democratic, welfare capitalist systems. In presenting this argument, I have to some extent followed certain positions adopted by Bell in his work on the cultural contradictions of capitalism and in his writing on fiscal sociology. Bell has of course seen status politics as the product of prosperity and class politics as the outcome of economic decline and decay, in the collection of essays on *The Radical Right* (Bell 1962). However, Bell has argued

> the sociological fact that, throughout the western world, the industrial working class is shrinking, relative to other classes, and one can say that, 'historically' it is moving off the stage of world history . . . in advanced industrial society, ignores the question of time. . . . The most important factor about the working class parties and trade unions is that they are still the best organised groups in the society, and in a society which is becoming increasingly amorphous, with the multiplication of structures and constituencies, that very fact of organisation gives the trade unions (like the military in under-developed societies) an enormous importance, particularly in a period of crisis.
>
> (Bell 1975: 173–4)

However, against Bell I have suggested that the solidaristic features of the working class may have been eroded, since Bell was analysing the American situation in the mid-1970s. With further industrial decline and with the persistence of a world recession, the economic basis of militant, working-class politics has been eroded significantly in most industrial societies. In the vacuum created by the decline of class politics, status-bloc politics have flourished as features of the new social movements with complex alliances in pursuit of some element of redistribution of privileges under the general slogans of equality of condition and democratic participation.

The consequences of status-bloc politics, as I have argued, are an increase in the service sector in response to the demands of disprivileged status communities, an increase in inflation because demands for redistribution tend to be expansionary, and finally an increase in the level of surveillance through state bureaucracies of the population as a whole. Following the works of Weber on bureaucracy and critical theory on instrumental rationality, the irony is that greater democratization brings about greater surveillance. The problem with the inflationary character of status-bloc politics is that, in a period of world recession, governments are in fact constrained in their capacity to respond to the demands of such communities for a redress of social privileges and for a redistribution of wealth. Democratic governments are caught between the pressures of political response to status communities and the limitations of capitalist economies in a period of global recession. The political result is, not so much the crisis of disorganized capitalism, but a permanent instability of governments caught between the pressures of economic inequality and political democracy. These contradictory pressures are intensified within those societies which we might regard as peripheral to the capitalist core. One theoretical conclusion of this discussion is that we need a greater emphasis on what might be called inter-societal analysis, since the dilemmas of peripheral democracies like Australia, New Zealand, and Canada cannot be understood without conceptualizing these nation-states within the framework of global capitalism.

CONCLUSION

Although this argument has been primarily concerned with the relationship between class and status as organizing concepts within a theory of social stratification, the conclusion of this argument leads us to reflect upon the preoccupations of European sociology with class and the importance of status in migrant societies which might be described more fully as white, colonial, settler societies — namely, North America, South Africa, Australia, and New Zealand. It has often been observed that, while European sociology has been fascinated by the problem of social class, North American sociology has far more extensively focused on issues of status and culture. These different emphases are of course bound up with the different role of Marxism and socialism in Europe and North America, but there are, I would argue, more profound causes for this different emphasis within the sociological traditions of North America and Europe.

The colonial societies of the southern hemisphere and to some extent the white settler societies of North America have had historical and cultural characteristics which sharply separate them from the culture and history of northern Europe. In particular, white colonial settler societies had no real experience of feudalism and therefore did

157

not undergo a transformation of feudal estates as the principal feature of stratification under the impact of markets, capitalism, and class formation. In this regard we might note the uniqueness of Australia as a convict settler society which not only had no history of feudalism but in a sense no history of civil society without the regulation of the state. The American War of Independence brought about the development of Australia as a convict settlement, providing a peculiar but important linkage between the history of the United States and that of the Australian colony (Albinski 1985). The problem of democracy in the white colonial societies was therefore connected not so much with the transition from feudalism to capitalism and the growth of social classes, but with migration, colonial autonomy, and the development of status blocs as a consequence of migration. These differences, of course, provided much of the thematic interest of de Tocqueville's account of democracy in the development of American social organization.

The white colonial settler societies furthermore became linked into capitalist development relatively late in the nineteenth century with the expansion of industrialism in Europe and the growing demand for raw commodities. As these agrarian structures were sucked into the global capitalist system, there was of course a significant development, first of a rural working class and much later of an urban working class. However, this class formation was developed alongside the emergence of status blocs as an effect of migration.

The problem of social order in these societies was inevitably bound up with racial conflicts, ethnic differences, and the problem of national identity, given the extreme cultural variation of the migrant groups which were the building blocks of the civil societies of colonialism. Hence, in these societies the problem of order was debated in the context of the problems associated with the melting pot, the notion of a mosaic society, and the issue of multi-culturalism (Glazer and Moynihan 1963).

Whereas in Europe the cultural unity of civil society was developed over a long historical trajectory out of feudalism (often under the regulation and control of the state with the emergence of nationalism), in white colonial settler societies based upon waves of migration, the problem of national identity and national unity is prolonged and retarded by the presence of status-bloc politics which create an inevitable confusion over national symbolism. A simple illustration of this problem is the difficulty of deciding upon a national flag and a national anthem in Australia in the contemporary period. Whereas the great conflicts of European social structure were consequences of the industrial and the French revolutions with the gradual collapse and erosion of feudalism both as an economic and as a cultural system, the problem of civil society in colonial settler systems is centred on the questions of national culture, cultural diversity, status-bloc politics, and the role of the state as an institution of social integration. These issues have been intensified in recent years as a consequence of the growth of citizenship, the claims for equal status, and the development of multi-culturalism as a cultural policy in such societies as Canada, Australia, and New Zealand. For reasons which have been outlined in this chapter, there are certain permanent contradictions between the democratic process which is inflationary and the economic constraints on colonial settler societies which have been marginalized within the global capitalist economy. The sharp decline of the value of raw commodities in the contemporary reces-sion of world capitalism, in particular, puts significant strains upon such societies as Argentina, Australia, and New Zealand, where the growth of status-bloc politics has put considerable pressure on modern governments to respond to the interests of culturally divided groups within civil society.

The theme of this chapter is that these contradictions are per-manent features of these societies, but they have been intensified within the contemporary global recession. The implication of this argument is to underline the theoretical and explanatory value of Weber's notion of status politics as a framework for the analysis of multi-cultural societies. Furthermore, the validity of status politics as a framework draws attention to the problems of conventional class analysis, given the erosion of the urban working class as an organized political force within contemporary capitalism.

Chapter Six

HAS CLASS ANALYSIS A FUTURE? MAX WEBER AND THE CHALLENGE OF LIBERALISM TO *GEMEINSCHAFTLICH* ACCOUNTS OF CLASS

Class has often been presumed dead or on the point of extinction (Nisbet 1959). Many of the propositions of class theory have proved false or inadequate, not least Marx's and Engels' celebrated expectation of proletarian revolution in the advanced capitalist world. And yet the language of class continues to be widely used in popular culture and political action as well as social theory.

The meaning of class terminology appears to vary considerably between the domain of popular culture (where it is often synonymous with status), and that of social theory (where it is usually treated as a *sui generis* component of social inequality linked to the structure of economic power). But there is little unanimity of definition or conceptualization in intellectual circles either. Meanwhile, political actors invoke class as a means of dramatizing their claims to be organic leaders of mass opinion. In this situation the persistence of the language of class may simply signify intellectual confusion, and the conflation of analysis with rhetoric, or perhaps conceptual piety to an enduring piece of intellectual artifice. A more likely interpretation of the persistence of class, however, is its powerful and multi-dimensional metaphoricality.

Ossowski (1963) was one of the first to explore the metaphoricality of class. Metaphors are figures of speech 'in which a name or descriptive term is transferred to some object to which it is not properly applicable' (*Oxford English Dictionary*). For Ossowski, metaphors function to combine intuitive understanding with routine application in a way that evades comprehensive and systematic definition. Class is one such metaphor, able to draw on a wide range of possible meanings or allusions. These include the methodological practice of categorizing, the labelling of cohesive social groups possessing a quality distinct from other social groups, and the use of spatial allusions to suggest distance between social groupings, as well as more rhetorical political allusions to the existence of organic agents of conflict and social change in society and world history. Class is simultaneously an objective feature of the world — 'something which in fact happens' (Thompson 1963: i) — and a subjective idea. Its metaphorical flexibility is also reflected in the proliferation of dichotomic, gradational, and functional class schema.

There are a number of further ways in which we can unravel the metaphoricality of class. One of these involves the serviceability of class concepts in both *Gemeinschaft*-based and *Gesellschaft*-based accounts of society. In other words, class is equally used to discuss community formation, as it is to refer to the distribution of individuals within roles available within structures of economic production and exchange. Developing this point it is possible to identify three typical idioms of class analysis on the *Gemeinschaft–Gesellschaft* spectrum. Speaking metaphorically, it is possible to specify a strong class idiom at the *Gemeinschaft* end of the spectrum, a weak class idiom at the *Gesellschaft* end, and certain intermediate positions.

The strong class idiom operates both as a structural account of relationships of power, inequality, and exploitation, and simultaneously an account of consciousness, group formation, and social movements as emancipatory social change. As in most conventional accounts of class, these relations derive in a fundamental sense from economic relations of production and exchange instituted in property rights. However, in the strong class idiom these relations are not only contained within the economy, but suffuse politics, culture, and so on. The strong class idiom presents a unitary account of society, whereby the theory of class is coterminous with the theory of society. Its most influential formulation is to be found in Marx's and Engels' emphasis on class as the motive force of history.

To describe the strong class idiom in terms of *Gemeinschaft* relations is more a metaphorical than a literal procedure. This is because the literal sociological usage of *Gemeinschaft* is generally related to pre-modern particularistic accounts of community tied together by blood, kinship, and locality. The classic Marxist account of class under capitalism takes as its starting point the cash nexus of the *Gesellschaft*, or society of 'free' individuals. Yet the strong class idiom is precisely an attempt to define the circumstances under which community may again triumph over individual atomization. In this sense, it is legitimate to describe the strong class idiom, metaphorically, as a *Gemeinschaftlich* view of class.

The 'weak' class idiom, by contrast, treats class as one of several patterns of power and inequality, which may exist in any given society. This idiom not only rejects a unitary account of class in society, but also argues against any necessary connection between class positions and the development of group formation, class communities, social change, and the course of world history. A typical formulation of this approach is to be found in Weber's tripartite account of the distribution of power in terms of class, status, and party. Here, class is again derived from economic relations, but the centre point of the approach concerns the character of class positions occupied by individuals. Social class formation is a contingent possibility, but there is room here for some sense of exploitation.

Weber's approach is typical of what might be called the radical liberal perspective on class. This accepts the *Gesellschaftlich* account of modern society as a given and seeks out dimensions of market-place exchange where power inequalities affect the life chances of individuals. There is an underlying commitment here to *Gesellschaft* relations as the foundation for equality of opportunity, but also space for justifications of class inequalities of condition, especially where these result from differences in marketable skill and human capital endowment. The metaphorical flexibility of class permits its continued usage in this very different context, though its provenance is restricted to the analysis of economic inequality and its contingent social consequences.

Between the strong and weak class idioms there has grown up a range of intermediate positions. These have generally arisen as a result of perceived weaknesses in the strong class idiom as originally formulated in the nineteenth century. Class continues to be seen as a major dimension to social inequality, and as having a connection with group formation, conflict, exploitation, and change. On the other hand, the strong claim for class as a unitary account of inequality, and as the motive force for history, is no longer advanced with confidence. Far more typically, class is projected as a manifestation of economic conflict within the work-place, which generally fails to achieve radical political expression. This goes further than the weak idiom in its continuing emphasis on conflict and collectivist organization, as well as in the elusive search for a more robust understanding of class politics. This search has, however, led some to abandon key elements of the older *Gemeinschaftlich* position, such as the labour theory of value, while still maintaining a critique of capitalism and liberalism as inegalitarian and exploitative.

The main aim of this chapter is to evaluate this relationship between *Gemeinschaft* and *Gesellschaft* elements in class theory in the light of Weber's earlier statement of the 'weak' *Gesellschaft* idiom. Although there are relatively few enthusiasts any longer for the strong class idiom, it remains clear that there has been some regrouping around a 'transitional' position on the *Gemeinschaft*–*Gesellschaft* spectrum. The argument of this chapter is, first, that the case for any kind of *Gemeinschaft* component of class theory is getting progressively weaker, and second, that much of the debate between neo-Marxists and radical liberals is now taking place on the terrain of the *Gesellschaft* idiom. This is particularly evident in the deployment of rational choice and game theory assumptions within Marxist and radical discourse. A third feature of my argument is that *Gesellschaft* theories of class offer limited justifications for retaining class analysis. The analysis of contemporary social structures, and relations between markets, households, organized interests, and the state, seems increasingly able to dispense with class analysis in all but a few residual *Gesellschaftlich* forms. Weber's radical liberal legacy has been of some use in encouraging social theorists in this direction, although Weber himself failed to follow through a thoroughgoing radical liberal account of market relations, linking production and distribution to consumption.

CLASS AND THE PROBLEM OF *GEMEINSCHAFT* IN WESTERN SOCIAL THOUGHT

It is important to re-emphasize that class has always been far more than a sociological concept debated amongst intellectuals. The language of class, and the social movements activated in the name of class, were a fundamental emergent feature of European capitalist industrialization (Briggs 1960; Williams 1976). In the process, the linguistic meaning of 'class' was massively extended and transformed. What began as a generic classificatory device became both a political and industrial rallying cry and a major discourse within social analysis. In both cases, issues of inequality and exploitation were linked with social conflict and the problem of how to overcome emergent social cleavages.

Until then, inequalities between social groups had generally been understood in terms of a complex status hierarchy of ranks, orders, and degrees. The new terminology of class now shifted attention to the 'economic' basis of social divisions and conflicts, and their expression in political action and cultural identity. This shift still left room for disagreement over precise specification of the nature of the economic processes involved. Of particular interest is the debate over the relative importance of inequalities of exchange relations in the distribution of income (as in Ricardianism), compared with the Marxist emphasis on inequalities in the social relations of production. None the less, the fundamental *formal* principle at stake in class theory was, and continues to be, the structural location of the causes of social inequality, exploitation, conflict, and change within socio-economic relations. However much such relations may influence or depend on political and cultural institutions, class theory is grounded in economic relations.

Having said this we immediately encounter a paradox, namely the perpetuation of evaluative, status-ridden, cultural values in popular, and much academic, language usage concerning class. It is not of course surprising to find that social classifications are value relevant. What is striking is the difficulty of making a sharp distinction between the ostensibly scientific, formal analytical procedures of class theory, on the one hand, and the value-concerns underlying class theory, on the other. This is particularly evident in the substantive class categories that have grown up since the early nineteenth century.

Many of the first social class categories deployed the distinction between 'industrial classes' and the rest. The preference for classification of this kind reflects a morally loaded distinction between those seen as socially 'productive', and the 'unproductive' social groups, such as *rentiers* and absentee landowners. The moralism of the language here rests on ideas of the dignity of labour, and the contention that rewards should be earned by direct labour rather than derived 'passively' from 'unearned' sources. To be productive was contrasted with idleness and parasitism. This language helped to dramatize the conflict between the dynamism of industrial society — the idea of 'industrial' being linked with notions of industriousness — and older forms of hierarchical status privilege based on birth and ascriptive evaluations of worth and value. The moral critique of idleness and parasitism depended on egalitarian and rationalistic conceptions of social organization, and centred on the productive part of the 'population', regarded as 'the people'.

Very soon, however, internal conflicts and cleavages were detected and expressed among the industrial classes themselves. The foremost of these was represented by a growing sense of class difference between labour and capital. Here again, however, we find moral and evaluative cultural assumptions built into the fabric of the language of class.

Most obvious perhaps is the distinction made between the working class or classes, and the capitalist class or classes, implying a cleavage between those who work and those who don't. Here we see the initial opposition to pre-industrial status privilege transferred on to the capitalists themselves. The suggestion is that some work, thereby permitting others to idle, and once again to effect superior status claims over others. In the demonology of class, the top-hatted capitalist, whose belly and general demeanour portray conspicuous luxury consumption, is far more popular a target than the cold, calculative meanness of an ascetic rationalistic Scrooge. Meanwhile, popular culture has continued to operate with notions of class as a form of status-bound distinction — that is, a form of exclusionary social prejudice — rather than a socio-economic mechanism of inequality and exploitation. In a more sophisticated way, this approach can be grounded in a labour theory of value. Here the claim is made that only labour can add value to commodities during production. It is but a very short route from the claim that labour adds value, to the claim that only the working class adds value, and hence that non-workers are non-productive and socially unnecessary.

There is of course a distinction to be made between the moral critique of personal luxury consumption and the Marxist critique of capital accumulation instituted within capitalist property relations. The former is in a certain sense an *ad hoc* or contingent moral adjunct to an argument about the structural imperatives of capital accumulation and labour exploitation under competitive capitalism. It is none the less difficult to evaluate this structural argument alone without reference to the moral presuppositions built into the very categories of value and surplus-value.

Marxist political economy is certainly not value-free. Marx's value theory, with its attempt to locate a universal equivalent with which to measure value, is constituted precisely to assert the need for a type of community to meet the social problems engendered by the alienation, atomization, and fetishism of commodities under capitalism.

Whereas the sphere of exchange appears constituted by individual atoms subject to a self-regulating allocation process beyond human intervention, Marx sees in the sphere of production an essentially co-operative enterprise — albeit currently conducted under highly exploitative conditions. The potential for social improvement comes not by emphasizing the market-place choices of the individual consumer, rich in needs, but through the creation of a community of free producers, individually autonomous, but collectively bound through an objective *Gemeinschaftlich* labour theory of value.

Marxist value theory, with its origins in medieval Christian theology and peasant communism, represents an attempt to replace the *Gesellschaftlich* categories of market exchange — price, wages, profits, and so on — each accruing to self-interested individuals, with an alternative account of social life grounded in co-operation among producers. For Marx, we need categories like value and surplus-value in order to demonstrate that the market is embedded within more fundamental social relations. Under some conditions the more fundamental relations of production may engender exploitation, but under others they may lay the basis for the transcendence of exploitation itself. This is not, however, a merely technical or scientific argument. For the categories of value and surplus-value contain a strong normative component. They assert the dignity of labour — to be more precise, productive labour — the parasitical character of non-productive occupations geared merely to the realms of market profitability, the exploitative character of private property rights which provide selective control over the necessities of life, the pathological nature of market-oriented consumption, and the need for an organic consensus about principles of just distribution.

All this assumes that there ought to be a communitarian basis upon which the different wants of individuals could be measured and made commensurable with one another. There is no suggestion that wants may be incommensurable, for to raise this spectre would undermine the search for an objective basis to value, and an objective grounding of the route to a reassertion of community over the 'fetishism of commodities' and reversal of the alienation of the producer. In all these respects Marx has a fundamental moral antipathy to *Gesellschaftlich* relations of individual exchange, where value is linked subjectively to the wants of individuals. He cannot accept that the conception of individuality involved could be anything other than an abstraction from social relations. Here Marx leaves no space for the possibility that liberalism could come up with a theory of socialized individuals, consistent with the existence of a social order. This position has been extremely influential, bequeathing to modern social theory the highly problematic axiom that market exchange cannot legitimize itself and has therefore to rely on sources of legitimacy that lie outside capitalist social relations (see, for example, Habermas 1976).

The value-relevant character of the labour theory of value is not in itself an argument against its sociological usefulness. There is, however, a second major problem with the theory: namely, its dubious status as a technical argument. Marx's argument, we may recall, is that wherever we find private property rights in the means of production and conditions of wage-labour, there is necessarily exploitation of labour through the extraction of surplus-value by capital. In other words, labour does not receive the full value it has added to potential commodities during the production process. Part of the value created is siphoned off as surplus-value. Without this, further capital accumulation would not be possible.

A major logical difficulty with this argument, as John Roemer (1982a) has pointed out, is that it can be made to apply to any resource utilized in economic activity. Any commodity is in fact capable of producing more value than it embodies through the value added during the production process. If we choose corn as a universal equivalent or measure of value, we can calculate the embodied corn values of commodities. From this we can prove that the economy can produce a surplus only if corn is exploited — that is, that the corn value of a unit of corn is less than one.

One consequence of this argument is that there is nothing unique about the status of labour as a universal equivalent. Marx's labour theory of value is therefore flawed. The significance of the theory concerns its value-relevance in that we are generally more interested in people and human labour than corn. The moral resonance of the theory arises from the belief that people should not be 'exploited', while there is widespread indifference to the exploitation of things. This humanism is given a *Gemeinschaftlich* expression in the notion of labour or the labour embodied in products as a universal equivalent.

If we want to reconstruct a *theory* of exploitation, according to Roemer, we must look elsewhere. His own strategy is to mobilize game-theoretic and rational choice assumptions of an inherently *Gesellschaftlich* character. Exploitation is said to exist where an individual or set of individuals could gain more if they withdrew from the current relations of production, compared with staying in. Here exploitation is linked not to the normative assumptions of a community of free producers but rather within the optimizing strategies of utility-maximizing individuals. The search is for that version of *Gesellschaft* which optimizes returns to individuals.

The uneasy combination of *Gemeinschaft* and *Gesellschaft* elements within Marx's class theory has been likened by Eugene Kamenka to the co-existence of technological scientism and anarchistic peasant communism in one and the same theory. Although Marx's pejorative comments on the peasantry and romantic backward-looking Utopian socialism are well known, it is equally the case that his moral standpoint is very much that of an idealized pre-capitalist association of direct producers. This is reflected in a number of ways.

First, and unlike liberalism, Marx's account of economic life is fundamentally supply-oriented, viewing the economy according to the problems of direct producers exchanging with other direct producers. This does not deny the demand-side problem of need–satisfaction, so much as subsume it within relations between producer–consumers. There is little scope here for differentiated relations between production and consumption, and hence little scope for recognition of modern arguments in favour of the market. While the market is regarded as a dynamic productive force — 'the cash nexus' — it is represented as a morally unacceptable, impersonal erosion of face-to-face community in the process of social co-operation. Instead of viewing market exchange and impersonality as functional to the universalization of access by the masses to utilities, Marx treats impersonality and individual atomization as exploitative and pathological mystification. His projection of the communist future not only assumes a solution to technical limitations achieved through the expanding dynamic of the productive forces, but also suggests that free producers can somehow get to know and co-ordinate exchanges to satisfy needs by something akin to instant inspection. There is no reference here to the co-ordination problems presented by the division of labour, or to the difficulties raised by the Austrian School of economics, that the division of labour may be congruent with a fundamental division of knowledge.

Second, Marx's distinction between productive and unproductive labour again reflects the moral hostility of producer *Gemeinschaften* to parts of the division of labour other than those linked with production.

Some care is needed here in rendering Marx's position accurately. For he did not wish to equate productive labour with manual labour as such or with production work excluding all services. Productive labour was defined instead in terms of labour which helped to create surplus-value for the capitalist. As Marx himself indicated, this could include the labour of a teacher in a private school as much as a sausage maker working in a sausage factory (Marx 1976: 644). Non-productive labour was therefore confined to occupations outside the commodity production–surplus-value extraction nexus, such as state workers, and those in administrative, managerial, and clerical positions paid out of revenue. The implication is that the non-productive positions are socially unnecessary and that they could be abolished under a different social system. Their function under capitalism is either to control the proletariat or simply parasitical.

While it is a mistake to interpret Marx's distribution between productive and non-productive work as a glorification of the status of manual work, it is very clear that his concern to draw some such distinction reflects a somewhat naïve attitude to the complex and extended division of labour characteristic of modern western societies. His critique of unproductive labour underestimates the necessity of managerial, administrative, professional, and clerical labour to the technical as much as the social division of labour, especially within large-scale bureaucratic organizations. Among other functions unexplored by Marx is that of marketing and the co-ordination of production with consumption. Marx's assumption seems to be that the future socialist and communist societies could be constituted simply through the inter-relations between direct producers. Such producers could somehow communicate needs to one another — 'rich' though they be (Heller 1976) — with no need for a specialized division of labour involving managerial supervision and marketing. The case for classifying certain occupations as unproductive does not in any way arise from a scientific account of the division of labour, but rather from a moralistic critique of social functions which lay outside the experience and understanding of the peasant-like *Gemeinschaft* of direct producers. Leaving free producers alone to get on with their lives is of course the ancient peasant dream.

Third, Marx's comments on the eventual 'withering away' of the state as socialism moved towards communism are again redolent of the anarchistic peasant *Gemeinschaft*. In Marx's view, post-capitalist free producers will require the state, as a body differentiated from the

Gemeinschaft, only if it is necessary to preserve their existence. Once this condition lapses with the productive upgrading of the post-revolutionary system, the need for a separate state will disappear. Once again we see a *Gemeinschaft* critique of excessive differentiation at work, though not of course a return to 'primitive' communism.

Within these *Gemeinschaftlich* parameters — with their minimal need for special differentiated bodies geared to the co-ordination of exchange, integration of the social fabric, state administration, and so on — the proletariat represents for Marx the emergent social force with the requisite community-like characteristics. It has been massed together in factories, and homogenized in condition by the imperatives of capital accumulation, most notably the rising organic composition of capital. This homogenization, and the consequent polarization of the class structure, encourages a collective interest in the abolition of private property rights in the means of production. Given the evaluative yardstick of the moral economy of free producers, social differentiation between owners and non-owners of capital, and the consequent hierarchical division of labour, is untenable since it breaks the *Gemeinschaft* aspirations and links between producers. Because capital requires wage-labour to function, contemporary proletarians cannot be emancipated as a class without destroying private property rights over the means of production. The revolutionary political mobilization of proletarian community is, however, synonymous with the conditions necessary to prepare a *Gemeinschaft* of humanity. Within the 1848 revolutions and the Paris Commune of 1871, Marx believed he detected the first stirrings of the imminent transition to socialism.

As is well known, Marx did not rule out the possibility that in Russia, the nineteenth-century peasant commune might provide the basis for a transition to socialism, bypassing capitalism altogether (Marx to Vera Sassoulitch, cited in McLellan 1977: 576–7). None the less, he did not in general align himself with peasant anarchism or anarcho-communism. There are two explanations for this. First is the wish to benefit from modern productive technique, at the same time as creating new community-like social relations. Given his historical materialism, Marx generally regarded the peasantry as a backward-looking force unable to generate socialized community. Second, Marx not only distrusted the true sociality of the peasantry — note the famous 'sack of potatoes' epithet — but also operated with a consistent suspicion of individualistic relations outside the sphere of production. Thus he was similarly dismissive of the urban 'lumpen-proletariat' as of the peasantry. Marx's celebrated moral castigation of the lumpen-proletariat of Paris in the *Eighteenth Brumaire* that 'whole indefinite disintegrated mass' — was directed against those living outside any recognizable *Gemeinschaft* bonds in what he believed to be a pathetic Bohemian sub-romantic world of vice and excess. Marx simply rejects the possibility that individuals in this world may be as 'rich in needs' as free producers. The alternatives are stark community or asocial egotism. Once again we find the characteristic nineteenth-century opposition between individual and society.

The implication of this discussion is that Marx's social theory, and especially his class theory, was in no way purged of evaluative status-like concern or with drawing social distinctions on the basis of moral criteria. Yet is is also true that Marx laid the basis for a tradition of class analysis which has developed rigorous structural conceptions of class. In this context it is still important to emphasize that the underlying function of his theory was to recast the centrality of *Gemeinschaft* bonds in the transcendence of conflict and exploitation, rather than to provide operational strategies for conducting class analyses. In this respect Marx was operating within a wider conservative discourse on the dislocating influences of capitalist industrialization (Nisbet 1970; Holton and Turner 1986).

Talcott Parsons has made the insightful general comment that the underlying normative basis of both nineteenth-century working-class and capitalist solidarity amounted to a perpetuation of the traditional *Gemeinschaft* orientations of the European peasantry and aristocracy respectively (Parsons 1967). It is not just that the proletariat, and its Marxist champions, legitimated its class aspirations through reference to the recreation of community. It is also that the model for capitalist class solidarity drew heavily on the search for status-like exclusive barriers between the wealthy and the rest. In short, much of the bourgeoisie came to ape its aristocratic forebears in the organiza-tion of social networks in business and at leisure — typified by the metaphor of membership of 'The Club'.

The question none the less remains open as to whether such connections are contingent or necessary. Many influential social theorists claim that capitalism and the market-place are not self-legiti-mating, and that legitimacy can only be secured by recourse to extra-capitalist (for example, pre-capitalist) or extra-market sources (Habermas 1976). An alternative possibility is that there are indeed successful legitimation claims associated with market capitalism, closely associated with a liberal-democratic world-view. This links individual autonomy with private property rights, individual choice, the impersonal, universalistic mechanisms of market exchange, and the normative sanctions of the market-place that reward purposive rationality. This world-view rests on an essentially *Gesellschaftlich* world-view. It is not at all self-evident that *Gesellschaften* cannot generate internal principles of legitimacy. What is unclear is whether such legitimation claims are a sufficient basis for overall societal legitimacy.

CLASS TERMINOLOGY AND BOUNDARIES

The language of class in the century since Marx has witnessed an increasingly dualistic development. On the one hand, status concerns have persisted in class categories, reflecting a continuation of the evaluative vocabulary of moral distinction. On the other hand, theorists have searched for a more sociologically grounded vocabulary linked with observable structural features of economic life, and with social movements. 'Class' has become a 'shorthand' concept we cannot seem to do without when discussing socio-economic groups, political action, and cultural behaviour, and yet the ambiguities in its meaning and intellectual function seem to be proliferating in an ever more confusing way than before.

The ubiquitous term 'middle class', which has emerged to prominence in class discourse since Marx's time, is a particularly graphic example of the conflation of status elements with the socio-economic characterization of structural locations within the division of labour. The middle class is often coupled with notions of 'upper class' and 'working class' in a three-class schema. Yet the nature and the boundaries of the middle class in this framework are never very clear. Is it meant to reflect a distinction between landowners (upper class), capital owners (middle class) and wage and salary recipients (working class)? Or is it that capital owners are the upper class, salaried workers such as professionals/managers and service providers the middle class, and wage-workers the working class?

It is very difficult to sort out these issues since the terminology itself is capable of interpretation both as a gradational status hierarchy (such as upper middle class, lower middle class, and so on) and as a structural account of qualitatively different socio-economic positions, albeit using terminology drawn from popular culture. The status connotations of the term 'middle class' are obvious since it allows occupancy of a position neither at the top nor at the bottom. Within a democratic society in which values of individual autonomy are prized, identification with this label avoids the connotation of being a 'snob', assuming the manners of older dominant status groups, while equally avoiding the status of a 'no-hoper' dependent on redistribution from others for social survival.

In order to avoid these connotations, some analysts have sought to retain the Marxist notion of a petty bourgeoisie as a description for positions and groupings that lie between capital and labour (Poulantzas 1975). This kind of conceptual stipulation may aid analytical clarity, but it still remains problematic as to why a three-class model should be preferred to any other kind. Given the notorious boundary problem that afflicts much structural class analysis of the middle class or petty bourgeoisie (old and new), it seems naïve to believe that such issues could be resolved by simple recourse to empirical data. The prior question is why we should in the first place wish to organize our understanding of the social structure in class categories, and in particular in categories which assert a link between structural position and group formation and mobilization. It is not sufficient to say that such classes really exist, since people think and act in class ways, and that analysts should get down to the task of measurement of their scale and coherence and organizational expression. This line of argument is unconvincing partly because popular class idioms are, as we have seen, very complex and often suffused with status connotations. It is also problematic because there is no a priori necessity that individual positions within the social division of labour have a unitary class character (see especially Wright 1978).

A further symptom of the persistence of status elements in the language of class is the use of the ostensible status labels 'white-collar' and 'blue-collar' as signifiers of the distinction between 'middle class' and 'working class'. It is not of course impossible that coherent socio-economic groupings (that is, economic classes) might use dress as one signifier of the boundary between two categories, and that status concerns embodied in dress might be used to consolidate and amplify class differences. At the same time it has again become harder in the liberal-democratic context of modern popular culture in dress to discern economic class differences from immediate inspection of distinctions in clothing. The 'collar and tie' test may help us to distinguish a motley group of higher civil servants, car dealers, football managers, and CID police officers from the rest, but the economic class significance of this cleavage is unclear. If it is claimed that the white-collar/blue-collar divide is merely symbolic, then the question arises, why choose this symbol? The most plausible answer is that we are dealing here with a latter-day version of the older historic distinction between manual and non-manual labour. Manual work was historically associated with routine toil and lack of freedom within a dirty environment, whereas non-manual occupations — those who think, pray, and organize others — have a higher status, associated with freedom and cleanliness.

While there is a good reason to believe that popular conceptions of class, and many class labels, include a strong element of evaluative status considerations, this does not rule out arguments in favour of structuralist accounts of class. Such accounts are justified to the extent that the set of positions available for individuals to enter arises independently of human volition. Within the strong class idiom, with all of its *Gemeinschaftlich* connotations, it is, however, very hard to aggregate the multiplicity of class positions into categories, without having recourse to evaluative cultural criteria. These criteria, as we have seen, embrace moral issues such as 'productiveness' as opposed to 'unproductiveness', or capacity to generate organic community as against simple collectivities of individuals. Considerations of what community should be like structure the ostensibly scientific discourse of what it is like. In the process, strong class theorists have now found themselves on the defensive as the *Gemeinschaftlich* preoccupations of nineteenth-century moral critics of market capitalism seem increasingly outmoded in late twentieth-century conditions of advanced *Gesellschaftlich* social relations.

THE EROSION OF THE STRONG CLASS IDIOM

The erosion of the strong class idiom in recent social analysis can be seen in three key areas. The first involves the increasing rejection of *Gemeinschaftlich* theories of class, in which classes are portrayed as having organic interests, expressed in specific 'class' agencies or institutions. The problem has been put very clearly by Hirst (1977). His claim is that classes as such do not act, and that politics is not conducted, in terms of the direct contact between classes. Instead, we find agencies such as political parties, campaign organizations, trade-union and employee organizations, riotous mobs, and so on, which are at best 'representative' of classes, though only indirectly. To say that particular organizations 'stand for certain economic classes is either simply to accept the claims of a party, organisation or apparatus to represent a certain class, or to argue that the party's programme and actions somehow correspond with the "interests" of that class' (Hirst 1977: 130).

To accept the former means accepting organizational rhetoric very naïvely at face value. To accept the notion of class 'interests' formed on the economic plane and then projected into politics assumes an organic homogeneity of interests, and that interests are somehow constituted independently of 'politics'. This last option represents a kind of unacceptable economism. Hirst's conclusion is that 'there is no necessary correspondence between the forces that appear in the political (and what they "represent") and economic classes. . . . Classes do not have "interests", apparent independently of definite parties, ideologies etc., and against which those parties, ideologies etc. can be measured' (ibid.: 130–1). This argument is not, however, directed to the construction of political/ideological definitions of class, or the location of class within the totality of relations that constitute 'class struggle' à la Poulantzas (1975). On the contrary, Hirst wishes to evaluate politics and political struggle from the viewpoint of the creation of a new social order rather than by locating that agency with the most progressive 'class' characteristics.

This challenge to organicist theories of class and of the organic connection between economic class and political action is very striking because it is advanced as an argument within Marxism, and yet it is critical of the overwhelming idiom of Marxist class analysis. For our present purposes it represents an attempt to avoid the assumption that classes are communities in a socio-political sense, while retaining a continuing sense of economic inequality and political conflict under capitalism. Elsewhere there are of course a range of arguments to the effect that economic inequalities at the point of production tend to generate sectional and instrumental conflict rather than outright political mobilization and radicalization (Goldthorpe *et al.* 1969; Mann 1973). Such criticisms have either led to a reconceptualization of class around non-organic *Gesellschaftlich* relations (Roemer 1982b; Wright 1985) or a historicization of class analysis around the few contingent moments when economic class has seemed to correspond with social class (Thompson 1963).

A second related development concerns the growing historical scepticism concerning 'ouvrierist' or rank-and-filist accounts of working-class social history. Although the study of rank-and-file community-level movements played an important role in correcting an earlier institutional bias in labour history (see especially Holton 1976), an over-preoccupation with this issue to the exclusion of sectionalism, instrumentalism, and non-economic social cleavages has created an over-romanticized distortion of working-class history. At its worst this genre has perpetuated the search for empirical instances of *Gemeinschaftlich* class relations, without testing for their typicality (see especially the work of the History Workshop movement in Britain). There are comparatively few studies like John Foster's magisterial *Class Struggle and the Industrial Revolution* designed to test the strength and limitation of class formation under different structural conditions (Foster 1974). There are also comparatively few studies of the 'un-making' of class communities on a par with Gareth Stedman Jones's seminal essay on working-class politics and culture in late nineteenth-century London (Stedman Jones 1974).

A third manifestation of the erosion of the strong class idiom is the declining support for the labour theory of value and the insistence on distinctions between productive and unproductive labour. The challenge here, as we have already seen, has been couched in terms of the overly moralistic and at times metaphysical character of the categories involved. This has been clearest in the self-styled 'no bullshit' theory of Marxism, which leaves aside Hegelianism, the labour theory of value, and organicist constructions of class in favour of models of rational choice and the critique of institutional frameworks which distort the achievement of individual interest.

Such changes in the intellectual climate can of course be connected with structural and cultural changes in modern western societies. First there is the decline of heavy industry and associated transport occupations, characteristically organized through occupational communities (for example, miners, shipyard workers, and dockers). The decline of occupational community is clearly linked with an erosion of *Gemeinschaftlich* views of class. This has been further accelerated with the shift to more organizationally diffuse forms of service work. In parallel with these changes is the diffusion of private home ownership, car ownership, and the general expansion of household privatism. Home ownership, alongside economic restructuring, has dissolved many of the older working-class communities.

Second, there is the erosion of class voting, and in certain western societies a decline in trade-union and left-wing political party membership (such as US trade unions, British trade unions, and parties of the left). New social movements such as feminism, the peace movement, and the ecology movement are neither work-centred (in the conventional sense of paid work outside the household) nor class-specific (Feher and Heller 1984; Gorz 1982). The feminist theorization of gender relations, personality development, and sexual politics within the household has been particularly corrosive of the largely male-centred work-place-oriented 'class' *Gemeinschaft*. Feminist theory has not only rejected the idea that women get their 'class' from their husbands/fathers (Allen 1982), but has in many cases gone further to deny that class is the central feature of women's experience and lives (Oakley 1974).

Such changes have also encouraged a more differentiated conception of propertized classes. There never was an entirely unitary ruling class with an organic solidarity (Abercrombie, Hill, and Turner 1980), but the continuing differentiation of propertized and credentialled social positions since the mid-nineteenth century has reduced the likelihood of this even further. The strong class idiom, with its increasingly polarized view of relations between the organic class communities of labour and capital has now been sharply revised. One prominent area of revision is to be found in New Class theory (Gouldner 1979) or service class theory (Renner 1953; Dahrendorf 1969). While earlier attempts to differentiate the capitalist class from a managerial class proved inconclusive, there is now a far greater weight of support for the need to differentiate between property-based and knowledge- or credential-based class positions or class strategies.

This debate has been encouraged in part by the realization that economic inequality and social stratification have also been evident in socialist as well as capitalist societies. If class is to be deployed as a means of understanding group formation under conditions of economic inequality, then it becomes necessary to develop a class analysis of socialism alongside that of capitalism (Djilas 1966).

It is evidently worth pursuing the possibility of a more generic theory of class, linked not merely to private property ownership, but also to the characteristics that make for inequality in socialist societies. This search led Dahrendorf to develop the neo-Weberian criterion of authority-relations as a generic basis for class divisions, whether under capitalism or socialism (Dahrendorf 1959). However, this advance was achieved by abandoning a concern for organic class community formation, in favour of the pursuit of class analysis within any 'imperatively co-ordinated organization'.

Communitarianism also disappears from Erik Wright's second 'class' model. This went beyond Wright's first class model based as it was on the fusion of property and authority relations. In the second model Wright sought to define class in different social systems by individual control over types of assets (private property under capitalism, organization under socialism) (Wright 1985).

The erosion of the strong class idiom has not led in any simple way to the decline of class theory itself. In spite of the exuberant claims of the New Right to be setting the terms of the intellectual and political agenda, there remain some striking attempts to reformulate an 'inter-mediate' or 'strong-as-possible' class theory short of objectionable elements and more appropriate to late twentieth-century conditions. And yet the challenge of the rejuvenated liberal social philosophies of some sections of the New Right is not so easy to evade in an era when 'the working population has developed institutions which reflect . . . individualism, egoism and economic calculation' (Marshall *et al.* 1985: 271).

This revival was, for one thing, completely unexpected by class analysts. Many still regard liberalism as a bizarre and outmoded atavism, which aims to restore a mythical world of sovereign indi-viduals that never existed even in the time of John Locke. This blanket rejection is, however, misconceived. In particular, it fails to comprehend the popular appeal of *Gesellschaftlich* ideologies designed to recognize individual autonomy and the differentiation of the private household from strong cultural and political controls. Popular culture simply does not experience the expanded public functions of the modern state as an unambiguous good, or as a timely rescue from the atomization of *Gesellschaft*. The alleged atomization of *Gesellschaft* is experienced by many as a kind of 'freedom' — notably freedom to determine one's own values and objectives.

In this context, it is important to scrutinize how robust reformu-lated versions of class theory may be in the light of the predominantly *Gesellschaftlich* characteristics of modern society. This brings into play the alternative credentials of what has here been called the 'weak' class theory. The intellectual coherence and explanatory power of this idiom is, however, difficult to grasp unless we are prepared to accept that liberalism offers genuine scientific insights into processes of economic inequality, social differentiation, cultural identity, and normative order. Marx's comments on commodity fetishism and the abstract character of liberal-democratic political theory do not represent the last and conclusive word on liberalism, yet they are often rehearsed as if they expressed enduring and self-evident truths. In this context, there is much merit in considering Max Weber's class theory and economic sociology as the classic statement of a liberalistic *Gesellschaftlich* view of class.

MAX WEBER, MARKET RELATIONS, AND THE TRANSITION TO *GESELLSCHAFT*

Max Weber's work represents a major turning point in the articulation of a 'weak' class idiom. Since there remains some misunderstanding of his position, it is important to clarify its core propositions. In the first place Weber's class theory sets out from a generic theory of the market-place — the classic locus of *Gesellschaft* relations — rather than the mode of production. Markets are social institutions in which scarce resources are allocated to meet a variety of ends, through the actions of individuals. The term '*Gesellschaft*' means a voluntary contractual association of individuals — and as such is used equally to describe a joint-stock company as a society characterized by voluntary exchange. Weber's conception of the market-place derives, as we have seen, in large measure from the Austrian neo-classicists, with whom he shared a profound methodological individualism (see above, Chapter 2).

The market-place is perhaps the classic example of instrumental purposive rationality, in so far as it is constituted as a disenchanted, impersonal realm dominated by the calculation of advantage through cost/benefit. Rather than seeing this merely as a heartless cash nexus, Weber's anti-organicist, non-romantic viewpoint led him to view the market as a modern rational device which is enabling as well as constraining. The differentiation involved in market activities between ends and means, values and technique, enables cost/benefit considerations to be calculated without constant intrusion of ultimate moral considerations. This not only enables the actor to establish the best means to reach a given end but also to choose more rationally between proximate ends. The structure of ends is, however, distributed among individuals rather than communities. With the 'death of God' and the predominance of this-worldly occidental rationalism, we are in a position of having to assert our own values, and then to pursue their successful attainment. No organic community can any longer determine values, and hence there is no objective basis upon which to ground a labour theory of value. Although individuals may come together in voluntary associations, they do so as individuals. This amounts to a radical subjectivism as to the validity of individual ends, but not a subjectivist understanding of the sources of ends. These arise in society. The constraints on economic action are therefore not merely technical — the problem of how to deploy scarce resources — but cultural: namely, what to choose.

Beyond this, as we have seen, Weber's 'social economics' sees the market-place as constituted through power relations. We are not simply dealing with an impersonal but efficacious rational device for allocating means to ends. For the market simultaneously enhances and constrains life chances as a result of inequalities in the distribution of power. For Weber such inequalities are conceptualized as class situations. Without this element of inequality in power there would be no need for class analysis, since different market outcomes could be ascribed either to variations in individual rationality (for example, differences in knowledge and errors of judgement) or to in-built differences in skill.

The lynch-pin of Weber's discussion of market power is the notion of differential life chances that arise as a result of inequalities in powers of ownership and control over marketable resources. The emphasis on individual life chances and individual mobility opportunities is of course entirely typical of a *Gesellschaft* construction of class. Inadequate attention has been given to the life-chance concept by most commentators on Weber. Most commentaries have insisted on a dichotomic classification of class theories centring either on production, or on exchange and/or distribution. Marx's class theory is taken as centring on production, while Weber's centres on exchange and/or distribution (see, for instance, Crompton and Gubbay 1978). There is room for a good deal of confusion here, however, when we try to establish exactly where market relations fit into this dichotomy.

Some commentators (such as Barbalet 1982) narrow Weber's market-centred theory of class to a concern merely with the *distributive consequences* of production. This approach is misleading, however, partly because Weber is more concerned with the markets for factors of production such as land, labour, capital, and entrepreneurship, than with the markets for commodities that individuals enter with differential resources derived from production (for a similar interpretation of Weber, see Marshall *et al.* 1985). It is true that his theory tries to fuse together a concern with factor markets, with distributive inequalities in life chances that derive from different types of market power. He does not, however, pursue such distributive consequences very far, as Giddens (1973: 109) points out, into an account of consumption itself.

Both Marx and Weber are in fact concerned with market relations in the constitution of class. (This is noted in Abercrombie and Urry 1983.) Marx, of course, took production to be prior to distribution or consumption, and explained exploitation in terms of production rather than exchange. Even so, his key concept of the social relations of production is not limited, as some like Braverman have supposed, to the 'labour process' itself. This is because the essential prerequisite for exploitation at the point of production is the wage-labour/capital relation, in which labour-power appears as a commodity. Marx certainly contrasted the 'free' exchange of the labour market with exploitation and the extraction of surplus-value at the point of production. It is none the less important not to read this completely literally, since the freedom of the market was constrained by unequal labour market power. Thus, although the site for the extraction of 'surplus-value' was the labour process, the institutional prerequisite for this activity is the unequal labour market relationship between capital and labour, including such phenomena as the reserve army of unemployed. This unequal relationship and the social division of labour in any given society are none the less constantly contested and re-negotiated, depending in part on changes in factor market conditions. These points, are, however, obscured if we focus exclusively on Marx's apparent verbal contrast between free markets in exchange and exploitative production.

Weber's concern for market exchange as more central than production does not therefore exclude a certain common ground with Marx. Both are interested in the significance of market inequalities for the distribution of power and income. Where Weber departs from Marx is first of all in regarding the market as central to class (Marshall *et al.* 1985). Second, Weber manages to do entirely without an objective *Gemeinschaftlich* value theory. In this sense, property rights in the production process, however unequal, need not necessarily be described as exploitative. Third, Weber follows through market-based power conflict in the allocation of resources to production, into distributive patterns of income and access to key life chances (for example, education) that result.

The substance of Weber's market-based theory focuses on the complexities involved in inequalities of power and ownership and control over resources. Two distinct types of inequality are involved. The first centres on the ownership dimension, in which variations in amounts of capital resources owned prescribe different life-chance situations (for instance, *rentier* versus propertyless worker). Weber's ownership criterion is similar to Marx's. The second dimension of Weber's discussion involves possession of marketable skills, around which commercial class positions form, analytically distinct from ownership class positions. In this second dimension, those with marketable skills, such as managers and professionals, are distinguished from unskilled workers. This has of course provided a major dimension missing in Marx's class theory — namely, the capacity to analyse a middle class of salaried possessors of marketable skills, distinct from both capitalist and working classes. It also pre-figures recent developments in New Class theory. The point to emphasize at this stage is that we are dealing with class positions, not classes as such. For Weber, such positions are arranged gradationally, and involve no necessary sense of dichotomy. This gradational pattern of individual power inequalities in the market-place is structured on an inherently *Gesellschaftlich* basis. It leaves room for the analysis of certain market-based inequalities as a function of differing human capital endowments between individuals, rather than manifestations of exploitation of the working-class community. In this respect Weber's analysis is inherently modern, relating to the achievement-oriented pursuit of individual goals.

Weber's concern to link power differentials in production *and* exchange to distributional outcomes arises because he rejects Marx's polarization theory of class structure. In this theory private capital accumulation so effectively polarizes society that distributional issues become of limited importance. The lot of all workers becomes increasingly homogeneous as advantages of skill and localism are undermined by the global structural determinism of capital. Judged by Marx's *Gemeinschaftlich* standards, the qualitative characteristics of the capitalist totality are thoroughly alienating. There is no interest in individual fates, as such, nor in the qualitative resources at the disposal of individuals within the market-place; hence the failure to leave any theoretical space for the analysis of social mobility as it is affected by the distributional dimensions of market inequality. Marx similarly leaves no space for an understanding of private consumer strategies, as they relate to saving and to the purchase of life-enhancing goods and services, such as homes, means of transport, travel, and so on.

Beyond this, Weber treats the problem of class-like *Gemeinschaft* formation as a contingent rather than necessary product of social change and historical development. 'Social classes' with some kind of solidaristic identity may form at points where sets of individuals share common mobility chances within a range of market opportunities. The four social classes Weber located in early twentieth-century Europe were:

(a) the working class;
(b) the petty bourgeoisie;
(c) the propertyless intelligentsia and specialists;
(d) the classes privileged through property and education (Weber 1978: 305).

Although Weber does not develop the discussion of social classes very far, the logical inference to be drawn is that there are at least two minimum conditions for social class formation:

1 common mobility chances of moving among a limited set of class positions;
2 power differentials blocking mobility into other positions.

In this way, Weber's social classes occupy a contingent and therefore somewhat precarious place in the social structure. Further structural changes in economic development may change opportunities for social mobility, leading to the possible corrosion of existing social classes and the possible development of new ones. There is no logical reason to guarantee that social classes will persist, and absolutely no place for teleological accounts of history in terms of the necessary 'mission' of particular classes.

The final dimension of Weber's account of class concerns the much misunderstood relationship between class, status, and party. (For clarification, see Giddens 1973: 41–52.) Commentators on Weber are now rather less prone to render this tripartite set of terms as class, status, and power. It is quite clear from the texts that Weber's intention was to distinguish between class, status, and party, not as differing bases of stratification, but rather as alternative bases for the distribution of power within a community.

It is also important to emphasize that the class–status–party framework did not emerge from micro-level empirical accounts of the complex basis of the modern social structure. It grew, rather, out of the historical orientation of German social thought, and from a sense of the dichotomous contrast between past and present. Tönnies' dichotomous presentation of this contrast in terms of the *Gemeinschaft/ Gesellschaft* contrast is paralleled in Weber's ideal-typical contrast between status-ordered societies and market-ordered societies. Here status order and market represent alternative bases of social organization. The former is based on ascriptive forms of cultural evaluation and action — strategies of social closure — the latter on the universalistic logic of calculative exchange among self-interested individuals structured through concentrations of market power.

The analytical distinction between class and status does not necessarily require their empirical separation as distinct entities. They may be intertwined in a most complex manner in the empirical world. Weber, however, refused to reduce all status concerns to class, as generations of Marxists have attempted to do. The theoretical underpinning of this anti-reductionist multi-dimensionality is the axiomatic proposition that individuals have both material and ideal interests, and that neither is epistemologically privileged. In this respect, it is equally possible for class positions in the labour market to be dominated by status interests (for example, racial and ethnic labourmarket closure) as for status divisions to be used to protect powerful class interests by strategies of divide-and-rule. In this way class and status may in certain circumstances be complementary.

Alexander (1983) makes the even stronger claim that Weber's classes must necessarily be associated with non-economic forms of social action (for instance, religion) in order to give material interest meaning. This interpretation is, however, difficult to sustain for the modern period, when disenchantment and rationalization impart a powerful *Gesellschaftlich* flavour to class relations, captured in notions of bargaining between self-interested agents.

Weber, of course, also posed the question as to whether class or status is likely to predominate in contemporary society. His rather undeveloped answer is that class will tend to predominate in periods of economic up-swing and expansion. At this time new wealth and new occupations disrupt the existing basis of market power. In periods of stagnation and recession, on the other hand, status is likely to predominate as individuals and groups seek status identity, and social closure to uphold their social standing. Where status divides persist in this way, so does the *Gemeinschaft*, and in this sense we might infer that the contemporary world is unlikely to become completely disenchanted. On the other hand, the association of status with stagnation and economic down-swing suggests a rather attenuated function for such power groups. They may under certain circumstances promote community in the face of modernity, but they cannot subdue the rise of economic rationalization.

Marx–Weber comparisons have certainly proved useful in clarifying and evaluating different options in class theory. They have also helped to consolidate the continuing prominence of class theory within social theory. Yet there is also a major danger of excessive theoretical piety and intellectual conservatism if we approach contemporary analysis by this route alone. Marx–Weber comparisons do not provide the sole vantage-point from which to assess Weber's impact on class theory, since they take insufficient account of attempts to extend and refine the Weberian legacy.

The most important recent attempt of this kind is the extension of Weber's concern with market inequalities and with the distributive consequences of the market for class structures, into the areas of housing and consumption. This line of argument represents a major extension of *Gesellschaftlich* versions of class theory — the weak class idiom — and a major setback for the attempt to defend an intermediate class idiom, able to retain as much of the strong class *Gemeinschaftlich* idiom as possible.

WEBER, DISTRIBUTION, HOUSING, AND CONSUMPTION

The first major breakthrough in this field came with the publication of Rex and Moore's study, *Race, Community and Conflict* in 1967. This seminal work on housing allocation, immigrant settlement, and political conflict in the English Midlands raised for the first time a neo-Weberian theory of 'housing classes'. The central proposition was that 'there is a class struggle over the use of houses and that this class struggle is the central process of the city as a social unit' (Rex and Moore 1967: 273). The allocation of housing, according to this view, represents a major determinant of life chances, yet the operation of the housing markets leaves some groups in positions of advantage and others in a state of massive disadvantage. Rex and Moore posited that such groups could be termed 'housing classes' in a Weberian sense in that their life chances were patterned unequally as a result of the possession or lack of possession of resources and assets relevant to the distribution of power within the housing market.

While recognizing that power in the housing market was in large measure a reflection of power in the labour market, Rex and Moore argued that occupancy of a particular class situation, defined in terms of production relations, did not necessarily prescribe any specific location in the housing market. This view is particularly significant in highlighting a major line of differentiation and potential power conflict within the large group of wage and salary earners conventionally grouped together as part of a propertyless class with respect to ownership of the means of production. Unequal property rights within the housing market, as distinct from the labour market, are located within differences in tenurial status; for example, between owner-occupiers, private tenants, and public housing tenants.

Moving from class structure to class conflict, Rex and Moore buttressed their argument with the assumption that there is a unitary value system in the community about the desirability of different patterns of tenure. Owner-occupancy is ranked first, while private tenancy is ranked last. Conflict arises as individuals with different amounts of market power struggle for access to the most desirable forms of housing.

The theory of housing classes has been criticized by many urban sociologists, not least by those sympathetic to neo-Weberian versions of class theory (Saunders 1981, 1984). Criticism has, for example been directed against the existence of a unitary value system relating to housing desirability (Davies 1972). Whatever force this particular point may or may not have, it would not necessarily invalidate the core proposition concerning class formation around structural positions defined by tenurial relations in the housing market. A far more damaging argument, advanced by Haddon (1970), is that tenurial status is an inadequate measure of market power. Thus it is possible for the private tenants category to include those too poor to achieve owner-occupation, as well as those members of the middle class who may choose private tenancy where it provides access to preferred situations, such as inner-city housing.

Another line of criticism is that structural positions in the housing market do not typically generate a sufficiently enduring sense of group identity and interest in contradistinction to other interests (Pahl 1975: 257). Hence class conflict of an overt kind is unlikely on the basis of housing market relations. Once again, this criticism may be of some validity, yet it is not so damaging to the weak *Gesellschaftlich* version of class theory which posits no necessary connection between structural position, class identity, and class conflict.

While Rex and Moore's original statement of the housing class theory finds few outright supporters, the ensuing debate has none the less stimulated discussion in a number of previously neglected areas, such as the sociology of consumption. One interesting argument is that Rex and Moore's ostensible housing classes, defined by property-relations in the housing market, were really Weberian housing status groups, defined in relation to consumption relations. Their salience is not therefore in the realm of market position and class inequality, but in the distribution of prestige and honour in consumer life-styles. The fragmentation of wage- and salary-earners between different forms of housing tenure might merely reflect the fragmentation of economic class by consumption relations and consumption cleavages both between owner-occupiers and tenants, and between public and private modes of housing consumption.

This debate is of particular significance in the erosion of the strong *Gemeinschaftlich* class theory. One of the fundamental tenets of the strong class idiom is the emphasis placed on working-class community — and especially working-class occupational community. This is seen as a central locus of cultural identity, political mobilization, and social change. This type of community is, moreover, generally associated with public rather than private housing, with collective rather than private consumption. The obverse of working-class community with its 'mutuality', 'solidarity', and 'militancy in pursuit of social justice', is generally taken to be 'middle-class' suburbia. Here, instead of mutuality and militancy we are told that atomized privatism, commodity fetishism, and social quiescence prevail. Notwithstanding this critique, the general trend in the western world since the Second World War has been in favour of the expansion of private housing, usually located outside any organic physical relationship with the work-place. These changes, based on market exchange and the private household, have implicated the working class in an increasing network of *Gesellschaftlich* relations including both housing, car purchase, and the consumption of other durable products. Where then do these developments leave housing class theory?

Peter Saunders, in a series of important contributions (see especially 1978, 1981, 1984) has provided a number of insights into the reality of increasingly privatized housing provision and its relation to class theory and consumption. In the earliest paper (Saunders 1978) he sought to re-formulate the original neo-Weberian housing class concept in a different framework. This centred on domestic property classes — a fundamentally *Gesellschaftlich* notion — rather than Rex and Moore's housing class. Domestic property classes arose as a result of the differential effects on life chances that arose from inequalities in the market-place between owners and non-owners of domestic property. This kind of differentiation has been particularly pronounced in his view during the post-war epoch, when house price inflation has been in excess of general inflation, creating potential capital gains for home-owners. It leads, however, to a conflict between owner-occupiers' interest in high house prices and low interest rates, and the interest of tenants in low house prices which produce low rents. Home-owners in Britain have also benefited from taxation subsidies reducing potential fiscal benefits for other groups.

The significance of this argument is twofold. First, that domestic property owners constitute a class in the Weberian sense in that they use domestic property ownership to generate returns in the market-place which in turn influences life chances. The second point, of major significance for the *Gesellschaftlich* theory of class, is that increasing numbers of wage and salary earners have in the post-war period taken up privatized home-ownership rather than remaining as tenants. This not only enhances private consumption and *Gesellschaft* relations over collective consumption and working-class *Gemeinschaft*; it also suggests ways in which changes in material interest in the sphere of domestic property may weaken organized class solidarities and class politics.

Although Saunders subsequently had second, more critical thoughts about the utility of the domestic property class concept, this has not lessened his concern — nor that of other commentators such as Pratt (1982) — with those forms of social inequality and social cleavage which do not originate from the character of property rights in the means of production. The main difficulty with the domestic property class notion is not the challenge to production-centred theories of class, but rather the insufficiently radical break with conventional class theory. Saunders suggests that to treat domestic property ownership merely as *one dimension* of class analysis is to narrow the significance of housing and home-ownership. His view is that inequalities in consumption relationships cannot be subsumed within the overall rubric of class theory without causing a fundamental elision between the analytically distinct spheres of consumption and production (Saunders 1984: 206).

In his recent work, Saunders (1984), following Dunleavy (1979) and others, now wishes to discuss housing within a broader framework than that available within class theory. Just as there are property relations in the means of production, the province of class theory, so there are property relations in the means of consumption, which are analytically separate from class divisions, and which may, following Dunleavy, be usefully termed 'consumption cleavages'.

For Saunders, the class concept is fundamentally grounded in 'the social organisation of production', and associated with the generation of class conflict. The provenance of class theory is restricted to the strong class idiom. Judged from this viewpoint, housing as domestic property is assigned to the non-class-like sphere of consumption, rather than the class-based sphere of production. The enhanced housing market power that home-owners may have represents not class power but a form of 'private ownership of the means of consumption' which functions to augment 'revenue'.

Saunders' conceptual move has two possible disadvantages. The first is that the capital accumulation function of house-ownership which Saunders previously emphasized has shrunk to the mere augmentation of 'revenue'. In this way Saunders appears to have been persuaded that power advantages in the housing market which are not of a production-based class-like nature are transitory or purely contingent. Whether such advantages are so easily explained away is not quite so clear-cut, however. As Pratt (1982) points out, empirical contingency is not in itself grounds for ruling out the housing class theory. What theory is not associated with large elements of contingency — Marxist class theory included! Pratt also challenges Saunders' belief that government tax relief to owner-occupiers is too general a market advantage to be germane to class conflict on the grounds that such advantages have considerable bearing on to desired spatial situations within the city. They are, in other words, fundamental to life chances. Pratt's critique suggests that Saunders has taken the intellectual credentials of conventional Marxist class theory on an a priori basis, discounting any other type of market-based class theory. One might add that Saunders missed an opportunity to assess a more *Gesellschaftlich* class theory.

A second possible disadvantage of Saunders' re-conceptualization is the failure to discuss the impact of capital gains in housing as capital for small businesses, whether directly or as security for credit. Given the reversal of the historical decline of small proprietorship in recent years, this market advantage is clearly of some importance in the possibility of capitalizing small businesses.

While there are some grounds for believing that Saunders' evacuation from the terrain of a neo-Weberian class theory seems premature, his underlying theoretical strategy, which separates production and consumption, is of major significance. Among other things it highlights an undeveloped element in Weber's sociology of the marketplace and of market society dominated, as it was, by a continuing concern for production over consumption.

Marx and Weber both emphasize the centrality of production to the constitution of class relations — though they do so, as we have seen, in rather different ways. For Marx, this emphasis on production leaves little place for consumption, especially consumption of commodities by private consumers. Given the predominance of exchange-value within the capitalist mode of production, any use-value characteristics possessed by commodities are merely contingent to the underlying logic of the system. For Weber, by contrast, consumption is given some attention, but within the discussion of 'status' rather than 'class'.

Giddens (1973: 109) has demonstrated that Weber's discussion of 'status' and 'status groups' conflates two analytically distinct elements. The first, and most clear-cut, is the development of differentiation and power relations based upon non-economic estimations of value. These typically involve positive or negative prestige associated with consumption activities. This mode of consumption-based power distribution, inherited from pre-capitalist status societies, is, however, distinct from a second, more generic type of consumption relation. This simply involves the existence of groupings based on common consumption characteristics — whether or not conscious evaluation of honour or prestige takes place. Giddens calls these 'distributive groupings'. His argument is that such groupings are a generic feature of social structures capable of influencing the 'structuration' of class relations.

Typical distributive groupings are based not merely on differentials in income, but also on differential access to housing, mortgages, and so on. This presumably gives us housing distributive groupings rather than housing classes. Giddens does not, however, pursue this interesting foray into the sociology of consumption very far. His primary concern is to show how the existence of distributive groupings may be contributory factors in explaining the circumstances under which economic classes (defined structurally) become social classes with community-like characteristics. Distributive groupings in housing provide one dimension to social class formation wherever segregation between 'working-class' and 'middle-class' neighbourhoods takes place. In the final analysis, then, class and the development of class communities takes precedence over concern for consumption.

Sociology has in general been very slow to develop an autonomous sociology of consumption. Instead, we generally find consumption issues reduced to the imperatives of production and economic socialization. This tendency was not only found within Marxist discourse, since Weber also emphasized the capacity of producers to dominate consumers, through superior market power and modern devices such as advertising (Weber 1978). Within Frankfurt School critical theory, the critique of consumerism at the level of personality, as well as structure and culture, became even more savage. This is best exemplified in Marcuse's scathing comments on the private household in *One Dimensional Man* (Marcuse 1964). It is only in the last few years that this situation has begun to break down with the rescue of the knowledgability of actors and the distinction between consumption and consumerism (Kellner 1983; Otnes 1988).

One reason for the breakdown in resistance to a sociology of consumption is the growing interest in the household and household activities as part of everyday life. This interest comes in part from the feminist critique of analysis which concentrates disproportionately on the formal, public, production-centred dimensions of society, at the expense of the social functions and conflicts evident within the domestic and informal sphere. This thrust embraces both the gender division of labour and household work, socialization processes connected with the household, and household consumption processes. The old reductionism which saw the household merely as functional

191

to the production and reproduction of economic life has now been overtaken by a more complex sense of the differentiation between household and work-place, between public and private.

Another reason for the growing interest in consumption is a concern for the fate of public or collective as against individual or private modes of consumption. This has been sparked by the contemporary challenge to welfare states by New Right policies of deregulation and privatization. The impact of such policies, in areas such as housing and health, has generated particular debate within urban sociology. Here an initial expectation of collective resistance by urban social movements to inroads into collective consumption (Harloe and Paris cited in Saunders 1984) has been undermined over time by the realization that private housing is actually very popular, and that desire for access to private health and private education is not restricted to middle-class elites.

There is a most fundamental issue at stake in the slow, painful, and protracted emergence of an autonomous sociology of consumption. This centres on the conservative resistance of sociologists to liberalism, and especially to economic liberalism. Sociology has always contained traditions hostile towards individualism and market exchange, and which advanced disbelief that the impersonal character of such relations could be consistent with community and social order. This is very closely linked with a preference for some kind of non-particularistic *Gemeinschaft* over and above the atomistic impersonality of *Gesellschaftlich* relations. Although twentieth-century sociology has increasingly accommodated itself to modern institutions, there is still, especially in European social thought, a massive scepticism or outright hostility to the liberal vision of a society of free-standing, morally responsible individuals. Such pejorative attitudes are sometimes expressed through an elitist disdain for popular culture and popular consumption activities. This is fairly typical of Frankfurt School critical theory, and in Marxisant critiques of consumers as cultural dupes.

Meanwhile, the intellectual basis of the critique of liberalism usually rests on one of two inadequate strategies. The first merely rehearses Marx's 140-year-old critique of liberalism as resting on an allegedly abstract formulistic account of the individual. Individuals have formal rights (such as citizenship) but they cannot actualize them in any *real* sense. 'Real' in this sense usually refers rather to the particular values that intellectuals would wish to see exemplified in popular culture, than an empirically grounded understanding of individual and household autonomy, reflected in day-to-day projects. These value preferences are none the less usually mystified as some kind of objective social ontology of humankind. This is simply to conduct a rearguard action on behalf of a communitarian *Gemeinschaftlich* world-view. The problem is that *Gemeinschaft* is dead.

The second strategy adopted in the critique of liberalism centres on the argument that a massive power imbalance between producers and consumers renders an autonomous sociology of consumption untenable. This argument is certainly empirically testable. It also has some empirical plausibility, in so far as it exposes a flaw in naïve liberal accounts of the actually existing market-place as an unambiguous system of natural liberty. Producer power cannot be so simply offset by 'sovereign' consumers, and indeed the notion of consumer sovereignty is itself misleading. Having said this, it does not follow that power in the market-place is always unilaterally structured in one direction. Recent evidence of successful consumer resistance to producer strategies indicates that consumers are very far from cultural dupes. And, more generally, consumers are clearly asserting demands about the content of the use-values they expect from commodities.

Commodity exchange under capitalism is not then simply dominated by exchange-value concerns to the exclusion of use-value issues. Against Marx, we can also go further to claim that maximization of use-values can be pursued within the *Gesellschaft* relations of the market-place. Such relations are impersonal and atomized, and this does represent a challenge to *Gemeinschaft* conceptions of face-to-face community. Impersonality and atomization are, however, enabling features of the market-place, in so far as they permit the liberation of individuals from oppressive community sanctions and the limits of access to resources set by face-to-face contacts. Individuals cannot, however, live merely as social atoms, so that the unit of analysis of the consumer side of the commodity market is better viewed as the household. This, though, makes little difference to the advantages that accrue from market impersonality and atomization between households.

Weber's liberalism induced a strong general sympathy with the notion of the free-standing, morally responsible individual, and with Austrian neo-classical economics. It did not, however, carry through into an analysis of the sociology of consumption under *Gesellschaftlich* conditions. This is partly because Weber felt obliged to point out the limits to market freedom set by property-based power relations, and partly because the consumer society was as yet poorly developed in early twentieth-century Germany. It is arguable that Simmel, in *The Philosophy of Money* (1978) and in his urban essays, went much further than Weber in outlining the social/philosophical and cultural configuration of *Gesellschaftlich* relations. In Weber's case, by contrast, nostalgia for an older world of religious certainty may also have retarded an extended discussion of the logic of *Gesellschaftlich* relations.

CONCLUDING REMARKS

The robustness of the strong class idiom has disintegrated in the last forty years. On an intellectual level, this process owes something at least to Weber's cryptic but influential articulation of a weak *Gesellschaftlich* conception of class. The weak class idiom has not, of course, gone unchallenged. Yet the attempt to stabilize an intermediate or 'strong-as-possible' class idiom has been purchased at the cost of an abandonment of the labour theory value, and, in some cases, the harnessing of rational choice theory to class analysis.

Even Giddens' (1973) more modest proposal to centre class analysis on the problem of transformation from economic class relations to social class formation seems increasingly redundant. As the full maturity of *Gesellschaftlich* relations is secured within contemporary consumerism and the extension of individual citizenship rights, there seems little place any more for social classes in the neo-Weberian sense of class communities. This is not to deny the salience of social conflict within the market economy or within structures of political authority. Yet this generally takes the form either of managed conflict between organized interest-groups (for example, organized trade unions, organized employers, and the state), or non-class protests by social movements over the environment, women's rights, and so on. All this appears to make class an increasingly redundant issue, except in the weak sense as a means of delineating forms of economic power relations which generate and reproduce social inequalities.

The Weberian legacy to class theory is not, however, exhausted by reference to Weber's own delimitation of class inequality to market-based societies. For an alternative strand in Weber's sociology centred on the generic problem of how authority is legitimized in any society. This raised issues beyond the material and ideal market-interests of social actors, extending to a concern for the differing bases of compliance to legitimate domination. This legacy has influenced class theory in one of two ways.

The first influence is felt in New Class theory. Here the influence of Saint-Simon and Hegel in treating rational knowledge as a basis for social organization distinct from private property, has been merged with Weber's interest in the relations and agents of legitimate domination. Gouldner's New Class theory (1979) and Szelenyi's account of the emergent socialist class of teleological redistributors both depend on some such fusion (Konrad and Szelenyi 1979).

This metaphorical extension of the private-property-based class concept has, however, run into difficulties in trying to delineate exactly what structural positions are involved, and in establishing their significance for political action — whether radical or conservative (see, for example, Bell 1979; Goldthorpe 1982). It is still too early, then, to accept New Class theory as a coherent extension of the repertoire of class analysis.

The second, neo-Weberian extension of class theory is to be found in Dahrendorf's attempt to subsume property-based inequalities within a wider, more generic set of structural inequalities dependent on authority relations. Here class inequalities arise within any 'imperatively co-ordinated organisation'. By this means the same over-arching framework is applicable in capitalist as in socialist societies.

One problem with this is that no unified account of class structure is possible, since classes are defined separately for each organizational unit. This creates insurmountable difficulties in deciding how to aggregate the array of authority relations in different organizational settings. A second problem is that the approach assumes the primacy of authority relations over market relations in the constitution of life chances. In other words, the focus is on legitimate domination and bureaucratic rationalization at the expense of market-based inequalities.

This position is not, of course, untenable a priori, because the limits of bureaucratic iron cage rationalization in the modern world are complex and subject to shifting boundaries. Since Weber regarded both the institutions of rational-legal domination and of the market-place as examples of rationalization, it is not entirely clear how he saw the fate of the market in relation to the development of bureaucracy. This does not make a neo-Weberian reconstruction of class theory any easier. None the less, Dahrendorf's primary intention is not piety to Weber, but a more incisive analysis of class and class conflict in the modern epoch.

It remains unclear, therefore, whether inequalities in market power can plausibly be subsumed under authority relations without conflating inequalities deriving from economic property rights with those deriving from managerial authority. Is there really much advantage in subsuming the former to the latter in an authority-based conception of class? Once again, the metaphoricality of class seems to prove analytically counter-productive, where too many distinct phenomena are subsumed under one heading. This also reflects the elusiveness of a generic theory of class.

Given the problems with Dahrendorf's theory there would seem to be little immediate hope for a major renewal of a generic form of class analysis. We are left, therefore, in a situation where the persistence of the class idiom is explicable more in terms of the metaphorical character of class rhetoric than any clear intellectual persuasiveness. And while a weak *Gesellschaftlich* version of class theory is defensible, this is by itself a rather slender basis upon which to construct an account of social inequalities and their connection with group formation and social change.

The historic *élan* of the strong class idiom is now dated in an epoch in which *Gesellschaftlich* and corporatist forms of social organization prevail. The liberalistic vision of a world of autonomous, morally responsible private individuals and households is not, however, redundant even in a world of massive state intervention and corporatism. The threat of the iron cage may be ever-present, but it is equally possible that Weber's liberal despair was premature and unduly defeatist.

BIBLIOGRAPHY

Abercrombie, N., Hill, S., and Turner, B. S. (1980) *The Dominant Ideology Thesis*, London: Allen & Unwin.

Abercrombie, N., Hill, S., and Turner, B. S. (1983) 'Determinacy and indeterminacy in the theory of ideology', *New Left Review* 142: 55–66.

Abercrombie, N., Hill, S., and Turner, B. S. (1986) *Sovereign Individuals of Capitalism*, London: Allen & Unwin.

Abercrombie, N. and Urry, J. (1983) *Capital, Labour and the Middle Classes*, London: Allen & Unwin.

Adler, Z. (1987) *Rape on Trial*, London: Routledge & Kegan Paul.

Albinski, H. (1985) 'Australia and the United States', *Daedalus*, Winter: 395–420.

Alexander, J. (1983) *Theoretical Logic in Sociology*, vol. 3: *The Classical Attempt at Theoretical Synthesis: Max Weber*, London: Routledge & Kegan Paul.

Alexander, J. (1984) *Theoretical Logic in Sociology, the Modern Reconstruction of Classical Thought: Talcott Parsons*, London: Routledge & Kegan Paul.

Alexander, J. C. (ed.) (1985) *Neofunctionalism*, Beverly Hills, Cal.: Sage.

Alexander, J. C. (1987) *Twenty Lectures, Sociological Theory Since World War Two*, New York: Columbia University Press.

Alexander, J. C. (1988) *Action and its Environments, Toward a New Synthesis*, New York: Columbia University Press.

Allen, S. (1982) 'Gender, inequality and class formation', in A. Giddens and G. Mackenzie (eds) *Social Class and the Division of Labour*, Cambridge: Cambridge University Press.

Antoni, C. (1959) *From History to Sociology*, Detroit, Mich.: Wayne State University Press.

Antonio, R. J. and Glassman, R. M. (eds) (1985) *A Weber–Marx Dialogue*, Lawrence, Kan.: University Press of Kansas.

Atkinson, A. B. (1975) *The Economics of Inequality*, Oxford: Clarendon Press.

Bagley, C. (1973) *The Dutch Plural Society*, London: Oxford University Press.

Barbalet, J. M. (1980) 'Principles of stratification in Max Weber: an interpretation and critique', *British Journal of Sociology* 1(3): 401–18.

Barbalet, J. (1982) 'Social closure in class analysis: a critique of Parkin', *Sociology* 16(4): 484–97.

Baudrillard, J. (1983) *Simulations*, New York: Semiotext(e).

Bean, P. and Whynes, D. (eds) (1986) *Barbara Wootton, Social Science and Public Policy, Essays in Her Honour*, London and New York: Tavistock.

Becker, G. S. (1976) *The Economic Approach to Human Behaviour*, Chicago: Chicago University Press.

Bell, D. (1961) 'The breakup of family capitalism', in *The End of Ideology, on the Exhaustion of Political Ideas in the Fifties*, New York: The Free Press.

Bell, D. (ed.) (1962) *The Radical Right*, New York: Doubleday-Anchor.

Bell, D. (1973) *The Coming of Post-Industrial Society*, New York: Basic Books.

Bell, D. (1975) 'Ethnicity and social change', in N. Glazer and D. P. Moynihan (eds) *Ethnicity, Theory and Experience*, Cambridge, Mass.: Harvard University Press.

Bell, D. (1976) *The Cultural Contradictions of Capitalism*, London: Heinemann.

Bell, D. (1979) 'The new class: a muddled concept', in B. Bruce-Biggs (ed.) *The New Class*, New Brunswick: Transaction Press.

Bell, D. (1986) 'Vorwort zur deutschen Ausgabe', *Die Sozialwissenschaften Seit 1945*, Frankfurt/Main, Campus Verlag: 7–12.

Bellah, R., Sullivan, W., Swidler, A., and Tipton, S. M. (1985) *Habits of the Heart, Individualism and Commitment in American Life*, Berkeley, Cal.: University of California Press.

Bendix, R. (1974) 'Inequality and social structure: a comparison of Marx and Weber', *American Sociological Review* 39(2): 149–61.

Bendix, R. and Lipset, S. M. (eds) (1953) *Class, Status and Power, a Reader in Social Stratification*, New York: The Free Press.

Bentham, D. (1977) 'From socialism to fascism: the relation between theory and practice in the work of Robert Michels', *Political Studies* 25: 3–24 and 161–81.

Berger, P. L. (1969) *A Rumour of Angels*, New York: Garden City, Doubleday.

Berman, M. (1982) *All That is Solid Melts into Air, the Experience of Modernity*, New York: Simon & Schuster.

Bourdieu, P. (1984) *Distinction, a Social Critique of the Judgment of Taste*, London: Routledge & Kegan Paul.

Brand, A. (1982) 'Against romanticism: Max Weber and the historical school of law', *Australian Journal of Law and Society* 1: 87–100.

Braverman, H. (1974) *Labour and Monopoly Capital, the Degradation of Work in the Twentieth Century*, New York and London: Monthly Review Press.

Briggs, A. (1960) 'The language of class', in A. Briggs and J. Saville (eds) *Essays in Labour History*, vol. 1, London: Macmillan.

Brittain, J. A. (1978) *Inheritance and the Inequality of Material Wealth*, Washington, DC: The Brookings Institution.

Browning, H. C. and Singelmann, J. (1978) 'The transformation of the US labour force: the interaction of industry and occupation', *Politics and Society* 8: 481–509.

Brubaker, R. (1984) *The Limits of Rationality, an Essay on the Social and Moral Thought of Max Weber*, London: George Allen & Unwin.

Canning, J. P. (1980) 'The corporation in the political thought of the Italian jurists of thirteenth and fourteenth centuries', *History of Political Thought* 1: 9–32.

Carchedi, G. (1977) *On the Economic Identification of Social Classes*, London: Routledge & Kegan Paul.

Clarke, S. (1982) *Marx, Marginalism and Modern Sociology*, London: Macmillan.

Cohen, J. L. (1982) *Class and Civil Society: the Limits of Marxian Critical Theory*, Amherst, Mass.: University of Massachusetts Press.

Cohen, S. (1972) *Folk Devils and Moral Panics*, London: Paladin.

Collins, R. (1986) *Max Weber, a Skeleton Key*, Beverly Hills, Cal.: Sage.

Corrigan, P. and Sayer, D. (1985) *The Great Arch, English State Formation as Cultural Revolution*, Oxford: Basil Blackwell.

Cottrell, A. (1984) *Social Classes in Marxist Theory*, London: Routledge & Kegan Paul.

Cousins, M. and Hussain, A. (1984) *Michel Foucault*, London: Macmillan.

Crompton, R. and Gubbay, J. (1978) *Economy and Class Structure*, London: Macmillan.

Dahrendorf, R. (1959) *Class and Class Conflict in Industrial Society*, Palo Alto, Cal.: Stanford University Press.

Dahrendorf, R. (1969) 'The service class', in T. Burns (ed.) *Industrial Man*, Harmondsworth: Penguin.

Davies, J. (1972) *The Evangelistic Bureaucrat*, London: Tavistock.

Davis, K. and Moore, W. E. (1945) 'Some principles of stratification', *American Sociological Review* 10(2): 242–9.

Davis, M. (1982) 'The political economy of late-imperial America', *New Left Review* 143: 6–38.

Djilas, M. (1966) *The New Class*, London: Allen & Unwin.

Donzelot, J. (1979) *The Policing of Families*, New York: Pantheon Books.

Dumont, L. (1983) *Essais sur l'individualisme*, Paris: Seuil.

Dumont, L. (1986) 'Collective identities and universal ideology: the actual interplay', *Theory, Culture and Society*, 3: 25–33.

Dunleavy, P. (1979) 'The urban bases of political alignment', *British Journal of Political Sciences* 9: 409–45.

Durkheim, E. (1978) *On Institutional Analysis*, Chicago and London: University of Chicago Press.

Eisen, A. (1979) 'Called to order: the role of the puritan *Berufsmensch* in Weberian sociology', *Sociology* 13: 203–18.

Elias, N. (1987) 'The retreat of sociologists into the present', *Theory, Culture and Society*, 4: 223–48.

Elster, J. (1982) 'Marxism, functionalism and game theory', *Theory and Society* 11: 453–82.

Elster, J. (1985) *Making Sense of Marx*, Cambridge: Cambridge University Press.

Esposito, J. L. (ed.) (1983) *Voices of Resurgent Islam*, New York: Oxford University Press.

Esposito, J. L. (1984) *Islam and Politics*, Syracuse, NY: Syracuse University Press.

Feher, F. and Heller, A. (1984) 'From red to green', *Telos* 59: 35–44.

Foster, J. (1974) *Class Struggle and the Industrial Revolution*, London: Weidenfeld & Nicolson.

Foucault, M. (1970) *The Order of Things*, London: Tavistock.

Foucault, M. (1977) *Discipline and Punish, the Birth of the Prison*, London: Tavistock.

Foucault, M. (1979) *The History of Sexuality: Vol. 1. An Introduction*, London: Tavistock.

Fugen, H. N. (1985) *Max Weber, mit Selbstzeugnissen und Bilddokumenten*, Hamburg: Rowohlt.

Gellner, E. (1969) *Saints of the Atlas*, London: Weidenfeld & Nicolson.

Gershuny, J. and Miles, I. (1983) *The New Service Economy, the Transformation of Employment in Industrial Societies*, London: Frances Pinter.

Giddens, A. (1973) *The Class Structure of the Advanced Societies*, London: Hutchinson.

Glazer, N. (1983) *Ethnic Dilemmas 1964–1982*, Cambridge, Mass.: Harvard University Press.

Glazer, N. and Moynihan, D. P. (1963) *Beyond the Melting Pot*, Cambridge, Mass.: MIT Press.

Goffman, E. (1967) *Interaction Ritual*, Harmondsworth: Penguin.

Goldmann, L. (1973) *The Philosophy of the Enlightenment*, London: Routledge & Kegan Paul.

Goldthorpe, J., Lockwood, D., Bechhofer, F., and Platt, J. (1969) *The Affluent Worker in the Class Structure*, Cambridge: Cambridge University Press.

Goldthorpe, J. (1982) 'On the service class, its formation and future', in A. Giddens and G. Mackenzie (eds) *Social Class and the Division of Labour*, Cambridge: Cambridge University Press.

Gordon, M. M. (1950) *Social Class in American Sociology*, New York: McGraw-Hill.

Gorz, A. (1982) *Farewell to the Working Class*, London: Pluto Press.

Gouldner, A. (1979) *The Future of Intellectuals and the Rise of the New Class*, New York: Seabury Press.

Habermas, J. (1976) *Legitimation Crisis*, London: Heinemann.

Habermas, J. (1984) *The Theory of Communicative Action*, vol. 1, London: Heinemann.

Haddon, R. (1970) 'A minority in a welfare society', *New Atlantis* 2: 80–133.

Hay, D., Linebaugh, P., Ruile, J. G., Thompson, E. P., and Windslow, C. (1975) *Albion's Fatal Tree*, Harmondsworth: Penguin.

Hayek, F. von (1973–9) *Law, Legislation, and Liberty* (3 vols), London: Routledge & Kegan Paul.

Hearn, F. (1985) *Reason and Freedom in Sociological Thought*, Boston, Mass.: Allen & Unwin.

Heller, A. (1976) *The Theory of Need in Marx*, London: Allison & Busby.

Hennis, W. (1988) *Max Weber, Essays in Reconstruction*, London: Allen & Unwin.

Hepworth, M. and Turner, B. S. (1982) *Confession, Studies in Deviance and Religion*, London: Routledge & Kegan Paul.

Hill, S. (1981) *Competition and Control at Work, the New Industrial Sociology*, London: Heinemann.

Hindess, B. and Hirst, P. Q. (1975) *Pre-capitalist Modes of Production*, London: Routledge & Kegan Paul.

Hirst, P. (1977) 'Economic classes and politics', in A. Hunt (ed.) *Class and Structure*, London: Lawrence & Wishart.

Hirst, P. Q. (1979) *On Law and Ideology*, London: Macmillan.

Hirst, P. Q. (1986) *Law, Socialism and Democracy*, London: Allen & Unwin.

Hodgson, G. (1986) 'Behind Methodological Individualism', *Cambridge Journal of Economics*, 10: 211–24.

Hoffman, J. (1984) *The Gramscian Challenge, Coercion and Consent in Marxist Political Theory*, Oxford: Blackwell.

Hollis, M. (1979) 'Introduction', in F. Hahn and M. Hollis (eds) *Philosophy and Economic Theory*, Oxford: Oxford University Press.

Holton, R. (1976) *British Syndicalism*, London: Pluto Press.

Holton, R. J. (1985) *The Transition from Feudalism to Capitalism*, London: Macmillan.

Holton, R. J. and Turner, B. S. (1986) *Talcott Parsons on Economy and Society*, London and New York: Routledge & Kegan Paul.

Homans, G. C. (1984) *Coming to my Senses, the Autobiography of a Sociologist*, New Brunswick, NJ: Transaction Books.

Hunt, A. (1978) *The Sociological Movement in Law*, London: Macmillan.

Hutchinson, T. W. (1973) 'Some themes from *Investigations into Method*', in J. R. Hicks and W. Weber (eds) *Carl Menger and the Austrian School of Economics*, Oxford: Oxford University Press.

Jameson, F. (1985) 'Postmodernism and consumer society', in H. Foster (ed.) *Postmodern Culture*, London and Sydney: Pluto Press, pp. 111–25.

Johnson, T. (1982) 'The state and the professions: peculiarities of the British', in A. Giddens and G. Mackenzie (eds) *Social Class and the Division of Labour*, Cambridge: Cambridge University Press, pp. 186–208.

Kaufmann, F-X. (1986) 'Religion und modernität', in J. Berger (ed.) *Die Moderne–Kontinuitäten und Zäsuren*, Göttingen: Otto Schwartz, pp. 283–307.

Kellner, D. (1983) 'Critical theory, commodities and the consumer society', *Theory, Culture and Society* 1(3).

Kellner, D. (1984) *Herbert Marcuse and the Crisis of Marxism*, Berkeley: University of California Press.

Kent, S. (1985) 'Weber, Goethe and William Penn: themes of marital love', *Sociological Analysis* 46: 315–20.

Kirzner, I. (1976) 'The theory of capital', in E. G. Dolan (ed.) *The Foundation of Modern Austrian Economics*, Kansas: Sheed & Ward.

Konrad, G. and Szelenyi, I. (1979) *The Intellectuals on the Road to Class Power*, New York: Harcourt Brace.

Kristeller, P. O. (1978) 'Philosophy and medicine in medieval and Renaissance Italy', in Stuart F. Spicker (ed.) *Organism, Medicine and Metaphysics, Essays in Honour of Hans Jonas*, Dordrecht: D. Reidel Co., pp. 29–40.

Kronman, A. T. (1983) *Max Weber*, London: Edward Arnold.

Lachmann, L. (1970) *The Legacy of Max Weber*, London: Heinemann.

Lakhdar, L. (1981) 'Why the reversion to Islamic archaism?', *Khamsin* 8: 62–82.

Lash, S. and Urry, J. (1987) *The End of Organized Capitalism*, Cambridge: Polity Press.

Lechner, F. J. (1985a) 'Modernity and its discontents', in J. C. Alexander (ed.) *Neofunctionalism*, Beverly Hills, Cal.: Sage, pp. 157–76.

Lechner, F. (1985b) 'Fundamentalism and socio-cultural revitalization in America: a sociological interpretation', *Sociological Analysis* 46(3): 243–60.

Lepenies, W. (1985) *Die Drei Kulturen, Soziologie zwischen Literatur und Wissenschaft*, München: Carl Hanser.

Levitas, R. (ed.) (1986) *The Ideology of the New Right*, Cambridge: Polity Press.

Löwith, K. (1982) *Max Weber and Karl Marx*, London: Allen & Unwin.

Luhmann, N. (1982) *The Differentiation of Society*, New York: Columbia University Press.

Luhmann, N. (1985) *A Sociological Theory of Law*, London: Routledge & Kegan Paul

Lukes, S. (1968) 'Methodological individualism reconsidered', *British Journal of Sociology* 19: 119–29.

Lyotard, J-F. (1984) *The Postmodern Condition*, Manchester: Manchester University Press.

Macfarlane, A. (1980) *The Rise of English Individualism*, Oxford: Blackwell.

Macfarlane, A. (1981) *The Justice and the Mare's Ale: Law and Disorder in Seventeenth-century England*, Oxford: Blackwell.

McLellan, D. (1977) *Karl Marx: Selected Writings*, Oxford: Oxford University Press.

Machlup, F. (1978) *Methodology of Economics and Other Social Sciences*, New York: Academic Press.

Macpherson, C. B. (1962) *The Political Theory of Possessive Individualism*, Oxford: Oxford University Press.

Mann, M. (1973) *Consciousness and Action among the Western Working Class*, London: Macmillan.

Maravell, J. A. (1986) *Culture of the Baroque, Analysis of a Historical Structure*, Manchester: Manchester University Press.

Marcuse, H. (1964) *One Dimensional Man*, Boston, Mass.: Beacon Press,

Marshall, G. (1980) *Presbyteries and Profits: Calvinism and the Development of Capitalism in Scotland, 1560–1707*, Oxford: Oxford University Press.

Marshall, G. (1982) *In Search of the Spirit of Capitalism*, London: Hutchinson.

Marshall, G., Rose, D., Vogler, C., and Hewby, H. (1985) 'Class citizenship and distributional conflict in modern Britain', *British Journal of Sociology* 36(2): 259–84.

Marshall, T. H. (1977) *Class, Citizenship and Social Development*, Chicago and London: Chicago University Press.

Marsland, D. (1987) *Bias Against Business*, London: Educational Research Trust.

Martin, D. (1978) *A General Theory of Secularization*, Oxford: Blackwell.

Marx, K. (1971) *A Contribution to the Critique of Political Economy*, London: Lawrence & Wishart.

Marx, K. (1976) *Capital*, vol. 1, London: Penguin.

Mill, J. S. (1977) *Essays on Politics and Society*, London: Routledge & Kegan Paul.

von Mises, L. (1934) *The Theory of Money and Credit*, London: Cape.

von Mises, L. (1935) 'Economic calculation in the socialist commonwealth', in F. Hayek (ed.) *Collectivist Economic Planning*, London: Routledge.

von Mises, L. (1960) *Epistemological Problems of Economics*, Princeton, NJ: Van Nostrand.

Mommsen, W. J. (1974) *The Age of Bureaucracy*, Oxford: Blackwell.

Mommsen, W. J. (1985) 'Capitalism and socialism: Weber's dialogue with Marx', in R. Antonio and R. Glassman (eds) *A Weber–Marx Dialogue*, Lawrence, Kan.: University of Kansas Press.

Mommsen, W. J. (1987) 'Robert Michels and Max Weber: moral conviction versus the politics of responsibility', in Mommsen and Osterhammel, *Max Weber and His Contemporaries*, London: Allen & Unwin, pp. 121–38.

Mommsen, W. J. and Osterhammel, J. (eds) (1987) *Max Weber and His Contemporaries*, London: Allen & Unwin.

Münch, R. (1981) 'Talcott Parsons and the theory of Action. 1. The structure of the Kantian core', *American Journal of Sociology* 86(4): 709–39.

Münch, R. (1982) *Theories des Handelns: zue Rekonstruktion der Beitrage von Talcott Parsons, Emile Durkheim und Max Weber*, Frankfurt: Suhrkamp.

Neuwirth, G. (1969) 'A Weberian outline of the theory of community: its application to the dark ghetto', *British Journal of Sociology* 20(2): 148–63.

Nisbet, R. A. (1959) 'The decline and fall of social class', *Pacific Sociological Review* 2: 11–17.

Nisbet, R. (1970) *The Sociological Tradition*, London: Heinemann.

Nozick, R. (1977) 'On Austrian methodology', *Synthese* 36: 353–92.

Oakley, A. (1974) *Housewife*, Harmondsworth: Penguin.

Offe, C. (1985) *Disorganized Capitalism*, Cambridge: Polity Press.

O'Malley, P. (1983) *Law, Capitalism and Democracy*, Sydney: George Allen & Unwin.

Ossowski, S. (1963) *Class Structure in the Social Consciousness*, London: Routledge & Kegan Paul.

Otnes, P. (ed.) (1988) *The Sociology of Consumption*, Atlantic Highlands, Humanities Press.

Pahl, R. (1975) *Whose City?*, Harmondsworth: Penguin.

Parkin, F. (1978) 'Social stratification', in T. Bottomore and R. Nisbet (eds) *A History of Sociological Analysis*, London: Heinemann, pp. 599–632.

Parkin, F. (1979) *Marxism and Class Theory, a Bourgeois Critique*, London: Tavistock.

Parkin, F. (1982) *Max Weber*, London: Tavistock.

Parsons, T. (1931) 'Wants and activities in Marshall', *Quarterly Journal of Economics* 46: 101–40.

Parsons, T. (1932) 'Economics and sociology: Marshall in relation to the thought of his time', *Quarterly Journal of Economics* 46: 316–47.

Parsons, T. (1934a) 'Some reflections on the nature and significance of economics', *Quarterly Journal of Economics* 48: 511–45.

Parsons, T. (1934b) 'Sociological elements in economic thought, I', *Quarterly Journal of Economics* 49: 414–53.

Parsons, T. (1935) 'Sociological elements in economic thought, II', *Quarterly Journal of Economics* 49: 645–67.

Parsons, T. (1937) *The Structure of Social Action*, New York: McGraw-Hill.

Parsons, T. (1963) 'Christianity and modern industrial society', in Edward A. Tiryakian (ed.) *Sociological Theory Values and Sociological Change: Essays in Honor of Pitrim A. Sorokin*, New York: The Free Press, pp. 33–70.

Parsons, T. (1967) *Social Theory and Modern Society*, New York: The Free Press.

Parsons, T. (1971) 'Value-freedom and objectivity', in O. Stammer (ed.) *Max Weber and Sociology Today*, Oxford: Blackwell, pp. 25–50.

Parsons, T. (1978) *Action Theory and the Human Condition*, New York: The Free Press.

Parsons, T. and Smelser, N. (1956) *Economy and Society*, London: Routledge & Kegan Paul.

Pashukanis, E. (1978) *Law and Marxism, a General Theory*, London: Ink Links.

Pfautz, H. W. and Duncan, O. D. (1950) 'A critical evaluation of Warner's work in community stratification', *American Sociological Review* 15: 205–15.

Poggi, G. (1978) *The Development of the Modern State, a Sociological Introduction*, London: Hutchinson.

Poggi, G. (1983) *Calvinism and the Capitalist Spirit, Max Weber's Protestant Ethic*, London: Macmillan.

Polanyi, K. (1977) *The Livelihood of Man*, New York: Academic Books.

Poulantzas, N. (1975) *Classes in Contemporary Capitalism*, London: New Left Books.

Poulantzas, N. (1978) *State, Power and Socialism*, London: New Left Books.

Prager, J. (1985) 'Totalitarian and liberal democracy: two types of modern political orders', in J. C. Alexander (ed.) *Neofunctionalism*, Beverly Hills, Cal.: Sage, pp. 179–210.

Prais, S. J. (1981) *The Evolution of Giant Firms in Britain*, Cambridge: Cambridge University Press.

Pratt, G. (1982) 'Class analysis and urban domestic property: a critical re-examination', *International Journal of Urban and Regional Research* 6: 481–502.

Prendergast, C. (1986) 'Alfred Schutz and the Austrian School of Economics', *American Journal of Sociology* 92(1): 1–26.

Przeworski, A. (1977) 'Proletariat into class', *Politics and Society* 7: 343–401.

Przeworski, A. (1985) *Capitalism and Social Democracy*, Cambridge: Cambridge University Press.

Raskin, M. G. (1986) *The Common Good, Its Politics, Policies and Philosophy*, New York and London: Routledge & Kegan Paul.

Renner, K. (1953) *Wandlunger der Modernen Gesellschaft. Zwei Abhandlungen über die Probleme der Nachkriegszeit*, Vienna: Wiener Volksbuchhandlung.

Rex, J. (1971) 'Typology and objectivity: a comment on Weber's Four Sociological Methods', in A. Sahay (ed.) *Max Weber and Modern Sociology*, London: Routledge & Kegan Paul.

Rex, J. (1986) *Race and Ethnicity*, Milton Keynes: Open University Press.

Rex, J. and Moore, R. (1967) *Race, Community and Conflict*, London: Oxford University Press.

Rinehart, J. W. (1971) 'Affluence and the embourgeoisement of the working class: a critical look', *Social Problems* 19: 149–62.

Robbins, L. (1935) *An Essay on the Nature and Significance of Economics*, London: Macmillan.

Robertson, R. and Chirico, J. (1985) 'Humanity, globalization and world wide religious resurgence: a theoretical exploration', *Sociological Analysis* 46(3): 219–42.

Roemer, J. E. (1982a) 'New directions in the Marxian theory of exploitation and class', *Politics and Society* 11(3).

Roemer, J. (1982b) *A General Theory of Exploitation and Class*, Cambridge, Mass.: Harvard University Press.

Rolph, C. H. (1978) *The Queen's Pardon*, London: Cassell.

Rorty, R. (1982) *Consequences of Pragmatism (Essays: 1972–1980)*, Brighton: The Harvester Press.

Roth, G. and Schluchter, W. (1975) *Max Weber's Vision of History: Ethics and Method*, Berkeley, Cal.: University of California Press.

Rubinstein, W. D. (ed.) (1980) *Wealth and the Wealthy in the Modern World*, London: Croom Helm.

Saunders, P. (1978) 'Domestic property and social class', *International Journal of Urban and Regional Research* 2.

Saunders, P. (1981) *Social Theory and the Urban Question*, London: Hutchinson.

Saunders, P. (1984) 'Beyond housing classes: the sociological significance of private property rights in the means of consumption', *International Journal of Urban and Regional Research* 8(2): 202–26.

Saunders, P. (1985) 'The New Right is half right', in A. Seldon (ed.) *The New Right Enlightenment*, Sevenoaks: Economic and Literary Books, pp. 163–72.

Schluchter, W. (1981) *The Rise of Western Rationalism*, Berkeley, Cal.: University of California Press.

Schumpeter, J. (1954) *Economic Doctrine and Method: an Historical Sketch*, New York: Oxford University Press.

Schutz, A. (1943) 'The problem of rationality in the social world', *Economica* 10(38): 130–49.

Schutz, A. (1953) 'Commonsense and scientific interpretation of human action', *Philosophy and Phenomenological Research*, 14: 1–38.

Schutz, A. (1954) 'Concept and theory formation in the social sciences', *Journal of Philosophy*, 51(9): 257–73.

Schutz, A. (1967a) *The Phenomenology of the Social World*, Evanston, Ill.: Northwestern University Press.

Schutz, A. (1967b) *Collected Papers*, vol. 1, The Hague: Nijhoff.

Scott, J. (1979) *Corporations, Classes and Capitalism*, London: Hutchinson.

Semmel, B. (1984) *John Stuart Mill and the Pursuit of Virtue*, New Haven and London: Yale University Press.

Sen, A. (1976) 'Rational fools: a critique of the behavioural foundations of economic theory', *Philosophy and Public Affairs* 6: 317–44.

Sigrist, C. (1971) 'The problem of pariahs', in O. Stammer (ed.) *Max Weber and Sociology Today*, Oxford: Blackwell, pp. 240–50.

Simmel, G. (1978) *The Philosophy of Money*, London: Routledge & Kegan Paul.

Spierenburg, P. (1984) *The Spectacle of Suffering: Executions and the Evolution of*

Repression: from a Preindustrial Metropolis to the European Experience, Cambridge: Cambridge University Press.

Srinivas, M. N. (1952) *Religion and Society Among the Coorgs of Southern India*, Oxford: Clarendon Press.

Srinivas, M. N. (1966) *Social Change in Modern India*, Berkeley, Cal.: University of California Press.

Stauth, G. and Turner, B. S. (1986) 'Nietzsche in Weber oder die Geburt des Modernen Genius in professionellen Menschen', *Zeitschrift für Soziologie* 15: 81–94.

Stauth, G. and Turner, B. S. (1988) *Nietzsche's Dance, Resentment, Reciprocity and Resistance in Social Life*, Oxford: Blackwell.

Stauth, G. and Zubaida, S. (eds) (1987) *Mass Culture, Popular Culture and Social Life in the Middle East*, Frankfurt/Main: Campus.

Stedman Jones, G. (1974) 'Working class culture and working class politics in London 1870–1900', *Journal of Social History* 7: 460–509.

Stigler, G. and Becker, G. S. (1977) 'De gustibus non est disputandum', *American Economic Review*, 67: 76–90.

Stone, G. P. and Form, W. H. (1953) 'Instabilities in status: the problem of hierarchy in the community study of status arrangements', *American Sociological Review* 18(2): 149–62.

Tenbruck, G. (1975) 'Das Werk Max Webers', *Kölner Zeitschrift für Soziologie und Sozialpsychologie* 27: 663–702.

Therborn, G. (1980) *The Power of Ideology and the Ideology of Power*, London: Verso.

Thompson, E. P. (1963) *The Making of the English Working Class*, London: Gollancz.

Tracy, N. (1983) *The Origins of the Social Democratic Party*, London and Canberra: Croom Helm.

Troeltsch, E. (1912) *The Social Teaching of the Christian Churches*, New York: Macmillan, 1931.

Trubek, D. (1972) 'Max Weber on law and the rise of capitalism', *Wisconsin Law Review* 3: 720–53.

Turner, B. S. (1974) *Weber and Islam, a Critical Study*, London: Routledge & Kegan Paul.

Turner, B. S. (1978) *Marx and the End of Orientalism*, London: Allen & Unwin.

Turner, B. S. (1981) *For Weber*, London: Routledge & Kegan Paul.

Turner, B. S. (1983) *Religion and Social Theory, a Materialist Perspective*, London: Heinemann Educational Books.

Turner, B. S. (1984) *The Body and Society, Explorations in Social Theory*, Oxford: Blackwell.

Turner, B. S. (1985) 'The practices of rationality: Michel Foucault, medical history and sociological theory', in R. Fardon (ed.) *Power and Knowledge, Anthropological and Sociological Approaches*, Edinburgh: Scottish Academic Press, pp. 193–213.

Turner, B. S. (1986a) *Equality*, London: Tavistock.

Turner, B. S. (1986b) *Citizenship and Capitalism, the Debate over Reformism*, London: Allen & Unwin.

Turner, B. S. (1986c) 'Simmel, rationalisation and the sociology of money',

Sociological Review 34(1): 93-114.

Turner, B. S. (1987) 'Marx, Weber and the coherence of capitalism: the problem of ideology', in N. Wiley (ed.) *The Marx – Weber Debate*, Newbury Park: Sage Publications, pp. 169-204.

Turner, B. S. (1988a) 'Individualism, capitalism and the dominant culture: a note on the debate', *Australian and New Zealand Journal of Sociology* 24: 47-64.

Turner, B. S. (1988b) 'Classical sociology and its legacy', *Sociological Review* 36(1): 146-57.

Turner, B. S. (1988c) *Status*, Milton Keynes: Open University Press.

Urry, J. and Wakeford, J. (eds) (1973) *Power in Britain: Sociological Readings*, London: Heinemann Educational Books.

Utton, M. A. (1979) *Diversification and Competition*, Cambridge: Cambridge University Press.

Vaughan, M. (1984) 'The constitution of liberty', in N. Barry (ed.) *Hayek's Serfdom Revisited*, London: ILEA.

Wagner, G. and Zipprian, H. (1986) 'The problem of reference in Max Weber's theory of causal explanation', *Human Studies* 9: 21-42.

Ward, W. R. (1987) 'Max Weber and the Lutherans', in W. J. Mommsen and J. Osterhammel (eds) *Max Weber and His Contemporaries*, London: The German Historical Institute, and Allen & Unwin, pp. 203-14.

Weber, M. (1908) 'Die Grenznutzenlehre und das psychophysische Grundgezets', *Archiv für Sozial Wissenschaft*.

Weber, M. (1930) *The Protestant Ethic and the Spirit of Capitalism*, London: Allen & Unwin.

Weber, M. (1949a) 'The meaning of ethical neutrality in sociology and economics', in M. Weber, *The Methodology of the Social Sciences*, New York: The Free Press.

Weber, M. (1949b) 'Objectivity in social science and social policy', in M. Weber, *The Methodology of the Social Sciences*, New York: The Free Press.

Weber, M. (1951) *The Religion of China*, New York: Macmillan.

Weber, M. (1958) *The Religion of India*, New York: The Free Press.

Weber, M. (1965) *The Sociology of Religion*, London: Methuen.

Weber, M. (1966) *The City*, New York: The Free Press.

Weber, M. (1971) 'Socialism', in J.E.T. Eldridge (ed.) *Max Weber: the Interpretation of Social Reality*, London: Michael Joseph.

Weber, M. (1975) *Roscher and Knies: the Logical Problems of Historical Economics*, New York: The Free Press.

Weber, M. (1976) *The Agrarian Sociology of Ancient Civilizations*, London: New Left Books.

Weber, M. (1977) *Critique of Stammler*, New York: The Free Press.

Weber, M. (1978) *Economy and Society*, 2 vols, Berkeley, Cal.: University of California Press.

Wenger, M. G. (1980) 'The transmutation of Weber's *Stand* in American sociology and its social roots', *Current Perspectives in Social Theory* 1: 357-78.

Whimster, S. and Lash, S. (eds) (1987) *Max Weber, Rationality and Modernity*, London: Allen & Unwin.

von Wiese, F. (1927) *Social Economics*, London: Allen & Unwin.

Wiley, N. (1967) 'America's unique class politics: the interplay of the labor, credit and commodity markets', *American Sociological Review* 32(4): 529–41.

Wiley, N. (ed.) (1987) *The Marx–Weber Debate*, London: Sage.

Williams, R. (1976) *Keywords*, London: Fontana.

Wilson, B. (1982) *Religion in Sociological Perspective*, Oxford: Oxford University Press.

Wright, E. O. (1978) *Class, Crisis and State*, London: New Left Books.

Wright, E. O. (1985) *Classes*, London: Verso.

Wrong, D. H. (1977) *Skeptical Sociology*, London: Heinemann.

Zeitlin, M. (1974) 'Corporate ownership and control, the large corporation and the capitalist class', *American Journal of Sociology* 79: 1073–119

Zola, I. K. (1972) 'Medicine as an institution of social control: the medicalizing of society', *Sociological Review* 20: 487– 502.

INDEX

This index does not contain a specific reference to Max Weber. Since there is a reference to Weber and his work on virtually every page of this text, a reference in the index would be superfluous.

209

INDEX